William J Fay

THE COMMUNITY OF THE BELOVED DISCIPLE

This study in Johannine ecclesiology reconstructs the history of that Christian community whose life from "the beginning" to "the last hour" is reflected in the Gospel and Epistles of John.

"This is what we proclaim to you: what was from the beginning"
(I John 1:1)

"It is the last hour. . . . Many antichrists have now made their appearance, and this makes us certain that it really is the last hour"
(I John 2:18)

THE COMMUNITY OF THE BELOVED DISCIPLE

Raymond E. Brown, S.S.

PAULIST PRESS
New York/Ramsey/Toronto

Nihil obstat:
Myles M. Bourke, S.S.L., S.T.D.
Censor Deputatus

Imprimatur:
Joseph T. O'Keefe
Vicar-General, *Archdiocese of New York*

Date:
January 4, 1979

Library of Congress
Catalog Card Number: 78-65894

ISBN: 0-8091-2174-3

Published by Paulist Press
Editorial Office: 1865 Broadway, New York, N.Y. 10023
Business Office: 545 Island Road, Ramsey, N.J. 07446

Printed and bound in the
United States of America

PREFACE

In early 1955 my first seminar paper as a doctoral candidate at the Johns Hopkins University in Baltimore was devoted to the Johannine Gospel and Epistles.[1] Little did I realize then that I was beginning a quarter-century love affair with the most adventuresome body of literature in the New Testament. If one counted my articles on John since 1955, I suppose they would average almost an article a year, in addition to a pamphlet commentary (1960), and the two-volume Anchor Bible commentary (1966, 1970) on the Gospel. (Research for the present book has necessitated a review and digest of much of the literature written on John since the completion of that commentary, and so it may help as an updating supplement for those who study the commentary.) And now I am preparing the Anchor Bible commentary on the Epistles which I hope to publish in 1981. Amid such a flow of words there is a real danger of losing perspective on the forest because of the trees, and so I have decided to attempt a short book that pulls together my view of Johannine Christianity. In this book I hope to impart both a love for John and an enthusiasm for the adventurousness of Johannine thought. It is a thought that marks a high point in early christology and ecclesiology, and yet offers frightening dangers even to this day.

The immediate origins of the book lie in the preparation and

---

1. Published as "The Qumran Scrolls and the Johannine Gospel and Epistles," *CBQ* 17 (1955) 403-19, 559-74.

research done for two special occasions.[2] In December 1977 I finished my term as president of the Society of Biblical Literature by giving the requisite presidential address to the meeting of that Society in San Francisco.[3] In February 1978 I delivered the Shaffer Lectures at Yale University,[4] a series previously graced by such distinguished Johannine scholars as R. Bultmann, C.H. Dodd, and E. Käsemann. The material presented on those two occasions has now been completely rewritten and greatly expanded to present a sequential history of the Johannine community, and I wish to offer this book as an expression of gratitude to the Society of Biblical Literature and to the Yale Divinity School Faculty for having provided me with the incentive to shape my vision of Johannine Christianity into a coherent picture.

It has often been argued that the Johannine writings[5] may be the most important piece in putting together the puzzle of Christian

---

2. The Johannine topics for those two occasions will be given in nn. 3 and 4 below; but preliminary to both of them was a commissioned article, "Johannine Ecclesiology—The Community's Origins," *Interpretation* 31 (1977) 379-93. That article deals with the pre-Gospel period of Johannine history; the *JBL* article in n. 3 below deals with the Gospel period; the Shaffer Lectures in n. 4 below deal with the post-Gospel period. The Paul Wattson Lecture given at the Catholic University in Washington, DC, in October 1977 (" 'That They All May Be One': Unity and Diversity in John's View of Christianity at the End of the First Century") was a mélange of the material ultimately printed in the *Interpretation* and *JBL* articles.

3. " 'Other Sheep Not of This Fold': The Johannine Perspective on Christian Diversity in the Late First Century," *JBL* 97 (1978) 5-22.

4. The title for these three lectures on the Epistles of John was "The Importance of Jesus for the Johannine Community in Its 'Last Hour.' " The lectures were given from notes, and so it is only in this much developed form that they are being published.

5. By "Johannine writings" I mean the Fourth Gospel and the three Epistles of John. More could be determined about Johannine ecclesiology through recourse to the Apocalypse (Revelation) with its seven letters to the churches, but the relationship of Revelation to the main Johannine corpus remains puzzling. E.S. Fiorenza, "The Quest for the Johannine School: The Apocalypse and the Fourth Gospel," *NTS* 23 (1976-77) 402-27, argues that the author of Revelation "appears to have been more familiar with Pauline than with Johannine school traditions." I accept the thesis that the author of Revelation is an unknown Christian prophet named John (not the son of Zebedee), but I find Fiorenza's hypothesis exaggerated both as regards Pauline similarities and Johannine dissimilarities.

origins—the keystone to the arch of the early Church. Patterns of first-century church history have been reconstructed from the corpus of Pauline literature, from Luke/Acts, and from Matthew; but it has not been easy to fit John into the overall picture. The Fourth Gospel is startlingly different from the other Gospels in its presentation of Jesus and startlingly different from the Pastoral Epistles and the Book of Acts in its view of ecclesiastical realities, so that scholars have theorized that the Johannine Christianity may have been a "backwater" sectarian phenomenon. I hope to show that it was not backwater but rather in mainstream confrontation with the synagogues and other churches, and that despite sectarian tendencies it still prayed for unity with other Christians. But it was a challengingly different and volatile Christianity—so volatile that it was destined to be swallowed up in larger Christian movements (to the right and to the left) that emerged from the first century.

I warn the reader that my reconstruction claims at most probability; and if sixty percent of my detective work is accepted, I shall be happy indeed. Moreover, in the reconstruction of community history I shall concentrate on relationships to other groups and on a life-situation that reflects both loves and hates, and so this book is not an overall Johannine theology with neatly balanced pros and cons. (It may well be all the more interesting because it shows a more frank picture of church life, "warts and all.") Consequently, I hope that for most readers this will *not* constitute their maiden voyage into troubled Johannine waters. I think the book is intelligible to any educated person, but I would much prefer that the beginner in Gospel study give priority to a commentary on John, however short, in order to get an overall picture of the beauty and depth of Johannine theology. Here I shall be reading the Gospel as a key to church life thirty to sixty years after Jesus' lifetime; and I shall be more at ease in doing so if the reader already knows what the Gospel tells us about Jesus himself. Here I shall be using the Epistles as a key to some of the dangers in the Gospel thought; and I shall be more at ease in doing so if the reader already appreciates the positive pastoral direction of the Epistles. With all those cautions let me confess that I find the material I present in this book exciting, and I wholeheartedly invite the reader to share my excitement in seeing familiar material come together in a new way.

CONTENTS

INTRODUCTION: Problem and Method in Discerning
Johannine Ecclesiology   13-24

PHASE ONE: BEFORE THE GOSPEL—
  Johannine Community Origins   25-28
  The Originating Group and a Lower Christology   26
      A. Description of the Originating Group of Johannine
         Christians   27
      B. The Role of the Beloved Disciple   31
  The Admission of a Second Group and a Higher
  Christology   34
      A. Description of the Second Group of Johannine
         Christians   36
      B. Resultant Conflict with "the Jews"   40
      C. The Higher Christology   43
      D. Corollaries for Johannine Theology   48
      E. Continuity with the Earlier Stage   51
  The Gentiles and a More Universalist Outlook   55

9

PHASE TWO: WHEN THE GOSPEL WAS WRITTEN—
Johannine Relations to Outsiders   59-91
Non-Believers Detectable in the Gospel   62
    Group I.   The World   63
    Group II. The Jews   66
    Group III. The Adherents of John the Baptist   69
Other Christians Detectable in the Gospel   71
    Group IV. The Crypto-Christians   71
    Group V. The Jewish Christian Churches of
               Inadequate Faith   73
    Group VI. The Christians of Apostolic Churches   81
Was the Johannine Community a Sect?   88

PHASE THREE: WHEN THE EPISTLES WERE
WRITTEN—
Johannine Internal Struggles   93-144
The Life-Situation Envisaged in the Epistles   97
    A. The Johannine Churches   98
    B. The Johannine School   99
    C. The Intra-Johannine Schism   103
The Areas of Dispute   109
    A. Christology   109
        1. Position of the Secessionists   110
        2. Refutation by the Author   120
    B. Ethics   123
        1. Intimacy with God and Sinlessness   124
        2. Keeping the Commandments   128
        3. Brotherly Love   131
    C. Eschatology   135
    D. Pneumatology   138

PHASE FOUR: AFTER THE EPISTLES—
Johannine Dissolution   145-164
The History of the Fourth Gospel in the Second Century   147
The Secessionists and Second Century Heterodoxy   151
The Author's Adherents and the Great Church   155
Reflection   162

SUMMARY CHARTS   165-169

APPENDIX I: Recent Reconstructions of Johannine
    Community History   171-182

APPENDIX II: Roles of Women in the Fourth Gospel   183-198

BIBLIOGRAPHICAL INDEX   199-200

SUBJECT INDEX   201-204

INTRODUCTION:
PROBLEM AND METHOD
IN DISCERNING JOHANNINE
ECCLESIOLOGY

The word "church" (*ekklēsia*) never occurs in the Fourth Gospel or in I and II John. When it does occur in III John, two of the three uses (vv. 9-10) are associated with Diotrephes, an ecclesiastical leader of whom the Johannine writer disapproves. While the Synoptic Gospels are filled with references to "the Kingdom of God (Heaven)," that terminology is noticeably absent from John (only 3:3,5; see 18:36). The concept of the people of God also seems to be absent from Johannine theology,[6] as is the term "apostle" in its proper sense (n. 150 below). Can one then speak of a Johannine ecclesiology? Or is the Johannine commu-

---

6. E. Schweizer, *Church Order in the New Testament* (SBT 32; London: SCM, 1961) 119 (11b), in a minimalist estimation of Johannine ecclesiology, comments: "In contrast to Paul's writings, however, the name 'Israel', indeed the designation 'saints' or "God's people', is no longer associated with Jesus' Church." (Schweizer fails to respect literary form—a Gospel is not so terminologically free as an Epistle—and his "no longer" assumes that John has eradicated earlier views, whereas such terminology may never have been employed in Johannine theology.) For corrections of Schweizer, see S. Pancaro, " 'People of God' in St. John's Gospel," *NTS* 16 (1967-68) 114-29; and F.-A. Pastor, "Comunidad y ministerio en las epistolas joaneas," *Estudios Eclesiásticos* 52 (1977) 39-71.

nity an association of Christian individualists, each united to Jesus as a branch on the vine (John 15) but not overly concerned with the salvific aspect of being united to one another?

Another challenge to Johannine ecclesiology is offered by a marked opposition to outsiders, whether to "the world," to "the Jews," or to other Christians. Has the association of Johannine Christians become a sect? This is a burning issue with implications both for Fourth Gospel studies and for our understanding of Christian origins.[7] To some extent the answer to the question depends on the definition of "sect." Does one define "sect" in terms of a stance over against another religious body (in this instance, either against parent Judaism or against other Christians), or of a stance over against society at large (against "the world")?[8]

Working in the context of the latter understanding of "sect," R. Scroggs[9] argues that the whole early Christian movement was sectarian, for it met the following basic characteristics of a sect: (1) It emerged out of an agrarian protest movement; (2) It rejected many of the realities claimed by the establishment (claims of fam-

---

7. It would also have implications for the nature of Scripture, since a sectarian understanding of the Johannine community might imply that within the one NT the church canonized the writings of groups who would not have acknowledged each other as true Christians.

8. W. Meeks, *JBL* 95 (1976) 304, distinguishes between Americans who are accustomed to use "sect" as a sociological term, and many European schlars who use the term only in a theological and church-historical sense. His own solution to the question is clear from the title of his article: "The Man from Heaven in Johannine Sectarianism," *JBL* 91 (1972) 44-72. Caution is inculcated by D.M. Smith, Jr., "Johannine Christianity: Some Reflections on Its Character and Delineation," *NTS* 21 (1974-75) 224: "If this [Johannine] sectarian or quasi-sectarian self-consciousness is not a matter of dispute, its roots, causes and social matrix nevertheless are. What thereby comes to expression? A Christian sense of alienation or separation from the world generally? From the Synagogue? From developing ecclesiastical orthodoxy?"

9. "The Earliest Christian Communities as Sectarian Movement," in *Christianity, Judaism and Other Greco-Roman Cults—Studies for Morton Smith at Sixty* (ed. J. Neusner; 4 vols.; Leiden: Brill, 1975) II, 1-23. He gives a bibliography on the sociology of "sect," as does R.A. Culpepper, *The Johannine School* (SBLDS 26; Missoula: Scholars Press, 1975) 259, n. 10.

ily, of religious institution, of wealth, of theological intellectuals); (3) It was egalitarian; (4) It offered special love and acceptance within; (5) It was a voluntary organization; (6) It demanded a total commitment of its members; (7) It was apocalyptic. Obviously, in such an understanding of "sect," the Christian community known to us through the Fourth Gospel and the Johannine Epistles was a sect, as part of the larger Christian sectarian movement.[10]

Even if one takes "sect" in a purely religious framework, the whole early Christian movement may have been considered a sect, or at least the Jewish Christian branch of it. In Acts 24:5,14 Jews who do not believe in Jesus describe other Jews who do believe in him as constituting a *hairesis*—the same word used by Josephus (*Life* 10) when he speaks of the three "sects" of the Jews: Pharisees, Sadducees, and Essenes. But my interest here is the applicability of the religious term "sect" to the Johannine community in its relationship to other Christian communities at the end of the first century. Was this community an accepted church among churches, or an alienated and exclusive conventicle? In this dialectic, the Johannine community would *de facto* be a sect, as I understand the term, if explicitly or implicitly it had broken communion (*koinōnia*) with most other Christians,[11] or if because of its theological or ecclesiological tendencies, most other Christians had broken *koinōnia* with the Johannine community.

Some have argued for Johannine sectarianism on the basis of the relatively quick acceptance of the Gospel by second-century gnostics.[12] The logic is that these "heretics" had correctly recog-

---

10. The Johannine community may fit certain of these characteristics better than do other Christian groups, e.g., #4; yet (at least as seen through the Fourth Gospel) it would fit poorly other characteristics, e.g., #7.

11. See S. Brown, "Koinonia as the Basis of New Testament Ecclesiology?" *One in Christ* 12 (1976) 157-67.

12. That the Fourth Gospel was first accepted by groups who could be classified as heterodox has been proposed by J.N. Sanders and by M.R. Hillmer; the opposite thesis has been defended by F.-M. Braun. See my Anchor Bible (AB 29, 29A) commentary, *The Gospel According to John* (Garden City, NY: Doubleday, 1966, 1970) I, LXXXI, LXXXVI; also E.H. Pagels, *The Johannine Gospel in Gnostic Exegesis* (SBLMS 17: Nashville: Abingdon, 1973).

nized the innate tendencies of Johannine thought. D. M. Smith,[13] however, correctly observes that Irenaeus was able to accept the Gospel as orthodox, so that second-century usage is not a clear criterion of the sectarian status of Johannine thought in the first century: "If there was a Johannine line of development [trajectory], it has not yet proved possible to identify it clearly in the second century and thus to follow it back to the first."

Still another argument for Johannine sectarianism has come from radical interpretations of the theology and ecclesiology of the Fourth Gospel. The likelihood that the Johannine community was a sect sharply different from most other Christians would be increased if the Fourth Gospel is anti-sacramental or decidedly non-sacramental;[14] or if the Gospel is anti-Petrine (with the understanding that Peter is symbolic of the larger church's interest in apostolic foundation);[15] or if the Gospel is anti-institutional, rejecting the presbyter/bishop structure that was emerging at the end of the century,[16] or if its christology is a naïve docetism, so that the church committed an error when it ultimately declared the Gospel to be orthodox.[17] While there is always some basis in the Johannine writings for such radical interpretations, there is enough evidence on the other side of the issue to make them unconvincing and to point toward a more nuanced interpretation

---

13. "Johannine Christianity" (n. 8 above), 225.

14. In my AB commentary, I, CXI-CXIV, I discuss various theories about sacraments in John, including R. Bultmann's thesis that a final editor (the Ecclesiastical Redactor) and not the main evangelist was responsible for sacramental passages like 3:5 ("water" = baptism) and 6:51-58 ("flesh and blood" = eucharist).

15. See G.F. Snyder, "John 13:16 and the Anti-Petrinism of the Johannine Tradition," *BR* 16 (1971) 5-15.

16. Schweizer, *Church Order* (n. 6 above) 127 (12c): "Here [in the Johannine Epistles in continuity with the Gospel] there is no longer any kind of special ministry, but only the direct union with God through the Spirit who comes to every individual; here there are neither offices nor even different charismata."

17. This is the thesis of E. Käsemann, *The Testament of Jesus* (Philadelphia: Fortress, 1968) 26. A serious challenge to Käsemann's thesis has been presented by G. Bornkamm, "Zur Interpretation des Johannes-Evangeliums," *Evangelische Theologie* 28 (1968) 8-25.

of Johannine christology and ecclesiology. At any rate, there is little to be gained by debating once more such points.

I would like to study the history of the Johannine community (which ultimately involves questions of church and sect) by using a fruitful approach that has been opened up in Johannine scholarship of the last ten years. This is based on the suggestion that the Gospel must be read on several levels, so that it tells us the story both of Jesus and of the community that believed in him.[18] Let me discuss that suggestion in general and then some of the cautions that must be kept in mind when one accepts such an approach. Wellhausen and Bultmann were pioneers in insisting that the Gospels tell us primarily about the church situation in which they were written, and only secondarily about the situation of Jesus which *prima facie* they describe. I would prefer to re-phrase that insight as follows. *Primarily*, the Gospels tell us how an evangelist conceived of and presented Jesus to a Christian community in the last third of the first century, a presentation that indirectly gives us an insight into that community's life at the time when the Gospel was written. *Secondarily*, through source analysis, the Gospels reveal something about the pre-Gospel history of the evangelist's christological views; indirectly, they also reveal something about the community's history earlier in the century, especially if the sources the evangelist used had already been part of the community's heritage. *Thirdly*, the Gospels offer limited means for reconstructing the ministry and message of the historical Jesus.[19]

The reader will note the limitation I have placed upon the secondary ecclesiastical information that comes to us from the Gospels—if the recoverable pre-Gospel sources or traditions

---

18. Although in principle this suggestion is not new, a thoroughgoing application of it to John was the contribution of J.L. Martyn, *History and Theology in the Fourth Gospel* (New York: Harper & Row, 1968; rev. ed., Nashville: Abingdon, 1979).

19. Roman Catholic readers may recognize behind my division the three stages of Gospel formation taught by the Roman Pontifical Biblical Commission's "Instruction on the Historical Truth of the Gospels" (1964). For the pertinent section of the Instruction, see the Appendix of my *Biblical Reflections on Crises Facing the Church* (New York: Paulist, 1975), 111-15.

were formed at an earlier stage in the life of the same community that received the final Gospel, they help us to detect that community's history; but if they were composed outside the community and imported to supplement (or even correct) the community's thought, they may supply very little ecclesiastical information about the community itself. In the instance of the Fourth Gospel, scholars have sometimes assumed that the evangelist used and corrected sources taken from outside the community, indeed even from non-Christian sources. Today, however, the dominant trend supposes a much closer connection between the detectable pre-Gospel sources/traditions/editions[20] and the Johannine community (or at least factions within that community).

While I accept in principle the ability to detect Christian community life beneath the surface Gospel story, I wish to be clear about the methodological difficulties of applying such a principle. Since the presentation of Jesus and his message is of primary interest, the deeds and words of Jesus are included in the Gospels because the evangelist sees that they are (or have been) useful to the members of his community. From that we gain general knowledge about the life situation of the community, but it is difficult to move to specifics. For instance, the author of Mark describes the members of the Twelve, and especially Peter, as not understanding Jesus and the need for him to suffer (Mark 8:17-21,27-33; 9:6,32; 14:37). Clearly this is a general lesson for Marcan Christians that it is difficult to arrive at true faith in Jesus and that such faith may be possible only by sharing in his cross, a demand that Mark places overtly in the context of describing the disciples' misunderstanding (8:34). However, are some modern scholars justified in going farther to detect a Marcan attack on the kind of Christianity preached after the resurrection by Peter and the Twelve, and a struggle within Marcan community life over the leadership of the Twelve? Did the Twelve, who claimed to be witnesses of miracles and of the risen Jesus, preach a christology

---

20. For various theories of pre-Gospel sources and editions proposed in scholarship up to 1966, see my AB commentary, I, XXVIII-XXXIV; for developments since then, see R. Kysar, *The Fourth Evangelist and His Gospel* (Minneapolis: Augsburg, 1975) 13-54.

which was based on the miraculous but which neglected the cross? To many of us this seems an unwarranted reconstruction based on evidence that allows a simpler explanation.[21] A presentation of some misunderstanding on the part of the Twelve during Jesus' ministry is not irreconcilable with a great respect for the Twelve in the church, as we see in Luke/Acts and Matthew. If one objects, correctly, that these later Gospels soften the Marcan portrait of the Twelve (while still portraying misunderstanding), that may mean that the older remembrance of misunderstanding during the ministry is being joined in these Gospels to the memory of post-resurrectional profession of faith and fidelity to Christ. All Gospels read the post-resurrectional situation back into the ministry, but Mark is the earliest example of the Gospel genre and tends to put less effort into retouching the dramatis personae surrounding Jesus. To take another example, if Mark presents a Mary (mother of Jesus) who was not a follower of Jesus during his ministry (3:21,31-35; 6:4),[22] is that simply a historical memory, still useful in Marcan catechesis for stressing that physical family has no particular privilege in the Christian movement? Or can one jump to the conclusion that Mark denies that Mary ever became a Christian and indeed is attacking the family of Jesus?

If these examples show that one must beware of overly imaginative deductions about ecclesiastical history from what the Gospels tell us, one must be even more cautious of the argument from silence, i.e., from what the Gospels do not tell us. For example, because Mark (ending at 16:8) narrates no resurrection appearances to the Twelve or to Peter, are those interpreters correct who see this as more evidence of Mark's downgrading the apostles?[23] Or is Mark once more exemplifying an early stage of the Gospel genre before resurrection-appearance *narratives* had

---

21. E. Best, "The Role of the Disciples in Mark," *NTS* 23 (1976-77) 377-401.

22. See *Mary in the New Testament* (ed. R.E. Brown *et al.*; New York: Paulist, and Philadelphia: Fortress, 1978) chap. 4.

23. Usually this involves a dismissal of Mark 16:7, or a contorted interpretation whereby it becomes a warning to Peter of judgment at the parousia.

been developed and attached to the ministry narrative? Sage indeed is M. de Jonge's warning, given while discussing development in Johannine Christianity:[24] "A Gospel may be used only with great circumspection as a historical source."

A further peril in reconstructing community history from the Gospels is to posit non-existent pre-Gospel sources and to determine the theological outlook of the evangelist (and his community) from the way in which he has corrected the source. In the instance of Matthew and Luke, one has some confidence about corrections of a source, for there is an existing pre-Matthean and pre-Lucan document, namely Mark. But in the instance of Mark and John, pre-Gospel sources are a pure reconstruction, and often one of the criteria for that reconstruction is to place in the source harmonious theological material. In other words, one begins to detect a pattern in what looks like pre-Gospel material, and then one joins other passages to that material on the basis of their being harmonious with it. It is no surprise then that the hypothetical source will emerge with the theological outlook which the exegete used as a criterion in the reconstruction. Admittedly I am oversimplifying here—yet the issue of circular reasoning calls into question judgments about the evangelist's relation to such a reconstructed source.

One cannot completely avoid such perils; but in my attempt to detect Johannine community life in and through the pages of the Fourth Gospel, I shall try to minimize the element of self-deception. First, I shall base my conclusions on the existing Gospel, not on any reconstructed sources.[25] Second, I shall stress those passages of John which are significantly different from the

---

24. *Jesus: Stranger from Heaven and Son of God* (SBLSBS 11; Missoula: Scholars Press, 1977) 199.

25. In my AB commentary, I, XXXIV-XXXIX, I posit at least two Johannine writers, the evangelist and the redactor; and so I accept a final redaction that has added material to what was the Gospel proper. However, I regard this added material (some of it ancient) as complementary to the Gospel, and I regard the redactor as a member of a Johannine "school" of writers (see p. 102 below). Therefore, in this book I feel justified in discussing the Gospel as it now stands without insisting on my ability (or anyone else's) to be certain what should be attributed to the redaction.

Synoptic Gospels and where the latter have a better chance of being historical. The Fourth Gospel makes a claim to eyewitness testimony (19:35; 21:24) and does contain some important historical tradition about Jesus. Therefore, a passage where John is clearly modifying the historical picture of Jesus' ministry[26] is probably a passage where Johannine theological interests have come to the fore. Third, when I argue from silence, I shall confine myself to silence about matters which John could scarcely have passed over accidentally. In disagreement with E. Schweizer (n. 6 above), I do not think it significant that John never used the word "church" (*ekklēsia*), since the use of that word by evangelists is a Matthean peculiarity—it is missing from Mark and Luke, as well as from John. I am cautious in making deductions from John's silence about the virginal conception of Jesus. Such a silence could be significant, representing a rejection of the idea as wrong or unimportant; however, the silence could just as easily indicate ignorance of that tradition (which appears in the NT only in Matthew and Luke). But when both Epistles and Gospel fail to use the term "apostle" (especially in reference to the Twelve), a term used by most other authors of the NT, that silence has a good chance of being deliberate and significant. Similarly the Johannine failure to mention Jesus' eucharistic action over the bread and cup at the Last Supper can scarcely be accidental, granted the tradition in the three Synoptics and Paul. By being careful about the criteria, I hope to increase the plausibility of my reconstruction.

---

26. Roman Catholic readers should be aware that their Church teaches a *qualified* historical estimation of the Gospels. In the 1964 Biblical Commission Instruction (n. 19 above), the Gospels are presented as being historical in the sense that their portraits of the ministry are firmly rooted in what Jesus said and did, as preserved by those who accompanied him during the ministry. But these memories, Catholics are told, underwent years of development through apostolic preaching and rewriting by individual evangelists, so that the end-products, the Gospels, "relate the words and deeds of the Lord in a different order and express his sayings not literally but differently." The truth of the Gospels is not affected by this fact, for "the doctrine and life of Jesus were not simply reported for the sole purpose of being remembered, but were 'preached' so as to offer the Church a basis of faith and morals."

In reconstructing Johannine community life I posit four phases. *Phase One*, the pre-Gospel era, involved the origins of the community, and its relation to mid-first-century Judaism. By the time the Gospel was written the Johannine Christians had been expelled from the synagogues (9:22; 16:2) because of what they were claiming about Jesus. Such an expulsion reflects the situation in the last third of the first century when the teaching center of Judaism was in Jamnia (Jabneh)—a Judaism that was dominantly Pharisee and thus no longer so pluralistic as before 70.[27] Indeed, the action of expulsion may be connected with the reformulation *ca.* A.D. 85 of one of the *Eighteen Benedictions* (*Shemoneh Esreh*) which were recited in the synagogues. The reformulation of the Twelfth Benediction involved a curse on the *minîm*, i.e., on deviators who seemingly included the Jewish Christians.[28] Although the Gospel was written after this point in time, the pre-Gospel history certainly included the controversies between Johannine Christians and the synagogue leaders which led up to it. In 11:48 there is a reference to the destruction of the Temple ("place") which took place in 70. The accurate references to Palestinian places and customs,[29] and the Samaritan recollections to be mentioned below suggest that some of the tradition was formed before the major upheaval in Palestinian Christianity brought about by the Jewish revolt against Rome in the 60s.[30] And so we may be wise to date Phase One, the pre-Gospel period of conscious Johannine history, to a span of several decades stretching from the mid 50s to the late 80s.[31]

---

27. Important on this point is the work of W.D. Davies, *The Setting of the Sermon on the Mount* (Cambridge Univ., 1964).

28. See the careful discussion in Martyn, *History* (n. 18 above).

29. My AB commentary, I, XLIII.

30. In his attempt to push the composition of the whole NT before 70, J.A.T. Robinson, *The Redating of the New Testament* (Philadelphia: Westminster, 1976), points to some pre-70 elements in John as proof of its early date. It is bad method to date a final composition on the presence of some early elements; a work cannot be dated earlier than its latest element. See the justifiedly critical reviews of Robinson's claims by D.M. Smith, *Duke Divinity School Review* 42 (1977) 193-205; and J.A. Fitzmyer, *Interpretation* 32 (1978) 309-13.

31. The Jesus tradition in the Gospel goes back farther, of course; and the Beloved Disciple, the hero of the community, may have been an

Phase Two involved the life-situation of the Johannine community at the time the Gospel was written. "Written" is an ambiguous term if one posits the activity of both an evangelist and a redactor (n. 25 above), but the period *ca.* A.D. 90 would date the main writing of the Gospel. The expulsion from the synagogues is now past but persecution (16:2-3) continues, and there are deep scars in the Johannine psyche regarding "the Jews." The insistence on a high christology, made all the more intense by the struggles with the "the Jews," affects the community's relations with the other Christian groups whose evaluation of Jesus is inadequate by Johannine standards. Attempts to proclaim the light of Jesus to Gentiles may also have encountered difficulty, and "the world" becomes a blanket term for all those who prefer darkness to the light. This phase is particularly informative about the place of the Johannine community in a pluralistic world of believers and non-believers at the end of the century.

Phase Three involved the life-situation in the now-divided Johannine communities at the time the Epistles were written, presumably *ca.* A.D. 100. By way of introduction I shall provide a transitional section that seeks to establish what happened between the Gospel and the Epistles to cause the kind of division recorded in I John 2:19. I shall work with the hypothesis that the struggle is between two groups of Johannine disciples who are interpreting the Gospel in opposite ways, in matters of christology, ethics, eschatology, and pneumatology. The fears and pessimism of the author of the Epistles suggest that the secessionists are having the greater numerical success (I John 4:5), and the author is trying to bolster his adherents against further inroads of false teachers (2:27; II John 10-11). The author feels that it is "the last hour" (I John 2:18).

---

eyewitness of the ministry of Jesus. But I posit that in the very early days Johannine Christianity was not really distinguishable from other Jewish Christianity, and that what gave it its peculiar cast and direction was the catalyst offered by the entrance into the community of a group of Jewish Christians of anti-Temple views and their Samaritan converts. Acts 6-8 suggests that that mission to Samaria began in the late 30s, and I am allowing some time for the Johannine meld to have produced a high christology that would cause Jewish concern. See also the dates suggested by M.-E. Boismard in his reconstruction of Johannine tradition (Appendix I below).

Phase Four saw the dissolution of the two Johannine groups after the Epistles were written. The secessionists, no longer in communion with the more conservative side of the Johannine community, probably moved rapidly in the second century toward docetism, gnosticism, Cerinthianism, and Montanism. This explains why the Fourth Gospel, which they brought with them, is cited earlier and more frequently by heterodox writers than by orthodox writers. The adherents of the author of I John in the early second century seem to have gradually merged with what Ignatius of Antioch calls "the church catholic," as exhibited by the growing acceptance of the Johannine christology of the pre-existence of the Word. However, this amalgamation must have been at the price of the Johannine acceptance of authoritative church teaching structure, probably because their own principle of the Paraclete as the teacher had not provided sufficient defense against the secessionists. Because the secessionists and their heterodox descendants misused the Fourth Gospel, it was not cited as Scripture by orthodox writers in the first part of the second century.[31a] However, the use of the Epistles as a correct guide to interpreting the Gospel finally won for John a place in the canon of the church.

Much of this recognition shows a community whose evaluation of Jesus was honed by struggle, and whose elevated appreciation of Jesus' divinity led to antagonisms without and schism within. If the Johannine eagle soared above the earth, it did so with talons bared for the fight; and the last writings that were left us show the eaglets tearing at each other for the possession of the nest. There are moments of tranquil contemplation and inspiring penetration in the Johannine writings, but they also reflect a deep involvement in Christian history. Like Jesus, the word transmitted to the Johannine community lived in the flesh.

31a. For cautions in employing the terms "heterodox" and "orthodox," see nn 203, 278 below.

PHASE ONE:
BEFORE THE GOSPEL
Johannine Community Origins

In Appendix I below I shall digest five different reconstructions of Johannine history offered by scholars in the last three years. Despite the diversity there is significant agreement on at least two stages in Johannine development. In the early period the Johannine community consisted of Jews whose belief in Jesus involved a relatively low christology.[32] Later there appeared a higher christology which brought the Johannine community into sharp conflict with Jews who regarded this as blasphemy, and this friction pushed the Johannine group to even bolder assertions. These two stages of Johannine development are part also of my reconstruction of pre-Gospel history, along with a third stage involving the entrance of Gentiles in numbers.

---

32. In scholarly jargon "low" christology involves the application to Jesus of titles derived from OT or intertestamental expectations (e.g., Messiah, prophet, servant, lord, Son of God)—titles that do not in themselves imply divinity. ("Son of God," meaning divine representative, was a designation of the king; see II Sam 7:14; "lord" need mean no more than "master".) "High" christology involves an appreciation of Jesus that moves him into the sphere of divinity, as expressed, for instance, in a more exalted use of Lord and Son of God, as well as the designation "God." By speaking of "relatively low" and "higher" I wish to indicate fluidity and the lack of exact demarcations.

THE ORIGINATING GROUP AND A LOWER CHRISTOLOGY

Already in the first chapter of John there are remarkable differences from the Synoptic picture of Jesus' ministry. All four Gospels show respect for John the Baptist (henceforth JBap), but the Fourth Gospel attributes to him a knowledge of Jesus' pre-existence (1:15,30)! Since the exalted christology of pre-existence never appears even on Jesus' lips in the other Gospels, its appearance in JBap's proclamation is surely the product of Johannine theology.[33] A second difference involves the first disciples. The three Synoptic Gospels have Peter, Andrew, James, and John called early in the ministry; the cast of characters in John 1:35-51 is somewhat different: Andrew, Peter, Philip, and Nathanael. But markedly different is the disciples' comprehension of Jesus as indicated by the awesome collections of titles they heap on him within three days (Rabbi, Messiah, the one described in the Law and the Prophets, Son of God, King of Israel). By contrast, in Mark no follower of Jesus confesses that he is the Son of God before his death, and in Matt 16:16-17 Peter is singled out as the recipient of divine revelation because in the middle of the ministry he recognizes Jesus as the Son of God! What is more startling, however, than the easy access to christological titles at the beginning of the Johannine ministry is the indication that Jesus regards these titles as inadequate and promises a greater insight—they will eventually see that it is in him that heaven and earth meet (1:50-51).[34] When the Fourth Gospel is read autobiographically as the history of the Johannine community, what does such a unique first chapter tell us about Johannine origins?

---

33. Notice that I do not contend that John has simply invented sayings about Jesus and placed them on the lips of JBap. In my AB commentary, I, 63-65, I suggest a more complicated process involving the reinterpretation of traditional JBap sayings.

34. There is a subtle mélange of history and theology in John. The Fourth Gospel is clearly less historical and more theological than the Synoptics in attributing all this christology to the first few days of Jesus' ministry; yet the Fourth Gospel may be more factual historically in describing the first followers of Jesus as former disciples of JBap and in having them called in the Jordan valley rather than at the Lake of Galilee.

A. Description of the Originating Group of Johannine Christians

J. L. Martyn detects in 1:35-51 that the Johannine community began among Jews who came to Jesus and with relatively little difficulty found him to be the Messiah they expected. I think he is perfectly right, and this challenges reconstructions of Johannine history which would place the origins among heterodox Jews, among Gentiles, or among Gnostics.[35] The fact that some of the same first disciples are the dramatis personae both in the Synoptics and in John and that the titles they give Jesus in John are titles known to us from the Synoptics, Acts, and Paul means that Johannine origins were not remarkably different from the origins of other Jewish churches, especially from those churches which would later associate themselves with the memory of the Twelve. Luke/Acts is particularly insistent on the place of the Twelve Apostles in church origins; and so it is interesting to compare the statement in John 1:45, "We have found the one described in the Mosaic Law and the Prophets," with Jesus' post-resurrectional statement in Luke 24:44: "Everything written about me in the Mosaic Law and the Prophets and the Psalms must be fulfilled." Eventually Johannine Christianity went its own way, as hinted in Jesus' promise of greater things, but the beginnings were unexceptional.

The same impression is gained from an analysis of the miracle stories ("signs") and discourses that make up the public ministry. In the case of the miraculous signs in chaps. 4, 5, 6, 9, and 11, one recognizes that the *underlying* miracle is the same type that one finds in the Synoptic Gospels: the healing of the sick, the lame, and the blind, the multiplication of loaves, and the raising of a dead man.[36] The different final form of the Johannine narrative does not

---

35. In Appendix I below compare the reconstructions of Martyn, Cullmann, and Langbrandtner.

36. Martyn believes that the converted Jews who stood at the origins of Johannine life gathered miracle stories and used them in an apologetic way to gain believers. Reconstructions of pre-Johannine and pre-Synoptic miracle collections have many similarities. See R.T. Fortna, *The Gospel of Signs* (SNTSMS 11; Cambridge Univ., 1970); W. Nicol, *The Sēmeia in the Fourth Gospel* (NovTSup 32; Leiden: Brill, 1972); P.J. Achtemeier, "Toward the Isolation of Pre-Markan Miracle Catenae," *JBL* 89 (1970) 265-91.

stem from the miracle but from the Johannine expansion of the miracle through interpretative theological dialogue. Similarly, C. H. Dodd[37] has shown that embedded in the very distinct Johannine discourses are sayings of Jesus quite like those found in the Synoptic Gospels. Again what is different is the development of those sayings by the fourth evangelist. For instance, while there is nothing in the Synoptics like John 6:53-58, the opening saying in John 6:51, "The bread that I shall give is my flesh for the life of the world," resembles Jesus' words over the bread in Luke 22:19, "This is my body which is given for you." The saying of Jesus in John 3:5, "Without being born of water and Spirit no one can enter the kingdom of God," resembles the saying in Matt 18:3, "Unless you turn and become like little children, you will never enter the kingdom of God."

Eventually in Johannine history Synoptic-like miracles and sayings were woven into unique Johannine scenes and discourses, but that very fact suggests that there was a continuity between Johannine origins and the later development of the community. The sacred material from the tradition of the original community became the source of reflection and expanded teaching in a later period as the community moved toward a higher christology and the promised "greater things." An outside catalyst may have prompted that motion, as we shall see in the next section; but all the signs are against a real disruption. The tendency among some scholars, especially in Germany, to see an opposition between the Johannine evangelist and his sources, and thus antithetical phases of community life in the pre-Gospel period, is in my judgment almost certainly wrong. The material that came from the origins of the community was taken over because it was agreed with, and the new Johannine ideas were understood (correctly or incorrectly) as the true interpretation of the original material.

Several other observations support this. John uses the concept of the Paraclete to justify the audacity of the Johannine proclamation. If there are insights in the Fourth Gospel that go beyond the ministry, Jesus foretold this and sent the Paraclete, the

---

37. *Historical Tradition in the Fourth Gospel* (Cambridge Univ., 1963).

Spirit of Truth, to guide the community precisely in this direction (16:12-13). Yet the Paraclete is portrayed not as speaking anything new but as simply interpreting what came from Jesus (16:13-15; 14:26). The final Gospel picture of a pre-existent Jesus admittedly goes beyond what Andrew meant when he acclaimed Jesus as the Messiah (Christ) in 1:41, and beyond what Nathanael meant when he acclaimed Jesus as Son of God in 1:49. Yet, at the end of the Gospel (20:31), the evangelist is perfectly happy to keep those terms to describe the Jesus of his exalted christology: "These things have been written so that you may have faith that Jesus is the *Messiah*, the *Son of God*, and that through this faith may have life in his name." For the Johannine evangelist, the higher christology of his community has brought out the true, deeper meaning of the original confessions.[38]

Continuity with origins is also suggested by the way the Fourth Gospel portrays JBap. In the next chapter, describing Phase Two of Johannine life, I shall suggest that when the Gospel was written the Johannine community was engaged in a dispute with followers of JBap who rejected Jesus and claimed that their master was the Messiah or at least *the* envoy of God. For that reason the Fourth Gospel goes out of its way to preclude such a wrong interpretation and aggrandizement of JBap's role (1:20: "I am not the Messiah"; 3:28: "I am not the Messiah but am sent before him"—statements of a type not made in the Synoptic tradition). But the Fourth Gospel does not take the easy polemic route of rejecting JBap. To the contrary, he was sent from God (1:6—terminology used of Jesus himself), and everything that he said about Jesus was true (10:41). Indeed, he is the only one in the first chapter to understand Jesus by Johannine standards, since he does not use of Jesus the traditional titles of early Christian preaching, as do the disciples, but acknowledges Jesus' pre-existence (1:15,30). This is historically explicable if some of the first Johannine Christians had come from the JBap movement, even as did some of the originators of the tradition represented in the Synoptic

---

38. The author of the First Epistle will stress that what is being proclaimed in his time is what was "from the beginning" (I John 1:1-2).

Gospels.[39] A sense of continuity with its origins would impel the Johannine community, as late as the time the Gospel was being written and despite conflict with other followers of JBap, to make the claim that its peculiarly exalted understanding of Jesus was in complete harmony with the testimony given by JBap,[40] even to the point that it has JBap speak as a Johannine Christian.

Parallels have been recognized between the Fourth Gospel and the thought of the Essenes who lived in a settlement at what is now called Qumran on the Dead Sea (n. 1 above). Despite exaggerated claims to the contrary, there is no convincing evidence that the Johannine writer knew the Qumran literature. Rather the relationship is indirect, and best explained if there was a conversion into the Johannine community of Jews who held the kind of ideas known to us from the Dead Sea Scrolls (a dualism of light/darkness, truth/falsehood; an angelic prince of lights or spirit of truth leading the sons of light against the sons of darkness; the Law as life-giving water). Later, in the second stage of Johannine development to be discussed below, when the high, pre-existence christology emerged, Jesus would have been interpreted in light of these ideas as the heavenly light descended from above, his followers as the sons of light, and his Spirit as the Spirit of Truth. The Jews who brought these ideas into the Johannine tradition may have been followers of JBap, whose ministry brought him into close geographical proximity to the Qumran settlement at a time when it

---

39. See W. Wink, *John the Baptist in the Gospel Tradition* (NTSMS 7; Cambridge Univ., 1968). Note the hint in Acts 1:21-22 where Peter discusses the Twelve (Eleven) as the group that has been with Jesus "beginning from the baptism of John."

40. D.M. Smith, Jr., "The Milieu of the Johannine Miracle Source," in *Jews, Greeks, and Christians* (W.D. Davies Festschrift; ed. R. Hamerton-Kelly and R. Scroggs; Leiden: Brill, 1976) 164-80, defends Bultmann's association of the early pre-Johannine miracle collection with Christians who had been converted from the following of JBap and who used it as a missionary tract to convert still more followers. In the same volume, J.L. Martyn, " 'We have found Elijah,' " 210, proposes that the author of the pre-Johannine collection wrote it for Jews who might be potential converts, allowing them "to behold a chain of Jews, expectant like themselves, proceeding to discover the fulfillment of their messianic hope not in the Baptist, but rather in Jesus of Nazareth."

flourished, and whose preaching had important common features with Qumran thought and practice.[40a]

B. The Role of the Beloved Disciple

A particular nexus between the followers of JBap and the later community may have been centered in the Beloved Disciple,[41] that mysterious figure who appears only in the Fourth Gospel and who is obviously the hero of the community. The thesis that he is purely fictional or only an ideal figure is quite implausible. It would mean that the author of John 21:20-23 was deceived or deceptive, for he reports distress in the community over the Beloved Disciple's death. The Disciple was idealized, of course; but in my judgment the fact that he was a historical person and a companion of Jesus becomes all the more obvious in the new approaches to Johannine ecclesiology. Later in community history when the Johannine Christians were clearly distinct from groups of Christians who associated themselves with memories of the Twelve (e.g., with the memory of Peter), the claim to possess the witness of the Beloved Disciple enabled the Johannine Christians to defend their peculiar insights in christology and ecclesiology. The "one-upmanship" of the Beloved Disciple in relation to Simon Peter in the Fourth

---

40a. See R. E. Brown, "The Dead Sea Scrolls and the New Testament," in *John and Qumran* (ed. J.H. Charlesworth; London: Chapman, 1972) 1-8, esp. 4-5. Some contributors to this volume would posit a direct relationship between John and Qumran as if the evangelist knew the Scrolls.

41. For a discussion of the Johannine information about the Beloved Disciple and various scholars' theories, see my AB commentary, I, XCII-XCVII. A recent and novel theory is that of H. Thyen: the Beloved Disciple was the presbyter of II-III John, who was not an eyewitness of the ministry of Jesus but had the particular role of distinguishing true interpretation from false; all the Beloved Disciple passages in John were added by the redactor as part of the struggle against the Diotrephes of III John 9-10—a traitor whom only the Beloved Disciple can discern (John 13:21-30). See his "Entwicklungen innerhalb der johanneischen Theologie und Kirche im Spiegel von Joh. 21 und der Lieblingsjünger Texte des Evangeliums," in *L'Evangile de Jean: Sources, rédaction, théologie* (BETL 44; ed. M. de Jonge; Gembloux: Duculot, 1977) 259-99.

Gospel illustrates this (see below pp. 84-87). But such a depiction would have been counterproductive if the Beloved Disciple were a purely imaginative symbol or if he had never been with Jesus, for the community's self-defense would surely have crumbled under such circumstances.[42] Indeed, if I may introduce I John into the discussion, the appeal of that author to eyewitness tradition (1:1-3) is needed to correct abuses within the community and to refute those who indiscriminately appeal to the Spirit (4:1). The author of the epistle was not himself an eyewitness, but his community is one that is aware of its roots in eyewitness tradition—an awareness that supports the thesis that the Beloved Disciple was part of Jesus' following. This has been perceived by D. Moody Smith:[43] "If the Johannine community which produced the Gospel saw itself in traditional continuity with Jesus, we are in a position to perceive in the 'we' of the prologues of both Gospel and Epistle, not the apostolic eye-witness *per se*, but a community which nevertheless understood itself as heir of a tradition based upon some historical witness to Jesus."

I would further suggest that the Johannine picture becomes more understandable if the Beloved Disciple, like some of the named disciples of John 1:35-51, had been a disciple of JBap, indeed perhaps the unnamed disciple of 1:35-40 (a passage which mentions two disciples and identifies one of them as Andrew). Thus the Beloved Disciple would have had a background similar to that of some prominent members of the Twelve, even as the Johannine community in the first stage of its existence consisted of Christian Jews who shared the messianic outlook which marked the beginnings of communities that would stem from the Twelve.

---

42. I am not claiming that every instance involving the Beloved Disciple is historically accurate. R. Schnackenburg, "On the Origin of the Fourth Gospel," *Perspective* 11 (1970—also entitled *Jesus and Man's Hope*, I) 239-40, has argued that the Beloved Disciple, although he was a historical companion of Jesus, was "certainly not present" at the Last Supper. I am not so certain, but clearly John has highlighted him to such a degree that his importance in Gospel scenes goes beyond the importance he would have had in the eyes of an outside observer during the ministry. Of course, for the evangelist, this is a matter of perception, not of deception.

43. "Johannine Christianity" (n. 8 above) 236. For the "we" passages of the two Prologues, compare John 1:14 and I John 1:1-3.

The proposed identification of the Beloved Disciple with the disciple of 1:35-40 has often been debated and rejected on the grounds that elsewhere, when the Fourth Gospel is speaking of the community hero, it clearly identifies him as "the Disciple whom Jesus loved,"[44] and no such clarification is found in 1:35-40. The objection loses its force if it is realized that the unnamed disciple of chap. 1 was not *yet* the Beloved Disciple because at the beginning of the Gospel story he had not yet come to understand Jesus fully—a christological development that would place a distance between him and the other named disciples of chap. 1 and would bring him uniquely close to Jesus. Consonant with the theory that the Gospel is giving us an insight into Johannine ecclesiological growth, I think it no accident that the Beloved Disciple makes his appearance by name only in "the hour" (13:1) when Jesus, having loved his own, "now showed his love for them to the very end." This does not mean that this Disciple was not present during the ministry, but that he achieved his *identity* in a christological context. During his lifetime, whether in the period of Jesus' ministry or in the post-resurrectional period, the Beloved Disciple lived through the same growth in christological perception that the Johannine community went through, and it was this growth that made it possible for the community to identify him as the one whom Jesus particularly loved.[45]

Parenthetically, I am inclined to change my mind (as R. Schnackenburg has also done) from the position that I took in the first volume of my AB commentary identifying the Beloved Disciple as one of the Twelve, viz., John son of Zebedee. I insisted there on the combination of external evidence and internal evidence which made this the strongest hypothesis. I now recognize that the external and internal evidence are probably not to be har-

44. See 13:23-26; 19:25-27; 20:2-10; 21:7,20-23,24; also n. 155 below.

45. Culpepper, *Johannine School* (n. 9 above) 265: "The actual founder of the Johannine school is more likely to be found in the figure of the Beloved Disciple . . . the role of the BD is the key to the character of the community." R. Schnackenburg, *Das Johannesevangelium* (HTKNT 4/3; Freiburg: Herder, 1975) III, 449-64, maintains that the Beloved Disciple is the authority behind the Gospel in whose spirit the Gospel was written but who had no immediate part in the composition of the work. Rather he is the supreme tradition-bearer and witness for the community.

monized.[46] By setting the Beloved Disciple over against Peter (p. 84 below), the Fourth Gospel gives the impression that he was an outsider to the group of best-known disciples, a group that would have included John son of Zebedee, if we may judge from Acts 3:1; 4:13; 8:14.[47] The external (late second-century) evidence identifying the Beloved Disciple as John is a further step in a direction, already visible in the NT itself, toward simplifying Christian origins by reduction to the Twelve Apostles. Cullmann, then, may be right in his long-held theory that we cannot know the name of the Beloved Disciple,[48] even though we can suspect: "He is a former disciple of John the Baptist. He began to follow Jesus in Judaea when *Jesus himself was in close proximity to the Baptist*. He shared the life of his master during Jesus' last stay in Jerusalem. He was known to the high priest. His connection with Jesus was different from that of Peter, the representative of the Twelve."[49]

THE ADMISSION OF A SECOND GROUP AND A HIGHER CHRISTOLOGY

In chaps. 2 and 3 of John there is a stress on the need to understand Jesus more fully than the surface appearance of his

---

46. Second-century information about the origins of the Gospels (often reflecting scholarly guesses of that period) has not held up well in modern scholarship. The First Gospel is surely not written by an eyewitness of the ministry, despite the information of Papias that Matthew (one of the Twelve) collected the sayings of the Lord in Aramaic. The attitude toward Peter in the Second Gospel makes it highly unlikely that a disciple of Peter, John Mark, wrote it. The distance of Luke/Acts from Pauline thought makes it unlikely that a direct disciple of Paul (Luke) wrote those works. There is a set tendency in the second-century information to oversimplify the directness of the connection between the evangelists and the eyewitnesses.

47. Since the first four of the Twelve (Peter, Andrew, James and John) figure the most prominently in the Synoptic tradition, the relative silence of the Fourth Gospel (only 21:2) about the sons of Zebedee, James and John, remains a mystery.

48. Other guesses at his identity (Lazarus, John Mark) are of little help in reconstructing Johannine history. The only important question is whether or not he was a widely known disciple.

49. *Johannine Circle* (n. 318 below in Appendix I). I remain firmly convinced, however, that Cullmann is wrong in identifying the Beloved Disciple as the evangelist, as I shall explain in Appendix I.

actions would warrant;[50] otherwise the material in those chapters has considerable similarity to Synoptic material. The changing of water to wine is not unlike the type of miracle involved in the multiplication of loaves, and the dialogue challenging the intervention of Jesus' mother (2:3-4) resembles the attitude of Jesus in Luke 2:48-49 and Mark 3:31-35. The cleansing of the Temple and the saying about its future destruction are found in the Synoptic tradition. The coming of the "ruler" Nicodemus, who is favorably inclined toward Jesus as a rabbi, and the question of entrance into the kingdom resemble the story of the ruler in Luke 18:18 who says to Jesus, "Good Teacher, what must I do to inherit eternal life?" The idea that the disciples of JBap did not understand Jesus (John 3:22-26) has a thematic resemblance to the scene in Luke 7:18-23 where JBap sends disciples to Jesus to ask him if he is the one who is to come or should they look for another. Of course, the thrust in the Johannine scenes is different, but chaps. 2–3 do not tell us much that is new about Johannine community origins. True, there is an unfriendly encounter between Jesus and the Temple authorities, but the hostility is no greater than in the Synoptic Gospels. What is significant is that the cleansing of the Temple, which for the Synoptic Gospels represents the highpoint of conflict at the end of the ministry, is placed by John at the beginning of the ministry and only starts the hostility. (As with the titles of Jesus in chap. 1, John seems to start where the others leave off, so that the body of the Gospel, after the initial chapters, will give us the autobiography of the community when it began to be different.) Otherwise, despite hints of distrust in 2:24 and 3:10, there is nothing that betrays a severe conflict between the earliest Johannine community and "the Jews."

It is in chap. 4 that John again significantly departs from what we know of Jesus' ministry in the Synoptic Gospels, for in 4:4-42 Jesus passes through Samaria and wins over a whole village of Samaritans to the belief that he is the Savior of the world. In Matt

---

50. In 2:1-11 there is a challenge to see the glory behind the signs; in 2:13-22 a saying about the replacement of the Temple can be understood christologically only after the resurrection; in 2:23-25 and in the Nicodemus story of chap. 3 it is clear that even those attracted by Jesus do not fully understand him.

10:5 Jesus forbids his disciples even to enter a Samaritan city. In Luke, despite two favorable references to individual Samaritans (10:29-37; 17:16-18), the Samaritans show themselves very hostile to Jesus (9:52-55). According to Acts 8:1-25, it was only some years after the resurrection that Christianity was brought to Samaria by the Hellenist preacher, Philip. Thus there is real reason to doubt that historically during his ministry Jesus converted many Samaritans to his preaching; and the appearance of such a story in John (like the story in Acts 8) may well reflect the post-resurrectional history of the Christian movement.[51]

A. Description of the Second Group of Johannine Christians

As we shall see in Appendix I, in Martyn's reconstruction of Johannine history, he offers no real explanation for the appearance of a higher christology in the "Middle Period" of pre-Gospel development. Richter, on the other hand, supposes a conflict between the earliest Johannine Christians of his Group I and the higher christologians of his Group II. I am not satisfied with either of these approaches, and I think that chap. 4 may help us with the problem. Immediately after that chapter we get the picture of a very high christology and sharp conflict with "the Jews" who charge that Jesus is being deified (5:16-18). Already in reference to Martyn's earlier work, D. Moody Smith[52] observed: "This extension of his thesis suggests connections through a sort of Jewish Christianity with less orthodox forms of Jewish life and thought." Following up this suggestion, I think evidence can be found in the

---

51. By not having the Samaritans leave Samaria to follow Jesus and by not calling them "disciples," John is sensitive to the fact that the following of Jesus during the ministry included no great number of Samaritans.

52. "Johannine Christianity" (n. 8 above) 240. I am uneasy about his use of the term "less orthodox," as will be seen in Appendix I in my objection to Cullmann's use of the term "heterodox." In the pluralistic first-century Judaism before 70, there were different views held by majority and minority groups, but no established orthodoxy. Only by the standards of the triumphant Pharisees of the post-70 period can we designate views of the earlier period as heterodox. Both Smith and Cullmann know this, so the dispute centers more on the convenience of terminology.

Gospel itself for the entrance into Johannine Christianity of another group which catalyzed the christological developments. The disciples of JBap from 1:35-51 constitute the main followers of Jesus until 4:4-42 when the large group of Samaritans are converted. This second group of believers is not converted by the first (4:38), and its appreciation of Jesus as "the Savior of the world" (4:42) differs from the standard OT expectations mentioned in chap. 1.[53] The fact that Jesus reconciles his disciples of chap. 1 to the Samaritan converts of chap. 4 (see 4:35-38) means that Richter is not correct in seeing a sharp hostility between the two Johannine groups. Rather the acceptance of the second group by the majority of the first group is probably what brought upon the whole Johannine community the suspicion and hostility of the synagogue leaders. After the conversion of the Samaritans in chap. 4, the Gospel concentrates on the rejection of Jesus by "the Jews." The Johannine Jesus (who undergoes the harassment suffered historically by the Johannine community) says that he has come forth from God (8:41), only to be challenged by Jews who exclaim: "Aren't we right, after all, in saying that you are a Samaritan?" (8:48). This suggests that the Johannine community was regarded by Jews as having Samaritan elements.[53a]

Does this imply that the second group which entered Johannine history consisted entirely of Samaritans? I think there are indications that the situation was more complex. When the Samaritans are being converted by Jesus (and not by his first disciples), he affirms a clear Jewish identity: "Salvation is from the Jews" (4:22). He deliberately rejects a distinctive tenet of Samaritan theology, for he denies that God is to be worshiped on Gerizim. At the same time (4:21) he assumes a peculiar attitude toward Jewish cult, for he predicts that God will not be worshiped in Jerusalem either. (This constitutes another difference from what we know of the

---

53. In the OT Yahweh is the salvation of Israel and of the individual Israelite, but the term "savior" is not associated with the expected king (although in the LXX of Zech 9:9 "saving" appears). Nowhere else is Jesus called "Savior" during the public ministry. The most that one can prove, however, from John 4:4-42 is the use by the Samaritans of a title that is not traditionally messianic—there is no hint of pre-existence.
53a. For the complexities of this passage, see pp. 76-78 below.

Christianity proclaimed by the Twelve [and perhaps by the first Johannine Christians], for Acts 2:46 and 3:1 associate the apostles with faithful Temple attendance.) Accepting these indications, one may posit that the second group in Johannine history consisted of Jews of peculiar anti-Temple views who converted Samaritans and picked up some elements of Samaritan thought, including a christology that was not centered on a Davidic Messiah.[54]

Several trends in modern Johannine exegesis reinforce this thesis. Wayne Meeks,[55] among others, has detected strains in John similar to Samaritan thought; and he argues that the Johannine church has incorporated members, Jewish and Samaritan, who had a high Moses piety. Cullmann has argued for "a very close connection, if not a complete identity," between those who convert Samaria in John and the Hellenists described in chaps. 6–8 of Acts.[56] Those Jerusalem Hellenists (i.e., Jews who spoke *only* Greek as distinct from Hebrews or Jews who spoke Hebrew or Aramaic) spoke strongly against the Temple (7:48-50); and when they were driven out of Jerusalem, they proclaimed Christ to Samaria. Many of us would not be so certain that one can make this identification as simply as Cullman does,[57] but the evidence of Acts shows that it is not at all implausible to postulate the group which I have reconstructed entering the Johannine community and serving as a catalyst in the break with the synagogue. The insistence of Acts 8:1 that the Jerusalem Jewish leaders were especially hostile to the Hellenists, while they tolerated the apostles, corres-

---

54. In my judgment Richter's reconstruction (Appendix I below) wrongly attributes to Group I a christology that belongs to Group II.

55. *The Prophet King: Moses Traditions and the Johannine Christology* (NovTSup 14; Leiden: Brill, 1967) 318-19. See also E.D. Freed, "Did John Write His Gospel Partly to Win Samaritan Converts?" *NovT* 12 (1970) 241-56; J.D. Purvis, "The Fourth Gospel and the Samaritans," *NovT* 17 (1975) 161-98.

56. *Johannine Circle* (n. 318 in Appendix I below). We remember that B.W. Bacon wrote of John as *The Gospel of the Hellenists* (New York: Holt, 1933).

57. Reviews of Cullmann by W. Meeks, *JBL* 95 (1976) 304-5; and by R.E. Brown, *TS* 38 (1977) 157-59. In a paper delivered at the 1976 SBL meeting in St. Louis, C.H. Scobie, "The Origin and Development of the Johannine Community," stressed the role of the Hellenists, while presenting a modified form of the Cullmann hypothesis.

ponds well with my reconstruction. Inevitably the combination of a different christology, opposition to the Temple cult, and Samaritan elements, which were characteristic of the second group that entered the mainstream of Johannine Christianity,[58] would have made the Johannine believers in Jesus particularly obnoxious to more traditional Jews.

It is unlikely in my judgment that the main body of Johannine Christians had permanent contacts with Samaria or lived there. The Samaritan converts are never mentioned after chap. 4, and Jesus never goes back to Samaria. Nevertheless, the constituency of the two groups that I have posited thus far (Jews of fairly standard messianic expectations, including disciples of JBap, plus Jews of anti-Temple persuasion who had converted Samaritans) certainly points to the Palestine area[59] as the original homeland of the Johannine movement.

Can one be more precise? Some scholars have studied the contrast between Galilee and Judea in the Fourth Gospel[60] and have argued that Galilee is the land of belief in Jesus, while Judea is the land of disbelief. Often, Jesus' testimony that a prophet has no honor *in his own country* (4:44) is taken as a reference to Judea (last mentioned in 4:3) rather than to Galilee (mentioned in the immediate context, 4:43,45)[61]—an interpretation that I think has

---

58. One would wish to know if this group was also responsible for the high pneumatology of the Fourth Gospel and its picture of the Paraclete. In Acts 6:5,10 Stephen is "full of the Spirit" and speaks with the Spirit; in Samaria the struggle between Simon Magus and Peter (who completes the work of Philip the Hellenist) concerns the Spirit. But most Christian figures in Acts are moved by the Spirit, and it is not possible to show that the Hellenists had a special pneumatology.

59. I use this vague term to include the Transjordan (Pella) and adjacent Syria. In Boismard's reconstruction (Appendix I below) he would place the first two editions of John's Gospel (Document C and Jean IIA) in Palestine, with the Samaritan passage at the beginning of the *first* edition. P. Parker, "Two Editions of John," *JBL* 75 (1956) 303-14, thinks that the first edition was done in Judea, and to it the tradition of Jesus in Samaria was added.

60. R.T. Fortna, "Theological Use of Locale in the Fourth Gospel," *ATR* sup. series 3 (1974) 58-95.

61. In the Synoptic tradition the saying clearly applies to the hill country of Galilee around Nazareth, but it is suggested that John is reversing the Synoptic picture.

little to recommend it. The fact that in Galilee the royal official and his whole household come to faith (4:53) is not really more significant than the fact that in Jerusalem the blind man comes to faith (9:35-39). Only in chap. 6 is there a long scene in Galilee, and certainly the Galilean crowds show no faith (6:26). Indeed, they are described in the same language used for disbelievers in Judea, namely, as "the Jews" who dispute Jesus (6:41,52).[62] K. Matsunaga[63] has diagnosed the situation thus: "In the Evangelist's congregation, which is primarily a Jewish Christian community, there are some Galilean converts, as well as Samaritan converts, who accepted the Kerygma of John's church and believed in Jesus Christ. Or near the Evangelist's church, there is a certain Galilean Christian community, as well as a Samaritan Christian community." I would agree with the first sentence, although I would insist that the conversion of Galileans never gets the attention given in John to the conversion of Samaritans. I doubt, however, that we have evidence for the second sentence.

B. Resultant Conflict with "the Jews"

I wish now to turn in more detail to the conflict with "the Jews" which dominates the pre-Gospel phase of Johannine community existence and which becomes a prominent motif in the Gospel after chap. 4 and the conversion of the Samaritans. I have suggested that the presence of the new group (anti-Temple Jews and their Samaritan converts) would make the Johannine community suspect to the Jewish synagogue authorities. It is fascinating to speculate whether the hostile Johannine style of speaking of "the Jews" may not have been borrowed from the Samaritans on whose lips (as non-Jews) it would have been quite natural. Most Gentile readers of today do not notice the strangeness of John's having Jesus and the Jews around him refer to other Jews simply as "the Jews"—for the Gentile reader the Jews constitute a different ethnic group and another religion (and often they think of

---

62. The verb *goggyzein* is employed in 6:41,43, which in the LXX of Exod 16:2,7,8 describes the murmuring of the rebellious Israelites of the Exodus.

63. "The Galileans in the Fourth Gospel," *Annual of the Japanese Biblical Institute* 2 (1976) 135-58.

Jesus more as a Christian than as a Jew!). But to have the Jewish parents of the blind man in Jerusalem described as being "afraid of the Jews" (9:22) is just as awkward as having an American living in Washington, DC, described as being afraid of "the Americans"—only a non-American speaks thus of "the Americans." What has happened in the Fourth Gospel is that the vocabulary of the evangelist's time has been read back into the ministry of Jesus. The Johannine Christians were expelled from the synagogues (p. 22 above) and told that they could no longer worship with other Jews; and so they no longer considered themselves Jews despite the fact that many were of Jewish ancestry. The Jesus who speaks of "the Jews" (13:33) and of what is written in "their Law" (15:25; see 10:34) is speaking the language of the Johannine Christian for whom the Law is no longer his own but is the hallmark of another religion.

In the evolution of the term it is helpful to note that John can refer interchangeably to "the Jews" and to the chief priests and Pharisees (compare 18:3 and 12; 8:13 and 22), and that John speaks of "the Jews" where the Synoptic Gospels speak of the Sanhedrin (compare John 18:28-31 with Mark 15:1). But this interchangeability is not to be interpreted benevolently as it is by those who wish to remove the term "the Jews" from the Fourth Gospel by substituting "Jewish authorities."[64] John deliberately uses the same term for the Jewish authorities of Jesus' time and for the hostile inhabitants of the synagogue in his own time. During Jesus' lifetime the chief priests and some of the scribes in the Sanhedrin were hostile to Jesus and had a part in his death—I would judge that bedrock history. Those who have expelled the Johannine Christians and are putting them to death (16:2) are looked on as the heirs of the earlier group. Thus, on the double level on which the Gospel is to be read, "the Jews" refers to both.[65] It would be incredible for a twentieth-century Christian to

---

64. Worse still is the substitution of an exotic term like "Judaite" or "Judaist," which means nothing, or "Judeans," which is inaccurate, e.g., as a designation for the Galilean group in 6:41,52.

65. This makes John guilty of offensive and dangerous generalizing, but he was not the one who began the process. In the first Christian writing, I Thess 2:14-15, Paul speaks of "the Jews who killed the Lord Jesus."

share or to justify the Johannine contention that "the Jews" are the children of the devil, an affirmation which is placed on the lips of Jesus (8:44); but I cannot see how it helps contemporary Jewish-Christian relationships to disguise the fact that such an attitude once existed.[66] And, unfortunately, one can surmise that the synagogue authorities who regarded themselves as the disciples of Moses and the Christians as "disciples of that fellow" (9:28-29) spoke no more gently than did the Johannine community.

What are we to make of the Johannine charge that "the Jews" were killing Christians as a service to God?[67] Martyn thinks that some Johannine Christians had been executed by the authorities of the local synagogues.[68] Certainly we know that in the first century Christians were put to death by Jews: e.g., Stephen (Acts 7:58-60), James son of Zebedee (Acts 12:2-3), and James "the brother of the Lord" (Josephus, *Antiquities* XX ix 1;#200). Mishnah *Sanhedrin* 9:6 acknowledges certain instances where zealots may slay people for religious offenses.[69] Nevertheless, I wonder if the situation may not have been more complex, especially since the putting to death is connected in John 16:2 with the expulsion from the synagogues. In the second century Justin, who was born in Palestine, accuses his Jewish opponents:

---

66. Always with the caution, however, that John's anti-Judaism is not the same as later anti-Semitism which has picked up ethnic, political, and economic coloring over the centuries.

67. In John 16:2 the tense is future, but that is from the viewpoint of Jesus' ministry. The expulsion from the synagogues had already taken place by the time the Gospel was written, and so presumably had the killing.

68. *History* (n. 18 above) 47 ff. The evidence for the killing of Christians is not only 16:2 but also passages in the Gospel where "the Jews" seek to kill Jesus (5:18; 7:1,19,25; 8:22,37,40; 11:53; see 12:10). Comparing John to the Synoptics, I would have to judge that the prolonged intensity of this attitude described in the Fourth Gospel reflects a period *after* the ministry of Jesus. (Cf. Mark 13:9 and Matt 10:17 which refer to the beating and flogging of Christians in synagogues.)

69. *Midrash Rabbah* xxi 3 on Num 25:13 remarks: "If a man sheds the blood of the wicked, it is as though he had offered a sacrifice." Need I add that Christians have a long history of putting one another to death for the love of God.

"Though you have slain Christ, you do not repent; but you hate and murder us also . . . as often as you get authority" (*Trypho* 133:6; 95:4). Now we know that in the second century the "killing" of Christians by Jews was most often not a direct action but by way of denunciation to the Romans. Judaism was a tolerated religion, and in principle the Jews were not forced to take part in public worship. As long as Christians were considered Jews, there was no specific legal reason for the Romans to bother them. But once the synagogues expelled them and it was made clear that they were no longer Jews, their failure to adhere to pagan customs and to participate in emperor worship created legal problems. Second-century Christians accused Jews of betraying them to Roman inquisitors. The *Martyrdom of Polycarp* 13:1 says that "the Jews were extremely zealous, *as is their wont*," in preparing material for burning the saint, a burning that was carried out by a Roman pro-consul *ca.* A.D. 155. Indirect participation in executions through expulsion from synagogues may have been part of the background for John's charges against "the Jews."

I have spent some time on this struggle; for only if we appreciate the bitterness of it will we understand the antagonistic overtones of Johannine christology. The battle between the synagogue and the Johannine community was, after all, a battle over christology.

C. The Higher Christology

By way of leading into a more detailed discussion of the peculiar Johannine christology, let me recall to the reader that I spoke of the entrance of a group of Jews of anti-Temple views and their Samaritan converts as a *catalyst* toward a higher christology. The term "catalyst" was carefully chosen because John 4:4-42 reveals among the Samaritans a different christology from that articulated by the first followers of Jesus in 1:35-51. I have already mentioned the title "Savior of the world" in 4:42 (n. 53 above). More attention needs to be paid to Jesus' acknowledgement that he was the Messiah in response to the Samaritan woman's affirmation that the Messiah was to come (4:25-26). For John *Messias* or *Christos* ("Anointed") is not a term with only one meaning. I have already pointed out that when it is used of Jesus by Andrew in John 1:41, it is not an adequate grasp of his identity (p. 26 above). Nor is it adequate on the lips of Martha in 11:27, for she has not really understood (11:40). Yet John writes his Gospel so that the readers may believe that Jesus is the *Christos* (20:31), and so the term can be an adequate description of Jesus. Seemingly it is true but inadequate if Jesus is looked upon as the anointed king of David's line, which is the most usual meaning of Messiah; it becomes adequate when it includes the notion that he is the one who has descended from God to reveal Him to men and women. Which sense, if either, does Messiah have in 4:25-26?

It is most unlikely that a Samaritan believer would have hailed Jesus as the Messiah in a Davidic sense, for the whole of Samaritan theology was directed against the claims of the Davidic dynasty and of Jerusalem, the Davidic city.[70] In fact, the term "Messiah" is said not to appear in Samaritan writing before the 16th century. Rather, the Samaritans expected a *Taheb* (the one who returns, the restorer), a teacher and revealer;[71] and it may have been in that sense that Samaritans accepted Jesus as "Messiah"—notice what the woman says in 4:25: "I know there is a Messiah coming; whenever he comes, *he will announce all things* to us." Very strong also in Samaritan theology was the concentration on Moses, so that sometimes the *Taheb* was seen as a Moses-returned figure. It was thought that Moses had seen God and then come down to reveal to the people what God had said. If Jesus was interpreted against this background,[72] then Johannine preaching would have drawn from such Moses material but corrected it: it was not Moses but Jesus who had seen God and then come down to earth to speak of what he had heard above

---

70. For background information on the Samaritans, see my AB commentary, I, 170-72.

71. J. Bowman, "Samaritan Studies," *BJRL* 40 (1957-58) 298-329; S. Sabugal, "El título Messias-Christos en el contexto del relato sobre l'actividad de Jesús in Samaría. Jn 4,25.29," *Augustinianum* 12 (1972) 79-105.

72. The dating of strata of Samaritan thought is extremely difficult, and so we are not sure what picture of the *Taheb* was popular in the first century. See Purvis, "Fourth Gospel" (n. 55 above), 182-90; and Meeks, *Prophet-King* (n. 55 above).

(3:13,31; 5:20; 6:46; 7:16—see also 6:32-35; 7:23). Thus the term *catalyst* applied to the newcomers into the Johannine community implies that they brought with them categories for interpreting Jesus that launched the Johannine community toward a theology of descent from above and pre-existence.[73]

In any case, it is a uniquely high christology that appears in the pages of the Fourth Gospel, reflecting the type of belief in Jesus that came to be accepted in Johannine Christianity. The Word that existed in God's presence before creation has become flesh in Jesus (1:1,14); coming into the world like a light (1:9-10; 8:12; 9:5), he can reveal God because he is the only one who has come down from heaven and has seen God's face and heard His voice (3:13; 5:37); he is one with the Father (10:30), so that to see him is to see the Father (14:9); indeed, he can speak as the divine I AM.[74] Johannine christology is very familiar to traditional Christians because it became the dominant christology of the church, and so it is startling to realize that such a portrayal of Jesus is quite foreign to the Synoptic Gospels. With justice Johannine christology can be called the highest in the NT.[75]

A parenthetical paragraph may demonstrate this. Sometimes, wrongly in my judgment, it is claimed that Paul proclaimed the same kind of pre-existence christology as John. Let me note the following points: (a) the most frequently cited pre-existence passages in the Pauline corpus are I Cor 8:6; Phil 2:6-7; and Col 1:15-16. Although I Cor 8:6 speaks of all things being "through Jesus," the text is not really clear about his personal pre-existence.[76] The hymn in Philippians is more clearly personal in

---

73. J.L. Martyn, "Source Criticism and Religionsgeschichte in the Fourth Gospel," *Perspective* 11 (1970—also entitled *Jesus and Man's Hope*, I) 248-72, esp. 258, points out that at the early period of Johannine history the miracle source showed no debates over Moses, so that the need to correct claims about Moses came later.

74. John 8:24,28,58; 13:19; see the Appendix on *egō eimi* (I AM) in my AB commentary, I, 533-38.

75. Origen, *On John*, I, 6, recognized this: "For none of these [Paul, Matthew, Mark, Luke] plainly declared Jesus' Godhead, as John does when he makes him say, 'I am the light of the world'; 'I am the way, the truth, and the life'; "I am the resurrection.' "

76. It could be a reference to the power of *new* creation given to Jesus. See J. Murphy-O'Connor, *RB* 85 (1978) 253-67.

its reference to Jesus; but many scholars today doubt that "being in the form of God" and "accepting the form of a servant" refers to incarnation. It may mean that, unlike Adam who was also in the image of God, Jesus did not rebel at being a servant—in which case the whole hymn would refer to the earthly life of Jesus. Colossians is more open to a pre-existence reading, but many scholars think the Epistle is post-Pauline. (b) The Colossians passage speaks of God's Son as the "first-born of all creation." The parallel designation in Col 1:18, the "first-born of the dead," means that Jesus was the first one to be raised from the dead. It is possible then that Col 1:15 means that Jesus was the first one to be created, so that there is nothing in the Pauline corpus to match John 1:1-2 on the pre-existence of the divine Word *before* all creation.[77] (c) The Pauline passages in Philippians and Colossians are in hymnic pattern,[78] partly modeled on the hymns about divine Wisdom who was also created at the beginning of God's work (Prov 8:22). The portrait of Wisdom was an imaginative personification, and it is not clear how Paul and his disciples related such hymnic language to the earthly Jesus during the ministry. It is John who crosses the bridge from the hymn genre with its Wisdom model (the Prologue) to the Gospel genre which describes the words and deeds of Jesus. The Johannine Jesus during his ministry says, "Before Abraham was, I AM" (8:58); it is the earthly Jesus who talks about the glory that he had with God before the world began (17:5). Indeed, only in John is the term "God" applied to all phases of the career of the Word: the pre-existent Word (1:1), the incarnate Word (1:18), and the risen Jesus (20:28).

Such a comparison may explain why the struggle with "the Jews" over the issue of blasphemy was so acute in Johannine history. The evidence in Acts 5:33-42 indicates that the Jewish

---

77. In Phil 2:9 God bestows on Jesus the divine name after the crucifixion and exaltation. That is not so high a christology as found in John 17:11,12 where Jesus is given or has the divine name during his lifetime—see my AB commentary, II, 759, for the reading: "your name which you have given to me."

78. The same is true of Heb 1:1-4.

authorities grudgingly extended tolerance to fellow Jews who proclaimed that Jesus was the Messiah risen from the dead, provided that they did not attack the Temple as did the Hellenists.[79] But John 5:18 shows that they were not willing to tolerate a Christian claim that presented Jesus as God's equal.[80] After all, it was the characteristic of Lucifer to make himself the equal of the Most High (Isa 14:14). The *Shemoneh Esreh* addressed God: "You support the living and revive the dead. . . . You bring the dead back to life"; but the Johannine Christians were attributing precisely that power to Jesus (John 5:21,25-29). In the eyes of "the Jews" the Johannine Christians were proclaiming a second God,[81] and thus violating the basic principle of Israelite identity: "Hear O Israel, the Lord our God, the Lord is one" (Deut 6:4). No wonder then that the Jewish authorities thought that such people should be expelled from the synagogues and even exterminated for their blasphemy. The words directed to Jesus are meant for the Johannine Christians: "We stone you . . . for blasphemy: because you, although a man, make yourself God" (10:33; 8:58-59; 19:7). Such persecution would have made the Johannine community even more adamant in insisting on the divine status of Jesus: in their community hymn, they sang, "The Word was God" (1:1), and in their confessions of faith, they hailed Jesus as "My Lord and My God" (20:28).

---

79. This tolerance lasted during the period of Roman control from the mid-30s to the early 60s (when a Jewish revolt against the Romans became a greater possibility). The execution of James son of Zebedee and the persecution of Peter (Acts 12:1-19) came during the short period of the Jewish kingdom under Herod Agrippa I (41-44).

80. Occasionally it has been argued that the Jewish charge in 5:18 ("making himself God's equal") is totally false in John's eyes. I would argue that it is false in the sense that Jesus did not *make* himself God's equal. Jesus has nothing of himself; everything has been given him by the Father (5:19-22). But John would certainly not think it wrong that Jesus should receive the same honor as the Father (5:23). The question of just how equal are Jesus and God the Father would be debated by Christians for centuries after it was raised formally in the Fourth Gospel. For more on "equal to God" christology, see nn. 92-93 below.

81. Martyn, *History* (n. 18 above) had rendered important service in focusing on the charge of ditheism.

D. Corollaries for Johannine Theology

Having had to make a choice between Jesus and Judaism, and having preferred the glory of God to the glory of men (12:43), the Johannine Christians derived from their choice important corollaries about the Judaism they left behind. In the earlier Christian preaching the idea of a "new covenant" had meant a renewed covenant between God and His Jewish people through and in Jesus—there was not the sense of the new totally replacing the old. After all, had not Jesus said (Matt 10:5-6): "Go nowhere among the Gentiles and enter no town of the Samaritans, but go rather to the lost sheep of the House of Israel." Acts show us that it was years before the missions to the Samaritans and the Gentiles were begun, and then by the Hellenists (8:5; 11:19-20), not by the Twelve. For all Paul's preaching to the Gentiles, his ultimate goal was to make the Jews jealous and thus save some of them (Rom 11:13-14); after all the Gentiles were just a wild branch grafted on to the olive tree of Israel (11:17). But this attitude has disappeared in Johannine Christianity, and the theme of replacement has come to the fore. Jesus came to his own, but his own did not accept him (1:11); and so he has formed a new "his own" (13:1) constituted of those who did accept him (1:12). "The Jews" are not the children of God but of the devil (8:44,47). Having refused to believe in Jesus, their guilt remains and they will die in their sins (9:41; 8:24). The real Israel consists of those who receive the revelation of Jesus (1:13,47), and so Jesus is the "king of Israel" (1:49; 12:13). "The Jews" had been the people of God through birth, but what is born of the flesh cannot inherit the kingdom of God—being begotten from above through belief in Jesus makes one the child of God (3:3-7; 1:12-13). Nicodemus may be a ruler of *the Jews* (3:1); but because he does not understand that begetting from above has replaced begetting of the flesh, he cannot be a teacher of *Israel* (3:11).

We see the working out of this theme of replacement in the Johannine attitude toward the Jewish cult from which the Christians had now been cut off. (Here again the anti-Temple Jews and their Samaritan converts who entered the Johannine community must have served as a catalyst.) The sacred cultic institutions of

Judaism are looked upon as having lost their significance for those who believe in Jesus.[82] In the great covenant scene at Sinai the glory of God filled the Tabernacle (Exod 40:34), but now the Word of God has "tabernacled" among us and we have seen his glory (John 1:14).[83] The two outstanding virtues of the covenant God, His *ḥesed* (gracious love exhibted in God's choice of an undeserving people) and His *emeth* (true fidelity to His choice), are now embodied in Jesus "who is full of grace and truth" (1:14). "While the Law was a gift through Moses, this grace and truth came through Jesus Christ" (1:17). The Temple of Jerusalem may have been destroyed, but it has been replaced by the body of Jesus which is the true Temple (2:19-21). The time has come when God is no longer worshiped in Jerusalem but in the Spirit and truth that have come through Jesus (4:21-24). The traditional feasts, Sabbath, Passover, Tabernacles, Dedication (Hanukkah), are no longer feasts for believers in Jesus but "feasts of the Jews" (5:1; 6:4; 7:2). In the outline of chaps. 5–10 given in my AB commentary,[84] I showed how John has Jesus make an appearance on each of these occasions and say something which shows that the feast has lost its significance in his presence. For instance, if the Sabbath is the day of rest, Jesus, like God, works on the Sabbath (5:17). If it is customary to pray for rain during the Feast of Tabernacles, those who are thirsty can now come to Jesus, for from within him shall flow rivers of living water (7:37-38). If Dedication (Hanukkah) celebrates the consecration of a Temple al-

---

82. Another example of a high christology leading to the replacement of Jewish cult is found in Hebrews. The exegesis of the psalm in Heb 1:8 employs the designation "God" for Jesus, and this is followed by a lengthy argument that Jesus had made otiose a cult centered on Tabernacle, priesthood, and sacrifice. C. Spicq, *L'Epître aux Hébreux* (2 vols.; Paris: Gabalda, 1952), I, 109-38, treats sixteen parallels between John and Hebrews. I am attracted by the possibility that, if we use the terminology of Acts 6-7, Hebrews is a Hellenist Christian tract addressed to Hebrew Christians, trying to convince them in the last third of the century that it is no longer possible to remain within Judaism, as it had been during the middle third of the century.

83. The Greek verb *skēnoun*, "dwell," is related to *skēnē*, "Tabernacle."

84. See I, CXLIV, 201-4.

tar, Jesus is now the one whom the Father has consecrated and sent into the world (10:36). Truly, Johannine Christianity has become a new religion separate from Judaism, a religion that self-defensively affirms that it is richer rather than poorer—what it has gained is greater than what it has left behind. On the other side of the street, the spurning of cult and feasts by the Johannine Christians after their expulsion from the synagogues served to make "the Jews" certain that they had done the right thing in rooting out such people.

The necessity to stress what had been gained may account for the development of a strong Johannine sense of realized eschatology. "Eschatology" involves the expectation of the last times; and all Christians were to some degree convinced that the last times had come, for Jesus had proclaimed that the kingdom of God was at hand (Mark 1:15). However, it was also recognized that final judgment, ultimate peace and blessings, and the triumph over the enemies of God had not come about with the resurrection of Jesus. And so in the early phase of preaching there was a strong *final* eschatology—Jesus would come a second time, and then he would bring about such things as had been predicted in the Law and the Prophets (Acts 3:21; I Cor 15:23-28). But by the time the Fourth Gospel was written, *realized* eschatology was dominant in Johannine thought—much of what had been expected at the second coming was already accomplished. Once more this change may reflect the impact of Johannine christology. Other Christians thought of Jesus as one who had walked this earth and then been taken to God; in the end he would come down from God as the Son of Man to exercise judgment and reward those who had shown faith in him (Luke 12:8-9). But in John's unique interpretation of the Son of Man,[85] during his earthly ministry Jesus had already come down from God to serve as a

---

85. See J. Coppens, "Le Fils de l'homme dans l'évangile johannique," *ETL* 52 (1976) 28-81, esp. 66-68; F.J. Moloney, "A Johannine Son of Man Discussion?" *Salesianum* 39 (1977) 93-102; B. Lindars, "The Passion in the Fourth Gospel," in *God's Christ and His People* (N.A. Dahl Festschrift; ed. J. Jervell and W.A. Meeks; Oslo: Universitet, 1977) 71-86, esp. 75-77; R. Kysar, *John, The Maverick Gospel* (Atlanta: Knox, 1976) 35-40.

judgment (3:13; 6:62; see 16:28). God had sent His Son into the world; and whoever believes in him is not condemned, but whoever does not believe has already been condemned (3:17-21).[86] For the Synoptic Gospels eternal life is a gift that one receives at the final judgment or in a future age (Mark 10:30; Matt 18:8-9); but for John it is a present possibility: "The one who hears my word and has faith in Him who sent me possesses eternal life . . . he has passed from death to life" (5:24). Obviously, such theology would be reassuring in face of persecution and execution by "the Jews"—the Johannine Jesus had promised: "Everyone who is alive and believes in me shall never die at all" (11:26). For Luke (6:35; 20:36) divine sonship is a reward in the future life; for John (1:12) the gift of being a child of God is granted here and now. The Johannine Christian did not think that one needs to wait until the second coming to see God: whoever has seen Jesus has seen the Father, as Jesus said, "From now on you do know Him and have seen Him" (14:7-10). The Johannine believers, therefore, were not orphaned when they were expelled from the synagogues, since they followed a Jesus who had told them, "Do not let your hearts be troubled and do not be fearful" (14:27); "I shall not leave you orphans" (14:18).

E. Continuity with the Earlier Stage

A perceptive reader may be wondering whether, in stressing the uniqueness of Johannine christology and its corollaries, I have not been contradicting my earlier claim that there was continuity in Johannine thought from its earlier stages and that the developments catalyzed by the presence of a second group within the community were not a violent disruption (pp. 28-30 above). I would still insist on that point and use it to explain one of the great anomalies in the Fourth Gospel, namely, that new insights are placed next to old insights, high christology next to low christology, realized eschatology next to final eschatology, individualism next to a stress on community, a sacramental understanding of

---

86. Contrast the scene of the *last* judgment in Matt 25: 31-33.

reality[87] in a Gospel that shows relatively little interest in the institution of individual sacraments, etc.[88] Many scholars have regarded these elements as contradictory and have sought to make the evangelist's thought uniform by attributing all the passages on the other side of a given issue to another writer.[89] This is a failure to recognize that the evangelist (the main Johannine writer) thought synthetically, not dialectically, and that in Johannine thought the new insights reinterpreted the old. This observation holds true even if one posits the evangelist's dependence on complete written sources.[90] Moody Smith[91] has summarized the situation well: "To the extent that the Gospel of John betrays evidence of redaction as well as tradition, there is added reason to suspect that it is the product of a distinctively Johannine church which played a contributive role in its inception and development. The redaction of a document likely takes place in a community in which that document is already valued or regarded as authoritative. Given other evidence for the origin of the Fourth Gospel in a Johannine community and tradition, it is natural to

---

87. By this I mean the use of the earthly to portray the heavenly: e.g., the gift of eternal life is described as begetting or birth (3:3-5); the life-giving flesh and blood of Jesus are described as food (6:51-58).

88. Kysar, *Maverick Gospel* (n. 85 above) 87-92, lists conflicting passages of this type: future condemnation (12:48) and present condemnation (3:18; 9:39); future eternal life (12:25) and present eternal life (3:36; 5:24); future resurrection (6:39-40,54) and present resurrection (5:21,24).

89. For instance, Bultmann attributes final eschatology to the Ecclesiastical Redactor (church censor). Bultmann popularized the notion of demythologizing which involves, not, as wrongly thought, the removal of mythical language, but the reinterpretation of older mythical language to make it more meaningful. It is strange, then, that he could not see a similar process at work in the juxtaposition of realized and final eschatology by the evangelist. See R. Kysar. "The Eschatology of the Fourth Gospel—A Correction of Bultmann's Reactional Hypothesis," *Perspective* 13 (1972) 23-33.

90. R.T. Fortna, "Christology in the Fourth Gospel: Redaction-Critical Perspectives," *NTS* 21 (1974-75) 489-504, sees considerable continuity between the christology of the "Signs Gospel," which he posits, and the christology of the evangelist. See p. 28 above.

91. "Johannine Christianity" (n. 8 above) 235.

see in the latest redactions the continuing influence of the community."

A. C. Sundberg has written several articles[92] pointing out the presence in John side-by-side of passages portraying Jesus as equal to God and passages portraying Jesus as subordinate to God. In 5:19,30, for instance, we are told that Son cannot do anything by himself, whereas in 5:26 Sundberg would see the autonomous self-existence of the Father extended to the Son.[93] A classic contrast is between 10:30, "The Father and I are one," and 14:28, "The Father is greater than I." It is the perdurance of such lower christological statements which shows that the Johannine community had not made a rival God out of Jesus, but it also shows that the christology of John still stands at quite a distance from the christology of Nicaea wherein the Father is not greater than the Son.[94] Another indication of the kind of continuity we have been discussing is the way in which John has preserved the *terminology* of an older, lower christology, while giving it new meaning. R. H. Fuller[95] points out that the motif of the Son of God being "sent" belonged originally to a prophetic christology which saw Jesus, the prophet of the endtime, in the lineage of the earlier prophets. We find this in the Parable of the Vinedressers where, after sending servants, the owner *sends* his beloved son (Mark 12:2-6). John keeps this language of sending, but now it is

---

92. "*Isos Tō Theō*: Christology in John 5:17-30," *Biblical Research* 15 (1970) 19-31; "Christology in the Fourth Gospel," *Biblical Research* 21 (1976) 29-37. Sundberg finds more low christology passages than high christology ones ("*Isos*" 24), and he thinks that John so elevates the Son that his theology is binitarian.

93. I think that Sundberg somewhat hardens the Johannine attitude by making the low christology too low (subordinationism is not the right category) and the high christology too high. On the latter point, John always perceives a distinction between the divinity of the pre-existent Son and that of the Father. If he states "The Word is God," he still speaks of the Word being directed toward God (*pros ton Theon*).

94. See also C.K. Barrett, " 'The Father is Greater than I' (Jo. 14:28): Subordinationist Christology in the New Testament," in *Neues Testament und Kirche* (R. Schnackenburg Festschrift; ed. J. Gnilka; Freiburg: Herder, 1974) 144-59.

95. "New Testament Roots to the *Theotokos*," *Marian Studies* 29 (1978) 46-64.

the sending of a pre-existent Son into the world.[96] Still another example is supplied by F. Hahn[97] who contends that, in describing Jesus as the source of "living water," John is reworking common Jewish Christian apocalyptic imagery in light of his own christology.

Similarly John does not discard the *scenes* of a lower christology but reinterprets them. In earlier Synoptic imagery it was revealed at the baptism of Jesus that he was God's Son, and this was symbolized through the descent of the Holy Spirit upon him—see the connection of Spirit and divine Sonship in Rom 1:4. John has obviated the need for that revelation through the Prologue which tells us of Jesus as "God the only Son, ever at the Father's side" (1:18). Nevertheless, John 1:33 obliquely preserves the memory of Jesus' being baptized with the Holy Spirit by means of a quotation from JBap, who combines this concept with that of pre-existence (1:30). The baptism is now just a step in the sending of the pre-existent Word. Another example is found in the appearances of the risen Jesus. In an earlier christology these appearances revealed the victory of Jesus after the rejection and abandonment involved in the crucifixion. John has reinterpreted the crucifixion so that Jesus is already victorious on the cross when he is "lifted up" (12:31-32—see pp. 118-19 below); the crucified Jesus has not been abandoned either by believers (19:25-27) or by his Father (16:32). Yet John does not dispense with the post-resurrectional appearances, even if he modifies their importance (20:29). Thus, despite the advances of Johannine christology, the community retains an imagery and vocabulary that it can share with other Christians.

---

96. Intermediary between John and the Synoptics on this point is Heb 1:1-4. The author sees the Son in the lineage of the prophets ("God spoke of old to our fathers by the prophets, but in these last days He has spoken to us by a Son"); nevertheless, he interprets the Son in the language of personified Wisdom (p. 46 above) by stressing that the Son reflects the glory of God and bears the stamp of divine nature.

97. "Die Worte vom lebendigen Wasser im Johannesevangelium." in the Dahl Festschrift (n. 85 above) 51-70, esp. 67.

THE GENTILES AND A MORE UNIVERSALIST OUTLOOK

The reconstruction of Johannine community history thus far has involved an originating group of Jewish Christians (including disciples of JBap) and a later group of Jewish Christians of anti-Temple persuasion with their Samaritan converts. Some reconstructions are content to stop here,[98] but there are clear signs of a Gentile component among the recipients of the Gospel.[99] For instance, the author stops to explain terms like "Messiah" and "Rabbi"—terms which no Jews, even those who spoke only Greek, would have failed to understand. The fact that such explanations are clearly parenthetical indicates that this effort towards comprehensibility for non-Jews was made in the last pre-Gospel period of Johannine life. I see a hint of what happened in 12:20-23 where the arrival of "some Greeks" serves Jesus as sign that his ministry has come to an end.[100] The evangelist then stops to reflect upon the rejection of Jesus by the Jews who had refused to believe in his signs, and he cites Isaiah about God's blinding their eyes and numbing their minds (12:37-40)—the classic OT passage used by Christians as an explanation for the Jewish failure to accept Jesus and as the rationale for turning to the Gentiles (Acts 28:25-28; see Matt 13:13-15). Since John associates this text with the expulsion from the synagogues (12:42), we may suspect that it was particularly when the Johannine Christians of Jewish descent were rejected by Judaism and no longer thought of themselves as "Jews" that they received numbers of Gentiles into the community.

Some have objected that, if there were an entrance of Gentiles into the Johannine community, there should be in the Gospel some signs of strife over this issue, such as those we see in Acts, Paul,

---

98. See the theories of Martyn and Richter in Appendix I below.

99. S. Smalley, *John: Evangelist and Interpreter* (Exeter: Paternoster, 1978) 67, cautions against using these indications wrongly: "The Hellenistic features of the Fourth Gospel tell us more about its final audience than about the background of its author or its tradition."

100. It leads Jesus to affirm, "The hour has come for the Son of Man to be glorified"; and "the hour" is the Johannine term for Jesus' return to his Father through passion, death, and resurrection (13:1).

and Matthew. However, I would contend that the development of Johannine theology would suggest just the opposite. The Johannine community had already taken a significant step outside Judaism in accepting Samaritans who proclaimed Jesus as "the Savior of the world" (4:42),[101] and in promoting a worship in Spirit and truth rather than on Gerizim or in Jerusalem (4:21-24). The struggle with the synagogue had led Johannine Christians to insist that entry into the kingdom was not based on human descent (birth of the flesh) but on being begotten by God (3:3,5) and that those who accept Jesus are the true children of God (1:12). We have seen that John reinterprets "Israel" to cover believers rather than those of Jewish birth (p. 48 above). In a careful exegesis of 11:48-52, S. Pancaro[102] has shown that John thinks Caiaphas prophesied truly when he said that Jesus should die for the people, but that John corrects Caiaphas' identification of the people with the Jewish nation—"not for the nation only but for the scattered children of God." All of this should have led to a peaceful and untroubled acceptance of Gentiles into the Johannine ranks.

Thus, in no stage of *pre-Gospel* history do I see evidence of sharp internal struggle within the Johannine community; its battles were with outsiders. This helps to explain the deep sense of "us" against "them" which we shall see in the next chapter when we study the Johannine relations with other groups at the time the Gospel was written. It also explains the intense shock and anger, seen in the Epistles, when internal dissent finally appeared.

Did the opening to the Gentiles involve a geographic move of the Johannine community (in whole or in part)? Many scholars have posited such a move in order to reconcile the evidence of Palestinian origins with the tradition of composition at Ephesus in Asia Minor.[103] Is there a hint of transplantation in John 7:35 where

---

101. I have explained that the anti-Temple Jewish Christians who were involved in the conversion of the Samaritans have some similarity to the Hellenists or Greek-speaking Jews of Acts 6-8 (p. 38 above). It is interesting that Acts 11:19-20 indicates that Hellenist missionaries were the first Christians to convert Gentiles in numbers.

102. "People of God" (n. 6 above) 121-22.

103. For theories about the place of composition of the Gospel, see my AB commentary, I, CIII-CIV, and the reconstruction by Boismard in Appendix I below.

"the Jews" wonder if Jesus is going off "to the Diaspora of the Greeks to teach the Greeks"? Some interpreters have read the genitive in this verse as explicative: "to the Diaspora which consists of Greeks, i. e., Greek-speaking Jews." However, why would Jerusalem Jews hint that Jesus would find a better and safer hearing among Jews who spoke another language? A more likely suggestion is that he could escape the Jewish efforts to destroy him by going among the Gentiles, with the genitive read as one of direction: "the Diaspora among the Greeks." This ironic proposal (which by the rules of Johannine irony unconsciously predicts what will happen) would have Jesus become a Diaspora Jew, living among the Gentiles and teaching them successfully. Is this also a portrait of the Johannine community?

An opening toward the Gentiles (with or without a geographic move) and the need to interpret Johannine thought to them involved much more than the occasional parenthetical note explaining Hebrew or Aramaic terms. It would have been necessary to adapt Johannine language so that it could appeal more widely. Kysar[104] reminds us that, while phrases like "Son of God" and "I AM" have a distinctive OT and intertestamental background, their usage in John could be appreciated by pagan Greeks. If this is true, the existence of "parallels" to Johannine terminology and thought in various bodies of Hellenistic and pagan literature may become more intelligible. It need not have been a case of John's borrowing from the other literature (or vice versa); rather, there may have been a Johannine attempt to make Jesus intelligible to another culture. G. MacRae[105] points in the same direction when he maintains that John may have been uniquely universalist in presenting Jesus in a multitude of symbolic garbs, appealing to men and women of all backgrounds, so that they understood that Jesus transcends all ideologies.

Such an opening would have carried the community a long way from its early origins among Jews, including disciples of JBap.

---

104. *Maverick Gospel* (n. 85 above) 40, 43.
105. "The Fourth Gospel and Religionsgeschichte," *CBQ* 32 (1970) 24: "John's message is that Jesus can be approached in many ways, but he can only be understood on Christian terms, not Jewish or Greek or Gnostic."

Nevertheless, in the Johannine mind even the proclamation to the Gentiles would be a continuation of what JBap had done when he revealed Jesus to Israel (1:31), as "Israel" was understood in the Fourth Gospel.

PHASE TWO:
WHEN THE GOSPEL WAS
WRITTEN
Johannine Relations to Outsiders

I have suggested that the pre-Gospel period of distinctive Johannine formation took several decades from the 50s to 80s (n. 31 above), and that the Gospel was written *ca.* A.D. 90. This chapter will discuss the Johannine outlook on various non-believers[106] and believers at the time the Gospel was written. In his reconstruction of Johannine history, Martyn (Appendix I below) proposed that at least four different groups, including the Johannine Christians themselves, could be detected as playing a role in the Fourth Gospel. I fear that I have virtually doubled his findings; but before I discuss my detection of seven groups (including the Johannine Christians), let me comment on the significance of the Johannine relationship to so many "outsiders."

At the end of the last chapter we saw the likelihood that the entrance of Gentiles into the Johannine community involved some adaptation of Johannine thought so that it might be more widely intelligible and appealing, and some openness to the implications of what the Johannine description of Jesus might mean to

---

106. "Non-believers" from the Johannine viewpoint where, if one does not believe in Jesus, one does not believe in God (5:38; 8:46-47).

those of other backgrounds. Universalism is certainly not absent from a theology that includes the statement: "God so loved the world that He gave His only Son that everyone who believes in him may not perish but may have eternal life . . . that the world might be saved through him" (3:16-17). Yet, as we see in the following verses (3:18-21), dualism is an important modifying factor in this universalistic outlook. The human race is divided into non-believers and believers, into those who prefer darkness and those who prefer light, into those who are condemned and those who already have eternal life. Since the Johannine community identifies itself with the believers, it is no surprise that most of those outside the community are looked upon as more or less shadowed by darkness. No other Gospel so lends itself to a diagnosis of community relationships in terms of opposition. Yet, if an inevitable stress on opposition gives this chapter of my book a somewhat somber tone, the reader must not forget the light which shines within the Johannine community of faith and which is the main emphasis of the Gospel.

I make this point because otherwise one might get the impression that the Johannine community had a negative self-identity.[107] As is apparent in the Epistles, the Johannine Christians tend to think of themselves as a communion (koinōnia: I John 1:3). There is a strong sense of family within this communion, and the address as "brother" (with "sister" implied) is common because the members are all children of God. The maxim "Love one another" is the chief commandment (John 13:34; 15:12), and this love brings joy and peace to those who share the same vision of Jesus (15:11; 14:27). The exalted Johannine christology is not some abstract test of orthodoxy that has nothing to do with community living. If it is crucial to believe that Jesus is the pre-existent Word of God who has come from God and is of God, it is because then we know what God is really like—He really is a

---

107. I greatly respect the work of Wayne Meeks, but it will become apparent that I give a different nuance to the Johannine situation. I share the hesitation of M. de Jonge, "Jewish Expectations about the 'Messiah' according to the Fourth Gospel," NTS 19 (1973) 264: "I am not sure that Meeks is right when he supposes that this social identity was largely negative."

God of love who so loved the world that He was willing to give of Himself, in His Son (3:16; I John 4:8-9), and not merely send someone else. And such an understanding of God and of Jesus demands that the Johannine Christian, who is the child of God, behave in a way worthy of his Father and of Jesus his Brother: "By this will all identify you as my disciples—by the love you have for one another" (John 13:35).

Some scholars object that this very sense of internal love and external opposition had made the Johannine community such an in-group that it developed a kind of esoteric language unintelligible to outsiders. Meeks[108] argues, "Only a reader who is thoroughly familiar with the whole Gospel or else acquainted by some non-literary means with its symbolism and developing themes . . . can possibly understand its double entendre and its abrupt transitions. For the outsider—even for the interested inquirer (like Nicodemus)—the dialogue is opaque." I think that this exaggerates the difficulty of Johannine literary artifices[109] and does not correctly situate the reader (presumably a Johannine Christian). I see a pedestrian parallel in the Sherlock Holmes stories where really there are *two* parties trying to understand the omniscient Holmes. He is quite opaque to the bumbling Dr. Watson; the reader is brighter and understands some of the clues that Watson overlooks; but the reader is still challenged by Holmes who is more penetrating than the reader. So too in the Johannine story the reader is brighter than the totally baffled person in dialogue with Jesus. The dialogue partner embodies the Johannine experience that there are many whose eyes are earthbound

---

108. "Man from Heaven" (n. 8 above) 57. Here he joins H. Leroy, *Rätsel and Missverständnis* (BBB 30; Bonn: Hanstein, 1968—see my review in *Bib* 51 [1970] 152-54) who maintains that the language of the Johannine community, as attested in the Fourth Gospel, is a special form of speech, a type of riddle-language, unintelligible to outsiders, and meant as a sort of self-congratulatory triumph over outsiders' failure to understand.

109. A short explanation of Johannine literary devices (irony, misunderstanding, double meaning) is found in my AB commentary, I, cxxxv. Good examples are 3:3-5; 4:7-15. Meeks' choice of Nicodemus may not be really supportive of Meeks' point of view; ultimately Nicodemus became a public adherent of Jesus (n. 128 below).

and who find Jesus quite incomprehensible. This judgment is found elsewhere in the NT (II Cor 4:4); and indeed, Johannine misunderstanding and double meaning had virtually the same effect on "outsiders" as the Synoptic parable (Mark 4:11-12). But John goes beyond the Synoptic Gospels, for the dialogue with Jesus is meant to challenge the Johannine reader to understand more than Nicodemus or the Samaritan woman does. The Gospel is not an in-group manifesto meant as a triumph over outsiders; its goal is to challenge the Johannine community itself to understand Jesus more deeply (20:31). Jesus is from God and therefore he remains above everyone's grasp. To that extent misunderstanding runs through the whole Gospel (not just a few literary passages) and is part of John's view of reality. As F. Vouga[110] puts it, the purpose of such misunderstanding is "to convince the believers to become Christians," to reveal the readers to themselves, and to strip away their self confidence.

The negative, then, does not dominate over the positive in the Fourth Gospel. The question most appropriate to the Gospel concerns the relation of the believers to God, through and in Jesus. In this chapter, however, we are not asking the question that the evangelist says he wrote to answer (20:31). We are asking a question about the relation of the Johannine believers to various shades of non-believers and other believers. This is a question the Gospel answers only indirectly through unhappy indications of polemic and conflict.

NON-BELIEVERS DETECTABLE IN THE GOSPEL

Before we finish this chapter we shall see that John regards as non-believers some who *say* that they believe in Jesus. However, in this section I plan to treat three groups of people who make no pretense of believing in Jesus: the world, "the Jews," and the adherents of JBap.

---

110. *Le cadre historique et l'intention théologique de Jean* (Paris: Beauchesne, 1977) 35-36. He devotes an important chapter (pp. 15-36) to correcting Leroy's concept of Johannine misunderstanding.

Group I. The World

Since the verse "God so loved the world that He gave His only Son" is very well known, the first impression is of a favorable Johannine attitude toward the world.[111] Actually, the term "world" becomes more common in John for those who reject the light, since those who accept it are for the most part within the Johannine community. And so we hear that Jesus' coming is a judgment on the world (9:39; 12:31), which is inhabited by sons of darkness (12:35-36); for the world is incompatible with Jesus (16:20; 17:14,16; 18:36) and with his Spirit (14:17; 16:8-11). In short, the world hates Jesus and his followers (7:7; 15:18-19; 16:20). Jesus refuses to pray for the world (17:9); rather, he overcomes the world (16:33) and drives out the Satanic Prince of this world (12:31; 14:30).

It has been proposed that there is virtual identity in John between the world and "the Jews." Often Jesus has a similar attitude toward both, e.g., if the Prince of this world is Satanic, the father of "the Jews" is the devil (8:44); if the world hates Jesus, "the Jews" seek to kill him. Nevertheless, the world is a wider concept.[112] The fact that the opposition to "the Jews" dominates chaps. 5–12 while opposition to the world dominates chaps. 14–17 suggests a chronology in the relationships. We saw that in the Gospel (12:20-22,37-43) the Gentiles come to Jesus at the same time that a definitive judgment is passed on the hopelessness of further appeals to "the Jews"; and I suggested that this means that Gentiles came into the Johannine community in numbers following the definitive break with "the Jews" because of expulsion from the synagogues. The shift in opposition from "the Jews" to the world may mean that now the Johannine Christians are encountering Gentile disbelief, even as formerly they faced Jewish disbelief. And the Gentile rejection of Jesus

---

111. Other benevolent references to the world include 1:29; 4:42; 6:33,51; 10:36; 12:47; 17:21. The fact that John leaves these alongside the many hostile references is another example of the fact that the community does not erase its past (pp. 51-53 above).

112. It includes Jews and Gentiles without distinction.

PHASE TWO: THE GOSPEL

64

may have involved factors that went beyond christology, as I
John 2:15-16 indicates: "Have no love for the world, nor for the
things that the world has to offer. If anyone loves the world, he
has no room for love of the Father. For all that the world has to
offer—carnal allurement, eye-catching enticement, the glamorous life—does not come from the Father."

That Jesus had come only to be rejected by "the Jews" in
particular and by the world in general has a tragic impact in
Johannine thought. There is a plaintiveness in the lapidary Gospel
statements: "To his own he came; yet his own people did not
accept him" (1:11); "God so loved the world that He gave His
only Son . . . but men preferred darkness to the light" (3:16,19).
Thus Jesus becomes a stranger on earth; he goes *home* when he
returns to the Father where he will have the glory that is appro-
priately his (17:5).[113] And if Jesus is "not of this world," the same
fate of rejection inevitably greets the Johannine Christians: "If
the world hates you, bear in mind that it has hated me before you.
If you belonged to the world, the world would love its own; but
the reason why the world hates you is that you do not belong to
the world, for I chose you out of the world" (15:18-19). Ultimately
the home of the Johannine community is in heaven too: "There
are many dwelling places in my Father's house . . . I am going off
to prepare a place for you; and when I do go and prepare a place
for you, I am coming back to take you along with me, so that
where I am you may also be" (14:2-3; also 17:24). The rejection of
the Johannine Gospel by "the Jews" and by the world has produced an increasing sense of alienation, so that now the community itself is a stranger in the world. At the time the Gospel is
written, internal love is enough to give joy and peace, as we have
seen. The real tragedy will come later when there is a split within
the community itself.

Can we diagnose more about the geography and chronology
of the Johannine community from its opposition to the world?
That the Johannine community would be detested by non-

---

113. The idea of the Johannine Jesus as a stranger has been developed by Meeks, "Man from Heaven" (n. 8 above), and is picked up in the
title of M. de Jonge's collected essays: *Jesus Stranger from Heaven* (n.
24 above).

believers who encountered it, we may well suspect. Later records show the extent to which pagans were infuriated by the inner intimacy of the Christians with their "brother" and "sister" language;[114] and the Johannine community was particularly vulnerable on that score. But had the struggle between the community and the world yet come to the point of persecution? Above (p. 43) I raised the possibility that the killing of Johannine Christians by "the Jews" (16:2) really involved denunciations of Christians to Roman authorities. F. Vouga[115] suggests that the Gospel was written in Asia Minor *ca.* A.D. 95-100 and that it reflects the persecution under Domitian. Since that is the period most frequently posited for the writing of the Apocalypse (Revelation), in his theory the two books would be closely related.[116] Nevertheless, the attitude toward the emperor and Pilate in the Gospel does not have the bitter tone toward Rome found in the Apocalypse, so that a massive confrontation with the empire seems unlikely. At most there may have been local harassment by Roman officials related to synagogue/church battles. What I would deduce from the Johannine references to the world is that, by the time the Gospel was written, the Johannine community had had sufficient dealings with non-Jews to realize that many of them were no more disposed to accept Jesus than were "the Jews," so that a term like "the world" was convenient to cover all such opposition.

Perhaps I may be permitted a paragraph of commentary on what the Johannine attitude toward the world means for Christians on a long-term basis. (I shall show in the next chapter what it ultimately meant for the Johannine community.) On the one hand, texts reflecting alienation from a hostile world have comforted inward-looking Christians, inclined to leave outsiders to their own devices if they are not attracted by God toward Christian truth. This has often produced a fortress mentality. On the other hand, these texts have annoyed Christians very conscious of a mission to the world, whether that mission be to infiltrate and

---

114. See A. Malherbe, *Social Aspects of Early Christianity* (Baton Rouge: Louisiana Univ., 1975) 40. He cites Tertullian, *Apology* 39; Minucius Felix, *Octavius* 9,2; 31,8.

115. *Le cadre historique* (n. 110 above) 10, 97-111.

116. See my remarks in n. 5 above.

change it, or to enable it to develop its own spiritual potentialities, or to win it for Christ. Certainly it is some facet of the latter mood that dominates in Christianity today, and especially in my own Roman Catholic community after Vatican II. Nevertheless, the Fourth Gospel remains a warning against naïveté. The world is not simply unplowed ground waiting to be sown with the Gospel; it is not simply neutral terrain. There is a Prince of this world that is actively hostile to Jesus, so that the maxim *Christus contra mundum* ("Christ against the world") is not without truth. Presumably it was with an initial conviction of God's love for the world that the Johannine community had turned to Gentiles from "the Jews," and the feeling that men of all sorts preferred darkness to light must have come after bitter experience. By all means Christians must keep trying in various ways to bear a testimony about Christ to the world, but they should not be astounded if they relive in part the Johannine experience.

Group II. The Jews

The expulsion from the synagogues had taken place some time before the Gospel was written; but, as discussed on p. 42 above, the Johannine Christians were still persecuted, nay, being put to death by "the Jews." This means that, even if they had moved (physically or theologically) into more contact with Gentiles, they still lived in a place where there were synagogues. Vouga[117] points out that, while there are occasional non-hostile references to "the Jews" in the Gospel, those to "the chief priests and the scribes" are uniformly hostile. Under that rubric the Johannine writer is probably lashing out at the synagogue *authorities* who have followed the leadership of Jamnia[118] in carrying out the expulsion of the deviators. There were many geographical regions with synagogues of sufficient significance to explain this continued hostile interaction; but it is interesting that the Apocalypse (Revelation), despite its massive concern about

117. *Le cadre historique* 66-70.
118. See p. 22 above. Scribes were usually of the Pharisee party, and at Jamnia the Pharisees succeeded to the authority formerly held by the priest-dominated Sanhedrin of Jerusalem.

the beast of Rome and emperor worship, takes time out to attack the synagogues in Asia Minor at Smyrna and Philadelphia (Rev 2:9; 3:9). Once again, then, the Ephesus location for the Johannine community remains attractive.

Because there are so many references to "the Jews," some[119] have thought that the Fourth Gospel was a missionary tract to be used in converting Jews and that an active conversion effort was still going on. I judge this position untenable—in citing evidence to support it, its proponents confuse the past history of the Johannine community with the situation when the Gospel was written. Certainly the Gospel shows traces of arguments between Christians and Jews, including topics known to us from other NT or early Christian writings: e.g., that Christians violate the Sabbath and thus violate the Law given by God to Moses (5:16; 7:19,22-24); that there was no resurrection of Jesus (2:18-22); that the eucharist is incredible (6:52); that Jesus was no great teacher (7:15) but could deceive only the uneducated (7:49). Nevertheless, these are only secondary issues; the dominant dispute echoed in the Gospel has been over the divinity of Jesus,[120] as we have seen. Ample Scripture arguments are offered to support the Johannine position (5:39-40,45-47; 6:31-33; 7:23; 8:34-57; 10:34-36). However, these are arguments that were honed in the earlier disputes between the Johannine Christians and the synagogue leaders, disputes which led to the expulsion from the synagogues.[121] If they are part of the Johannine heritage, it is not because there is still a formal effort to convert "the Jews." I do not mean that Johannine Christians would refuse converts from

---

119. K. Bornhäuser, *Das Johannesevangelium: eine Missionsschrift für Israel* (Gütersloh: Bertelsmann, 1928); J.A.T. Robinson, "The Destination and Purpose of St. John's Gospel," *NTS* 6 (1959-60) 117-31; W.C. van Unnik, "The Purpose of St. John's Gospel," *Studia Evangelica* I, 382-411.

120. S. Pancaro, *The Law in the Fourth Gospel* (NovTSup 42; Leiden: Brill, 1975), shows that even the battles over the Law and the Sabbath had become christological battles, for the sovereign attitude of the Johannine Jesus comes from his being above and beyond the Law.

121. Martyn, *History* (n. 18 above), is excellent in pointing out how a midrashic interpretation of Scripture was the weapon with which the battles between the Johannine community and the synagogue were fought.

the non-believing Jews; I am questioning whether they were sending into the synagogues missionaries armed with the Fourth Gospel. (If the Johannine community lived near synagogues, the missionary efforts may have been in the opposite direction—the
synagogue authorities and relatives seeking to win back the
Johannine apostates.) The insistence of the Johannine Jesus in
speaking to "the Jews" that it is not possible to come to belief
unless it be granted by God (6:37,39,44,65) is a sign that there was
no real hope in Johannine circles for such people. I see other
reasons for the inclusion of scriptural arguments that had been
used in times past. First, any religious group that has split off
from another group will preserve in its arsenal arguments that
justify the stance it took. They serve for the education of the next
generation lest there be backsliding, even if there is no hope
whatsoever that the erstwhile opponents will be convinced by the
arguments.[122] Second, as we shall see below (under Group IV),
there were believers in Jesus still hidden away in the synagogues;
and the Johannine writer seriously desired to embolden these to
confess Jesus, even if it meant that they would be thrown out of
the synagogues. The arguments in the Gospel gave the Johannine
Christians ammunition to be used in winning over those whom
they knew to be Crypto-Christians.

Perhaps, once again, it might not be out of order for me to
include a short paragraph reflecting on the significance today of
the Johannine attitude toward "the Jews." In different areas and
different times in the first century there were varied relations
between Jews who believed in Jesus and Jews who did not, and
these relations were not always hostile. In Johannine Christianity, because of its peculiar history, we see one of the most hostile
relationships, and by the second century such extreme hostility
became normal—a situation that has continued through the centuries. (Tragically, in those later centuries the situation of John
16:2 was reversed, and Christians put Jews to death thinking they
were thus serving God.) We can only be grateful that in the mid-

---

122. English Protestant colonists brought to the New World remembered refutations of Romanism, even though there would be no foresee-
able encounter with Roman Catholics here.

twentieth century, partly out of revulsion for the holocaust, the situation has changed; and a sincere effort at understanding is being made on both sides. However, I have an uneasy feeling that the basic Johannine difficulty still faces us. To Jews disturbed by Christian attempts to convert them, the Christian question comes back, which may be phrased in the words of John 9:22: Why have they agreed that anyone who acknowledges Jesus as Messiah can no longer be part of the synagogue? Christians have ceded to that decision by converting Jews *away from* the synagogue. Both parties, today as then, need to wrestle with the question of believing in Jesus and remaining a practicing Jew—a question that ultimately reflects upon the compatibility of Christianity and Judaism. This question was raised inchoatively when Jesus spoke of his own proclamation and its hostile reception by the Pharisees: "No one puts new wine into old wineskins; if he does, the wine bursts the skins" (Mark 2:22).

Group III. The Adherents of John the Baptist

John portrays the first followers of Jesus as disciples of JBap, and the Johannine movement itself may have had its roots among such disciples (especially the Beloved Disciple—see p. 32 above). Therefore, it is surprising to find in the Fourth Gospel such a large number of negative statements pertinent to JBap. He is not the light (1:9); he does not antedate Jesus (1:15,30); he is not the Messiah, nor Elijah, nor the Prophet (1:19-24; 3:28); he is not the bridegroom (3:29); he must decrease while Jesus must increase (3:30); he never worked any miracles (10:41). These fit into a portrayal of JBap's whole ministry as one of giving testimony to Jesus and of revealing him to Israel (1:29-34; 5:33—not that Jesus needed such human testimony [5:34]). All of this becomes intelligible when we hear in 3:22-26 that some of the disciples of JBap did not follow Jesus (contrast 1:35-37) and jealously objected to the number of people who were following him. If once more we read the Gospel partly as an autobiography of the Johannine community, we are led to suspect that Johannine Christians had to deal with such disciples and that the negations are meant as an apologetic against them.

G. Baldensperger suggested this at the end of the last century, and at times the anti-Baptist motif has been greatly exaggerated in the interpretation of the Fourth Gospel.[123] Nevertheless, the exaggerations should not lead us to overlook the evidence. No Synoptic Gospel has such a cautious attitude toward JBap or such a set of negations. Moreover, we do have other evidence of followers of JBap who did not immediately follow Jesus. The scene common to Matthew (11:2-16) and Luke (7:18-23) where JBap sends disciples to ask if Jesus is the one to come hints at difficulties about Jesus among JBap's followers.[124] In Acts 18:24–19:7, Luke tells us about Apollos and a group of twelve at Ephesus (the traditional site for the composition of the Fourth Gospel) who had been baptized only with JBap's baptism. Apollos already believed in Jesus, but the others needed to be instructed (19:4). In the Pseudo-Clementine *Recognitions*, a third-century work drawn from earlier sources, we are told that sectarians of JBap claimed that their master and not Jesus was the Messiah.[125] This limited evidence, while not probative, makes it at least feasible that the Johannine community was in dispute with non-Christian followers of JBap.[126] The fact that they are refuted in the Gospel, not by

---

123. As part of his tendency to see gnosticism everywhere, Bultmann posited that the evangelist had been one of the gnostic sectarians of JBap.

124. To understand why JBap's followers would find acceptance of Jesus difficult, it is useful to discern between the historical preaching of JBap (which may not have referred to Jesus directly) and the Christian reinterpretation of that preaching. For a brief treatment, see my *The Birth of the Messiah* (Garden City, N.Y.: Doubleday, 1977) 282-85.

125. There are problems about this reference; see my AB commentary, I, 47.

126. Purvis, "Fourth Gospel" (n. 55 above) 191-98, connects the JBap group with Samaria and suggests that they were Dosithean gnostics. (Dositheus is supposed to have been a disciple of Simon Magus of Samaria [Acts 8:9].) In any case, I think that the JBap group was still active in Johannine history when the Gospel was being written. The negations about JBap are not just in the opening chapters which reflect earliest community origins. John goes out of his way in 10:40-42 to bring JBap back at the end of the ministry: he is a true witness to Jesus but not one who could work miracles as Jesus did. Many scholars think that the Prologue was a late addition to the Gospel; if they are right, even at that late stage care was taken against exaggerations about JBap.

direct attack upon them as non-believers, but through careful correction of wrong aggrandizements of JBap may mean that the Johannine Christians still held hope for their conversion, a hope that the scene in Acts just quoted would make plausible. The scene in John 3:22-26 attributes to the non-believing disciples of JBap envy of Jesus and a jealous regard for the prerogatives of their master, but it does not portray them as hating Jesus in the manner in which "the Jews" and the world hate him. Perhaps their own origins in the JBap movement made the Johannine Christians less severe toward their former brethren who had not preferred darkness to the light but had simply mistaken a lamp for the light of the world.[127]

OTHER CHRISTIANS DETECTABLE IN THE GOSPEL

In the purview of the Johannine writer, clearly there are some who say they believe in Jesus but who, in fact, are no longer true believers. He speaks explicitly of "Jews who had believed" but whom Jesus rejects (8:31ff.) and of "disciples who broke away and would not accompany him any more" (6:66). Other, milder references to Christians who do not have the same understanding of Jesus as the Johannine community seem to be implicit in the characterization of a disciple like Philip who has been with Jesus a long time and still does not know him (14:9). From such indications I think that overall one can detect at least three non-Johannine groups of Christians, which can be added as IV, V, and VI to the three groups of non-believers.

Group IV. The Crypto-Christians (Christian Jews within the Synagogues)

John 12:42-43 supplies the clearest reference to a group of Jews who were attracted to Jesus so that they could be said to believe in him, but were afraid to confess their faith publicly less they be expelled from the synagogue. (See above p. 22 for this expulsion.) John has contempt for them because in his judgment

---

127. It is stressed in 1:8 that JBap was not the light—that is Jesus' privileged role (also 8:12). But 5:35 has Jesus describe JBap as "the lamp, set aflame and burning bright" in whose light people exulted.

they prefer the praise of men to the glory of God. He tells the story of the blind man in chap. 9 as an example of someone who refuses to take the easy way of hiding his faith in Jesus and is willing to pay the price of expulsion for confessing that Jesus is from God (9:22-23, 33-38). This blind man is acting out the history of the Johannine community, a community that would have had little tolerance for others who refused to make the difficult choice that they had had to make. John's negative comments about "the Jews" who did not believe in Jesus would have been broadly applicable to the Crypto-Christians as well; for in John's judgment, by not publicly confessing Jesus, they were showing that they too really did not believe in him. Like "the Jews," the Crypto-Christians had chosen to be known as disciples of Moses rather than as disciples of "that fellow" (9:28). Yet John seems to be making an implicit appeal to them as if he still hopes to sway them. As I suggested above, the inclusion in the Gospel of so many Scripture arguments against Jewish positions may have been part of an attempt to persuade the Crypto-Christians to leave the synagogues.

From the Johannine mirror-view of the Crypto-Christians it is difficult to reconstruct the details of their christology and ecclesiology.[128] We may guess that in their view the Johannine

---

128. In the reconstruction I confine myself methodologically to clear references to those who believe in Jesus but refuse to confess him publicly. I disagree with those who treat Nicodemus as a Crypto-Christian, a tendency in the otherwise significant article by M. de Jonge, "Nicodemus and Jesus," *BJRL* 53 (1971) 337-59, reprinted in his *Jesus* (n. 24 above), 29-47. Nicodemus' role is not to illustrate or personify the attitudes of a contemporary group in the Johannine experience, but to show how some who were attracted to Jesus did not immediately understand him. Presumably some never came to understand him (the Jerusalemites of 2:23-25), but some like Nicodemus did. When he first came to Jesus by night (3:2), he was afraid; and it was soon shown that he did not understand Jesus at all (3:10). But we see him later speaking up indirectly for Jesus to the Pharisees (7:50). His final appearance illustrates the word of Jesus in 12:32-33:" 'And when I am lifted up from the earth, I shall draw all men to myself'—This indicated the sort of death he was going to die." Nicodemus comes forward publicly after the crucifixion of Jesus to bury Jesus (19:39). He is joined to Joseph of Arimathea who had been a secret disciple of Jesus "for fear of the Jews," but who, in asking for the body of Jesus, is now making his faith public (19:38).

Christians had unnecessarily and tragically brought about the synagogue action against themselves. Presumably they would not have shared the high christology of the Johannine group; for, like the recipients of the Epistle to the Hebrews, they may have felt no need to exalt Jesus over Moses and to have their whole cultic heritage negated. They would have had little taste for Johannine polemics against the leaders of the synagogue. It is interesting to read John 9 from their point of view: to them the blind man may not have been a hero but rather an insolent enthusiast who was rude to those who questioned him and enjoyed repartee at the price of real communication. Over against the Johannine urging to leave the synagogues, the Crypto-Christians could recall that Jesus was a Jew who functioned *within* the synagogue, as also were James and Peter. In their judgment the expulsion of the Johannine Christians may have been just as much the fault of their radicalism as it was of synagogue intransigence. In keeping silent they would not in their own eyes have been guilty of cowardice but were exemplifying prudence. They would stay and work from within to bring the offended synagogue leaders back to a tolerance toward Christians that had previously existed.

History has shown that their strategy had no future, for the Christian movement continued in the path blazed by John, away from the synagogue. Without such hindsight, however, the choice between confrontation and compromise may not have been a clear issue to many in the late first century. And indeed, in subsequent Christianity there have been many times when it was not easy to decide whether for the sake of the Gospel one should split from the establishment or should stay and work stubbornly within it, striving for change. On the long road which position really exhibits more courage?

Group V. The Jewish Christian Churches of Inadequate Faith

Virtually all scholars acknowledge the existence of the Crypto-Christians in the Johannine ecclesiastical spectrum, but now I argue for the existence of a group that has had less recognition. I think that there were also Jewish Christians who had left the synagogues (or had been expelled), who were publicly known as Christians, who formed churches, and yet toward whom John had a hostile attitude at the end of the century. Their existence is indicated by the presence in the Gospel of Jews who were *publicly* believers or disciples but whose lack of real faith is condemned by the author.[129] The first clear instance of this is in 6:60-66. The immediately preceding discourse on the bread of life was given in a synagogue (6:59); and there we saw the utterly hostile objection of "the Jews" to Jesus' claim to be the bread of life, whether that be understood as divine revelation descended from heaven (6:41-42) or as his eucharistic flesh and blood (6:53). But then Jesus *leaves the synagogue* and engages in dialogue with those whom John calls his "disciples." Previously in the Gospel this term has designated those who went about publicly with Jesus, and indeed we discover in 6:67 that among the disciples are the Twelve. (If John presents some of these disciples unfavorably, then, he gives us no reason to think that he means Crypto-Christians in the synagogues.) Some of these public disciples of Jesus complain that what he has been saying in the synagogue is hard to take and deserves no attention. Presumably their distress particularly concerns the last things Jesus said, namely, that the bread of life is his flesh which must be eaten, even as his blood must be drunk, so that the recipient may have life.[130] In reply Jesus insists that his words are both Spirit and life, and he warns that some of the disciples do not really believe. The choice of those who come to him and believe is under the Father's control. "At this," John 6:66 reports, "many of his disciples broke away and would not accompany him any more." I suggest that here John refers to Jewish Christians who are no longer to be considered true believers because they do not share John's view of the eucharist.[131]

---

129. I would now modify my *JBL* article (n. 3 above) by being more precise about the distinguishing marks of this group. Jesus distrusts the Jerusalemites of 2:22-25 who believed in him on the basis of signs, but I am not sure that they would come under the group I am now discussing.

130. Clearly in this scene John has moved out of the historical ministry into the life of the church, and John's choosing to introduce eucharistic teaching into the bread of life discourse has some ecclesiological significance for the Johannine community.

131. Some would interpret this scene in light of the internal struggle portrayed in I John, so that the passage is attacking a view of the eucharist

Another instance of Jewish Christians of inadequate faith may be the brothers of Jesus in 7:3-5, We are told that they urge Jesus to go up to Judea to perform his miracles there, instead of doing them in relative hiding. [132] John equates this with an invitation for Jesus to display himself to the world, and so he comments that even his brothers did not believe in him. This statement, appearing in a Gospel written at the end of the century, is somewhat surprising. [133] It was well known that James the "brother of the Lord" had received a vision of the risen Jesus (I Cor 15:7) and had been an apostle who had served as leader of the Jerusalem church (Gal 1:19; 2:9; Acts 15; 21:18); indeed, in both Jewish and Christian tradition he had died as a martyr in the early 60s. [134] Later tradition had other brothers of the Lord succeed him in the Jerusalem leadership, and the relatives of Jesus were reputed to be prominent in the churches of Palestine into the second century. [135] In light of this, John's claim that the brothers of Jesus, who want him to go to *Jerusalem*, did not really believe in him cannot be facilely dismissed as a simple historical memory that at first some of Jesus' family did not react well to his ministry (see Mark 3:21; 34-35; 6:4). John gives a somewhat unfavorable picture of the interference of the mother of Jesus at Cana (2:1-11), a scene that has parallels to

---

held by the Johannine secessionists to be discussed in Phase Three below. However, the whole context in John 6 concerns the outsider groups ("the Jews"; the Twelve representing the Apostolic Churches), so that I assume this is an outsider group too. I shall mention Ignatius; I believe that he fought on two fronts (n. 303 below) and that the eucharistic aberration I shall mention here belonged to his Jewish Christian enemies rather than to his docetic enemies (who also had eucharistic difficulties).

132. Granted the Johannine antagonism toward signs as wonders, their request is a sign of disbelief (see 2:23-24; 4:48; also Mark 8:12; Matt 12:39).

133. Their lack of faith in 7:5 continues a sequence of reactions to Jesus begun in 6:66: some disciples would no longer accompany Jesus (6:66); Simon Peter as a spokesman for the Twelve continues to believe in Jesus (6:68-69); Judas, one of the Twelve, will betray him (6:71); and his brothers do not believe in him (7:5).

134. Josephus, *Antiquities* XX ix 1; ##200-3; Eusebius, *History* II xxiii 11-19 (from Hegesippus).

135. Eusebius, *History* III xi, xx, xxxii; IV xxii 4.

7:1-10 and the interference of the brothers.[136] But John takes pains to "redeem" the image of the mother of Jesus by showing her as a believer at the foot of the cross (19:25-27), while he shows no such courtesy to the brothers.[137] Indeed, the implication of 19:25-27 is that the real brothers of Jesus are believing disciples (see also 20:17-18) since the mother of Jesus becomes the mother of the Beloved Disciple.[138] Therefore, I would argue that John's hostile picture of the brothers is meant to have perduring significance. This fits into the present discussion when it is remembered that James, the brother of the Lord, was followed during his lifetime by a number of Jewish Christians in Jerusalem who were more conservative than Peter and Paul (Gal 2:12), and that after his death he became the hero par excellence for the Jewish Christians of the second century who gradually separated from the "Great Church."[139]

Still another Johannine reference to Jewish Christians of inadequate faith is more problematical. In 8:31 there begins a long dialogue between Jesus and "Jews who had believed him." One should take this designation literally and not argue that, because *pisteuein* is used with the dative rather than with *eis* ("in"), lesser faith is intended. The whole attempt of some (I. de la Potterie and others) to diagnose Johannine theology on the exact use of prepositions is, in my judgment, untenable; and in this particular instance C. H. Dodd[140] is right in classifying the variation as meaningless. One should take seriously that John describes these Jews as "believers," at least in their own view.[141] The discourse raises the

---

136. In both instances a request by relatives is rebuked because it is not Jesus' hour or time, but the request is granted later on.

137. An example of how knowledge of the positive role of James might have caused John to modify the harshness of his comments about the brothers is found in Luke/Acts. There the favorable picture of James in Acts brings Luke to modify the negative Gospel picture of Jesus' relatives which comes from Mark: for instance, Luke omits Mark 3:21; his scene in 8:21 (following 8:15) is more positive than Mark 3:33-35; and Luke 4:24 is not offensive when compared with Mark 6:4.

138. See my discussion of this scene at the end of Appendix II below.

139. In his book on the Jewish Christians, *The Church from the Circumcision* (Jerusalem: Franciscans, 1971) 70-78, B. Bagatti devotes a section to the "Exaltation of James."

140. *RHPR 37* (1957) 6.

theme of whether such Jewish believers are slaves or truly free
and whether they are the "seed" of Abraham. Antagonism in-
creases as Jesus charges that the devil is their father (8:44), and
they accuse him of being a Samaritan (8:45). It closes with Jesus'
making the christological claim, "Before Abraham even came
into existence, I AM," and their attempt to stone him. Some
would classify these believers as Crypto-Christians, even though
nothing in the text suggests that they hid their faith in Jesus. It is
more tempting to theorize that they are Jewish Christians who
strongly resent the Johannine community because of its high
christology and its admixture of Samaritan elements. "Seed of
Abraham" seems to have been a term frequently used in debates
between conservative Jewish Christians and their less conservative Christian opponents,[142] with the more conservative group
interpreting the term as physical descent. The Samaritan component in the Johannine community would make Jewish Christians
doubt that the Johannine Christians were really descended from
Abraham (see II Macc 6:2), while in Johannine eyes descent
through the flesh from Abraham would not guarantee that those
Jewish Christians who insist on it are the true and free seed of
Abraham. After all, Ishmael was physically descended from Abraham but was slave-born and was illegitimate in contemporary
Jewish estimation.[143] When in the course of the debate christology emerges as the real issue, the "believing" Jews (the Jewish

---

141. In my AB commentary, I, 354, I argued that 8:31 is an editorial
insertion and that the discourse was originally addressed to the dis-
believing Jews of 8:22. I still think that may be correct; but I should have
come to grips with the problem that whoever did the editing had a purpose in shifting the audience of the discourse to "believing" Jews. The
commentator must explain the final text, no matter what its prehistory.

142. It occurs relatively infrequently in the OT, not at all in intertestamental literature, and with moderate frequency at Qumran. But it is
prominent in Paul's debates with the Judaizers (Gal 3:16ff.; Rom 4:13ff.;
9:7ff.; 11:1; II Cor 11:22), and also Heb 2:16. Here I am indebted to B.E.
Schein who allowed me to read the chapter on John 8:31-59 in his unpublished Yale doctoral dissertation *Our Father Abraham* (1972)—see the
brief extract in SBLASP (Atlanta, 1971) S159, pp. 83-84.

143. Schein points out that the debate in John becomes intelligible if
one knows first-century midrashic tradition about Ishmael and Isaac.
Ishmael was looked on as a threat to Isaac's life (Josephus, *Antiquities* I
xii 3: #215), and Philo (*On Sobriety* II #8) calls Ishmael illegitimate. In

Christians) think it blasphemy that Jesus is said to have existed before Abraham and that he is given the divine name "I AM." In Johannine eyes such a failure to recognize the true character of Jesus means that these are "Jews who had believed" but are now no better than "the Jews." At the end of the debate we are told that they tried to kill Jesus. Because this attempt follows implicit references to Ishmael and to Cain (see 8:44), two men who killed or threatened their *brothers*, the author may be hinting that the Jewish Christians are acting in the same way toward their brother Christians, the Johannine community—perhaps by approving the actions of the synagogue authorities against them (see also 11:45–46).

The final passage in John to which I would turn (but with admitted uncertainty) is the criticism of hirelings who do not protect the sheep against wolves (10:12). These are not the Pharisees (synagogue leaders) of 9:40 who in 10:1 are called thieves and bandits. The hirelings are shepherds of the sheep, which means leaders of Christian groups,[144] perhaps of Jewish Christian churches. They have not distanced their flocks sufficiently from "the Jews" who are trying to take them away (i.e., back to the synagogue), for they have not really accepted the Johannine thesis that Judaism had been replaced by Christianity.

How can these four passages be put together if they all refer to Jewish Christian churches distinct from the synagogue but of whom John disapproves? Such churches would contain those who claimed the patronage of James and the brothers of the Lord, who insisted on the importance of physical Jewish descent, who had a low christology, and who rejected a highly sacramental under-standing of the eucharist.[145] Is the existence of such churches

---

John 8:39-41 Jesus says to the "believing" Jews that, if they were really Abraham's children, they would not be seeking to kill him; and they respond that *they* are not illegitimate.

144. Once again the public character of their task makes me think that John is not referring to Crypto-Christians. Would the latter, who were hiding their identity, have been so organized that they had shepherds or pastoral leaders?

145. That the Jewish Christians could accept the eucharist but not necessarily a Johannine understanding of the eucharist makes it necessary for me to comment on John's contribution to eucharistic theology. The

plausible at the end of the first century? It is clearly demonstrable in the second century where patristic references become increasingly hostile to the Jewish Christians because of their close adherence to some of the tenets of Judaism, their low christology, and their separateness from the Gentile Christian churches. Somewhere within the second century they begin to be treated as heretics. We have already seen that James was their patron. Epiphanius (*Panarion* XXX 1xi 1) tells us that Jewish Christians imitated the eucharistic mystery of the church once a year, using bread and water.[146] If one can trace all the features criticized by John to some period in the second century, even more important is the evidence from the letters of Ignatius of Antioch at the beginning of the century and within twenty years of the putative date of John's Gospel. In writing to the churches of Asia Minor, he attacks Jewish Christians particularly in the letters to the Magnesians and the Philadelphians. If I may quote from a recent study of Ignatius' charges against them,[147] "They reverenced Jesus as a teacher, but perhaps were not prepared to allow his person to upset the unity of the Godhead.... They adopted the sacred meal . . . and thought of it in terms of fellowship rather than as a sacrament on Ignatian lines." In John we may have a picture of such groups (in Asia Minor also?) two decades earlier, precisely because the peculiar empha-

---

Synoptic and Pauline passages about the Last Supper associate the eucharistic words of Jesus with the commemoration of his death ("Do this in memory of me"; "You proclaim the death of the Lord until he comes"). Jews might understand a meal that recalls or makes present again (by *anamnēsis*) a great salvific action of the past, for the Passover meal recalled the deliverance from Egypt. But John divorces the eucharist from the Last Supper context and interprets it as the food and drink that gives eternal life (6:51-58). Water baptism for John is a new birth or begetting which gives eternal life; eating the flesh and blood of Jesus nourishes that life. He has launched Christianity on the road to a distinctive sacramental theology whereby visible elements are signs communicating divine realities.

146. I am indebted for this reference to Robert L. Wilken.

147. C.K. Barrett, "Jews and Judaizers in the Epistles of Ignatius," in the Davies Festschrift (n. 40 above) 220-44, esp. 242. The eucharist was for Ignatius, as for John, the *flesh* and blood of Jesus, and also the medicine of immortality (*Eph.* 20:2), "that we should not die but live forever" (cf. John 6:58).

ses of Johannine theology brought about conflict between the Johannine Christians and such Jewish Christians earlier than it occurred elsewhere.[148]

Once again a few words on the relevance of this ancient struggle may be appropriate. When the charge of heresy is raised in Christian communities today, there is a tendency to associate that stigma with wild-eyed radicals proposing new ideas. In Christian history, however, some of the most significant heresies have been conservative rather than radical—the tendency to hold on to old theological answers when new questions have caused the main body of Christians to move on to new answers. The Jewish Christians, as we detect their presence in John and know their presence in the second century, were holding on to older and more primitive views on such subjects as christology, the eucharist, and relations to Judaism, views that were widely held early in the first century but were now no longer deemed to be adequate expressions of truth. At the Council of Nicaea (A.D. 325) the lower christology of Arius was more primitive than the higher christology of Athanasius. Arius was content with the scriptural formulations of Jesus' identity, e.g., "In the beginning was the Word," which meant for him that the Word had a beginning. Athanasius had to persuade the Council to accept newer, non-Scriptural formulas, e.g., true God of true God, coeternal with the Father. But he did this with insight: the Scripture answers were no longer adequate because now a question was being asked that had not been asked in NT times, and the new answers he proposed were true *to the direction* of the Scriptures. "Orthodoxy," then, is not always the possession of those who try to hold on to the past. One may find a

148. Second-century, non-gnostic Jewish Christians may have had a special loathing for Johannine thought. In the Pseudo-Clementine writings we hear the voice of a Jewish Christian community (presumably at Pella in the Transjordan) which honors James. In his study of them J.L. Martyn, "*Clementine Recognitions* 1, 33-71, Jewish Christianity, and the Fourth Gospel," in the Dahl Festschrift (n. 85 above), 265-95, states the possibility (288) "that the presence in the Fourth Gospel of polemics against Jewish Christians may in fact have caused the Gospel to be studiously avoided by Jewish Christians who lacked the connecting bridge of gnostic thought forms." This article is reprinted in Martyn's *The Gospel of John in Christian History* (New York: Paulist, 1979).

truer criterion in the direction toward which Christian thought has been tending, even if that direction suggests that past formulations of truth have to be considered inadequate to answer new questions.

Group VI. The Christians of Apostolic Churches

Distinct from the Johannine Christians themselves, still a third group of Christians may be detected. They are represented by Peter and other members of the Twelve (Andrew, Philip, Thomas, Judas-not-Iscariot, Nathanael[149]), and for that reason I call them "Apostolic." John would not have used that title, presumably, since he avoids the term "apostle";[150] but they may well have thought of themselves thus, for the idea of the Twelve Apostles was widespread in the last third of the first century.[151] The Johannine choice of Peter and the Twelve to represent a group of Christians suggests that this group was Jewish Christian in origin, but not necessarily still so in constituency.[152] Philip and Andrew are involved in the scene in 12:20ff where the Greeks come to Jesus, a scene which I have interpreted above (p. 55) as symbolic of an opening to the Gentiles.[153] Probably there was no important ethnic

---

149. I do not suggest that Nathanael is to be identified with anyone in the Synoptic lists of the Twelve, e.g., with Barnabas, as was done in times past. However, since the three Synoptics are not in agreement on who should be named among the Twelve (*JBC* art. 78, #171), Nathanael may have been counted in the never-given list of the Twelve accepted in Johannine tradition.

150. *Apostolos* appears only in the non-technical sense of "messenger" in 13:16. (If one would argue that it should be translated "apostle" there, then the verse becomes a "put-down" of apostles by Jesus: "No apostle is more important than the one who sent him.") The verb *apostellein*, "to send," appears in John interchangeably with *pempein*; but the sending is scarcely confined to those who are considered apostles in other NT documents (see n. 333 in Appendix II below).

151. Mark 3:14; Matt 10:2; Luke 6:13; Rev 21:14. See n. 162 below.

152. In Martyn's reconstruction (Appendix I below), he sees on the Johannine horizon various communities of *Jewish* Christians who had been expelled from the synagogues. Here he comes close to the groups for whom I am using an ethnically neutral designation.

153. Peter is remembered as the member of the Twelve most active in the admission of Gentiles to the church (Acts 10-11; Gal 2:9).

difference between the community of the Beloved Disciple and the communities represented in the Fourth Gospel by the Twelve. Both were mixed, Jewish and Gentile.

How do we know that John wishes to symbolize a special group of Christians by the figures of Peter and the Twelve? A prime indicator is found in 6:60-69 where two groups among Jesus' disciples are sharply contrasted. The first group consists of those who left the synagogue with him but then drew back over his claims that the bread of life was his flesh (and blood) which in turn was the nourishment of eternal life. They are representative of the Jewish Christian churches of inadequate faith, as we have just discussed. The other group consists of the Twelve (6:67) for whom Peter is the spokesman (6:68). They refuse to abandon Jesus: "Lord, to whom shall we go? It is you who have the words of eternal life." It is not illogical to conclude that we are hearing here the voice of Christians of a more adequate faith for whom Peter and the Twelve are appropriate symbols.

But how do we know that Peter and the Twelve do not stand for *all* Christians (outside the Crypto-Christians and the Jewish Christians of inadequate faith), rather than for a group of Christians distinct from the Johannine community? The key to that question is the consistent and deliberate contrast between Peter and the Beloved Disciple, the hero of the Johannine community.[154] In five of the six passages where he is mentioned, the Beloved Disciple is explicitly contrasted with Peter: in 13:23-26 the Beloved Disciple rests on Jesus' chest, while Peter has to signal to him for information; in 18:15-16 the Beloved Disciple can accompany Jesus into the high priest's palace, while Peter cannot enter without his help;[155] in 20:2-10 the Beloved Disciple outruns Peter to the tomb, and only he is said to believe on the basis of what he sees there; in

---

154. It is no accident that John speaks of this hero as a disciple, not as an apostle. Discipleship is the primary category for John; and closeness to Jesus, not apostolic mission, is what confers dignity.

155. In 18:15 John speaks simply of "another [*allos*] disciple" without further identification, while "the other [*ho allos*] disciple" of 20:2 is specifically identified as the Beloved Disciple. That 18:15 also refers to the Beloved Disciple is convincingly shown by F. Neirynck, *ETL* 51 (1975) 115-51. For the unnamed disciple of 1:35-40 see pp. 32-33 above.

21:7 the Beloved Disciple recognizes Jesus standing on the shore of the Sea of Tiberias and tells Peter who it is; in 21:20-23 when Peter jealously inquires about the Beloved Disciple's fate, he is told by Jesus, "Suppose I would like him to remain until I come, how does that concern you?" In a sixth passage (19:26-27), where the Beloved Disciple appears at the foot of the cross, the contrast is implicit: Peter is one of those who have scattered, abandoning Jesus (16:32). Such contrasts cannot be accidental, especially since in several scenes John seems to have added the Beloved Disciple to establish the contrast.[156] In counterposing their hero over against the most famous member of the Twelve, the Johannine community is symbolically counterposing itself over against the kinds of churches that venerate Peter and the Twelve[157]—the Apostolic Churches, whom other scholars call the "Great Church" (a term I prefer to hold for the church of the second century when the Apostolic Churches were bound more closely together by an increasingly common structure of episcopate and presbyterate in mutual recognition).

What is the Johannine attitude toward the Christianity of the Apostolic Christians? The scene mentioned in diagnosing their presence (6:60-69) suggests a fundamentally favorable attitude. The Apostolic Christians are clearly distinct from the Jewish Christians who no longer follow Jesus. The presence of the Twelve at the Last Supper (13:6; 14:5,8,22) means that the Apostolic Christians are included in Jesus' "own" whom he loves to the very end (13:1). Their forebears were among those who kept Jesus' word (17:6) and for whom he prayed (17:9,20) since they were hated by the world (17:14). They saw the Risen Lord (20:19,24;

---

156. The three Synoptic Gospels have Peter alone follow Jesus to the high priest's courtyard; and Luke 24:12 has Peter alone run to the tomb (yet see the plural in 24:24). This raises acutely the problem of historicity; see n. 42 above.

157. The Beloved Disciple was no less a real human being than was Simon Peter, but the Fourth Gospel uses each of them in a paradigmatic capacity. See D.J. Hawkin, "The Function of the Beloved Disciple Motif in the Johannine Redaction," *Laval Théologique Philosophique* 33 (1977) 135-50, esp. 146: "The Johannine *Einzelkirche* (the Beloved Disciple) has an equal claim to that of the *Gesamtkirche* (Peter).''

21:2); and their most prominent spokesman, Simon Peter, glorified God by his death in the following of Jesus (21:19).

Nevertheless, in the Fourth Gospel these named disciples do not seem to embody the fullness of Christian perception, as may be seen when the named disciples in general and Simon Peter in particular are compared with the Beloved Disciple. The others are scattered at the time of Jesus' passion, abandoning him (16:32), while the Beloved Disciple remains with Jesus even to the foot of the cross (19:26-27). Simon Peter denies that he is a disciple of Jesus (18:17,25), a particularly serious denial granted the Johannine emphasis on discipleship as the primary Christian category; and so he needs to be rehabilitated by Jesus who three times asks whether Peter loves him (21:15-17). No such rehabilitation is necessary and no such questioning is even conceivable in the case of the Disciple par excellence, the Disciple whom Jesus loved. Closer to Jesus both in life (13:23) and in death (19:26-27), the Beloved Disciple sees the significance of the garments left behind in the empty tomb when Peter does not (20:8-10); he also recognizes the risen Jesus when Peter does not (21:7). The Johannine Christians, represented by the Beloved Disciple, clearly regard themselves as closer to Jesus and more perceptive than the Christians of the Apostolic Churches.[158]

The one-upmanship of the Johannine Christians is centered on christology; for while the named disciples, representing the Apostolic Christians, have a reasonably high christology, they do not reach the heights of the Johannine understanding of Jesus. Andrew, Peter, Philip, and Nathanael know that Jesus is the Messiah, the fulfiller of the Law, the Holy One of God, and the Son of God (1:41,45,49; 6:69);[159] but they are told that they are yet to see

---

158. Cullmann, *Johannine Circle* (n. 318 in Appendix I below) 55: "Its members were probably aware of the difference which separated them from the church going back to the Twelve and also saw that their particular characteristics laid upon them the obligation of a special mission, namely to preserve, defend and hand on the distinctive tradition which they were sure had come down from Jesus himself."

159. Since I think that the figure who *became* the Beloved Disciple was the unnamed disciple of 1:35-40, I find no difficulty in using 1:35-50 to

greater things (1:50). As Jesus says to Philip at the Last Supper, "Here I am with you all this time and you still do not know me?" (14:9)—a rebuke precisely because Philip does not understand the oneness of Jesus with the Father.[160] When later on the disciples make the claim, "We believe that you came forth from God," Jesus' skepticism is obvious: "So now you believe? Why, an hour is coming, and indeed already has come, for you to be scattered, each on his own, leaving me all alone" (16:29-32). Even after the resurrection, the scene with Thomas indicates that the faith of the Twelve can stand improvement (20:24-29). In fact, Thomas' delayed confession of Jesus as "My Lord and my God" may be paradigmatic of the fuller understanding of Jesus' divinity to which, John hopes, the Apostolic Christians may ultimately be brought.

We may make an informed guess that the precise aspect of christology missing in the faith of the Apostolic Christians is the perception of the pre-existence of Jesus and of his origins from above. Both Apostolic and Johannine Christians say that Jesus is God's Son; yet Johannine Christians have come to understand that this means that he is ever at the Father's side (1:18), not belonging to this world (17:14), but to a heavenly world above (3:13,31). Once again the christology I attribute to the Apostolic Christians is not a pure hypothesis based on an interpretative reading of the Fourth Gospel. From the Gospels of Matthew and Luke we know of late-first-century Christians who acknowledged Jesus as the Son of God through conception without a human father; but in whose high christology there is no hint of pre-existence. They know a Jesus who is king, lord, and savior from the moment of his birth at

---

detect the christology both of Apostolic Christians and of the *original* Johannine community. However, as I explained on pp. 43-47 above, the Johannine community (and the Beloved Disciple) moved beyond this christology by accepting into their midst another group of anti-Temple Jews and Samaritans who catalyzed a higher, non-Davidic christology.

160. M. de Jonge, "Jesus as Prophet and King in the Fourth Gospel," *ETL* 49 (1973) 162: "Jesus' kingship and his prophetic mission are both redefined in terms of the unique relationship between Son and Father, as portrayed in the Fourth Gospel." This redefinition constitutes the difference between Apostolic and Johannine Christians.

Bethlehem, but not a Jesus who says, "Before Abraham even came into existence, I AM."[161]

A difference in ecclesiology may also have separated Johannine Christians from Apostolic Christians. The same NT works of the late first century, Matthew and Luke/Acts, show that continuity with Peter and the Twelve was becoming an important factor in church identity and self-security.[162] The Fourth Gospel, however, gives virtually no attention to the category of "apostle" (n. 150 above) and makes "disciple" the primary Christian category, so that continuity with Jesus comes through the witness of the Beloved *Disciple* (19:35; 21:24).[163] Furthermore, Matthew, Luke/Acts, and the Pastorals all testify to the increasing institutionalization of churches toward the end of the century, with a

---

161. John's lack of interest in Jesus' Davidic origins and birth at Bethlehem, as reflected in the debates with the Jews (7:41-42), may constitute a correction of the kind of christology we find in Matthew and Luke, a christology which (in John's eyes) puts too much emphasis on a matter of Jewish concern. Similarly John's exaltation of Jesus on the cross relativizes the importance of resurrection appearances and so implicitly corrects a christology which associates divine sonship with the resurrection (Acts 2:32, 36; 5:31; 13:33; the pre-Pauline formula of Rom 1:4). As M. de Jonge points out (*NTS* 19 [1972-73] 264), in the debates described in the Fourth Gospel, "Johannine christology is developed not only in contrast with Jewish thinking but also with other christological views."

162. Matthew (16:18) thinks of a church built upon Peter in which Peter and the Twelve have the power to bind and to loose (16:19; 18:18). Acts describes the Twelve at the origins of the Christian movement, approving every major step taken. In this discussion of "Christians of Apostolic Churches" I am not dealing with Pauline Christianity, precisely because Peter and the Twelve would not have served the Pauline churches as primary apostolic models. (For differences between Pauline and Johannine christology, see p. 45 above.) C.K. Barrett, "Acts and the Pauline Corpus," *Exp Tim* 88 (1976-77) 2-5, shows that different kinds of Gentile Christianity may be detected from reading Acts and Paul, and that Peter and Paul would have been followed by different groups of Christians.

163. C.K. Barrett, *The Gospel of John and Judaism* (Philadelphia: Fortress, 1975) 75, following Edwyn Hoskyns, catches the paradoxical Johannine attitude well: "John intended to bind the church to apostolic witness; but in other respects he meant to leave it free." John gives prominence to women disciples to the point that they seem to be on the same level as members of the Twelve; see Appendix II below.

developing interest in ecclesiastical offices. On the one hand, I oppose the assumption by E. Schweizer and others that the Johannine community had no special ecclesiastical ministries (n. 16 above)—we simply do not know that, and there are contrary indications in the Johannine Epistles. On the other hand, there is much in Johannine theology that would relativize the importance of institution and office at the very time when that importance was being accentuated in other Christian communities (including those who spoke of apostolic foundation). Unlike Paul's image of the body and its members which is invoked in I Cor 12 to accommodate the multitude of charisms, the Johannine image of the vine and branches places emphasis on only one issue: dwelling on the vine or inherence in Jesus.[164] (If John was interested in diversity of charism, he could have written of branches, twigs, leaves, and fruit, even as Paul wrote symbolically of foot, hand, ear, and eye.) The category of discipleship based on love makes any other distinction in the Johannine community relatively unimportant, so that even the well-known Petrine and presbyteral image of the shepherd[165] is not introduced without the conditioning question, "Do you love me?" (21:15-17).

The greatest of the named apostles in the NT, Peter, Paul, and James of Jerusalem, all died in the 60s; and afterwards the churches which invoked their names solved the teaching gap that resulted from these deaths by stressing that the officials who succeeded the apostles should hold on to what they were taught without change (Acts 20:28-30; Titus 1:9; II Pet 1:12-21). But the Fourth Gospel, which knows of the problem of the death of the Beloved Disciple (21:20-23), stresses that the teacher is the Paraclete who remains forever within everyone who loves Jesus and keeps his commandments (14:15-17); he is the guide to all truth (16:13).[166]

---

164. J. O'Grady, "Individualism and Johannine Ecclesiology," *BTB* 5 (1975) 227-61, esp. 243: "As with the flock, the point of interest [in the vine and the branches imagery] is the relationship between Jesus and the individual believer." Yet a community is presumed by such a collective image.

165. Acts 20:28; I Pet 5:1-5; Matt 18:12-14.

166. For the Paraclete as the Johannine answer to the problems

Finally, unlike Matt 28:19 and Luke 22:19, John has no words of Jesus commanding or instituting baptism and the eucharist just before he left this earth. The image of Jesus instituting sacraments as a final action tends to identify them with the sphere of church life, while for John the sacraments are continuations of the power that Jesus manifested *during his ministry* when he opened the eyes of the blind (baptism as enlightenment) and fed the hungry (eucharist as food).[167] In summary, let me stress that I do not interpret these Johannine ecclesiological attitudes as aggressively polemic, for there is no clear evidence that the Johannine community was condemning apostolic foundation and succession, church offices, or church sacramental practices. The Fourth Gospel is best interpreted as voicing a warning against the dangers inherent in such developments by stressing what (for John) is truly essential,[168] namely, the living presence of Jesus in the Christian through the Paraclete. No institution or structure can substitute for that. This outlook and emphasis would give Johannine ecclesiology a different tone from that of the Apostolic Christians known to us from other late first-century NT writings—a Johannine ecclesiology the peculiarity of which reflects the peculiarity of Johannine christology.

WAS THE JOHANNINE COMMUNITY A SECT?

A seventh group can be detected in the Gospel, the Johannine community itself. By contrasting this group with other groups, I

---

raised by the death of the first generation of Jesus' followers who had been community founders, see my AB commentary, II, 1142. Also below pp. 139-40.

167. For this approach to Johannine sacramentalism, see my AB commentary, I, CXIV. Cullmann, *Johannine Circle* (n. 318 below in Appendix I) 14: "In each individual event of the life of the *incarnate* Jesus the Evangelist seeks to show that *at the same time* the *Christ present in his Church* is already at work."

168. O'Grady, "Individualism" (n. 164 above) 254: "It may very well be true that the Johannine community and its spokesman saw its contribution to early Christianity mainly as emphasizing purpose and meaning as the Church found itself in need of structure, organization and ritual expression." See also the balanced treatment by O'Grady, "Johannine Ecclesiology: A Critical Evaluation," *BTB* 7 (1977) 36-44.

have already delineated much of what was unique about the Johannine Christians. But there remains the question which I posed in the Introduction to this book: Did the Johannine Christians constitute a sect, which had broken communion (*koinōnia*) with most other Christians? In answering this, let us recall the Johannine relationships with some of the groups already discussed. The Johannine Christians were not the only Christians hostile to the synagogue and its leaders (Group II: "The Jews"),[169] even though the bitterness attested in John may be more acute than in other NT works. The sectarian element in the Johannine picture would be the peculiar sense of estrangement from one's own people (1:11). As for the attitude of the Johannine Christians toward the Crypto-Christians (Group IV) and the Jewish Christians (Group V), once more they were not the only NT Christians to condemn other Christians as false.[170] But, more than others, John's community may have moved toward clearly excluding their opponents from Christian fellowship, e.g., by counting the Crypto-Christians as aligned with "the Jews" (12:42-43) and by charging that the Jewish Christians who were associated with the brothers of the Lord followed Jesus no longer and did not really believe in him (6:66; 7:5).

Besides these specific rejections of Groups II, IV, and V, there is much that is sectarian in John's sense of alienation and superiority. As we saw, the Johannine Jesus is a stranger who is not understood by his own people and is not even of this world. The Beloved Disciple, the hero of the community, is singled out as the peculiar object of Jesus' love and is the only male disciple never to have abandoned Jesus. Implicitly then, the Johannine Christians are those who understand Jesus best, for like him they are rejected, persecuted, and not of this world. Their christology is more profound, and they can be sure that they have the truth because they are guided by the Paraclete. To some extent even the literary style of the Fourth Gospel reflects Johannine peculiarity, with its

---

169. See n. 65 above for Paul's attitude. The attitude toward the Pharisees in Matt 23 is very hostile.

170. The fear in Acts 20:30 is almost typical among Christians in the last third of the century: "There will arise from your own ranks people who speak perversity to mislead disciples after them."

abstract symbolism (life, light, truth) and its technique of misunderstanding (see pp. 61-62 above).

Nevertheless, despite all these tendencies toward sectarianism, I would contend that the Johannine attitude toward the
Apostolic Christians (Group VI—probably a large group of
Christians in many areas) proves that the Johannine community,
as reflected in the Fourth Gospel, had not really become a sect.
They had not followed their exclusivistic tendencies to the point
of breaking communion (*koinōnia*) with these Christians whose
characteristics are found in many NT works of the late first century. If we can judge from the presence of Simon Peter and the
other named disciples at the Last Supper, the Johannine Christians
looked on the Apostolic Christians as belonging to Jesus' own to
whom they were bound by the commandment: "As I have loved
you, so must you love one another" (13:34). Their hopes for the
future may be expressed by 10.16, if that verse is a reference to the
Apostolic Christians, as J. L. Martyn[171] has argued: "I have other
sheep, too, that do not belong to this fold. These also must I lead,
and they will listen to my voice. Then there will be one sheep herd,
one shepherd." Even more probable is the suggestion that at the
Last Supper (where Simon Peter and the Beloved Disciple are both
present), when Jesus prays for those who believe in him through
the word of his disciples, "That they all may be one" (17:20-21),
he is praying for the oneness of the Apostolic and the Johannine
Christians. Here the Johannine attitude is just the opposite of the
outlook of a sect.

Ah, one may object, the Johannine prayer for unity with the
Apostolic Christians carried a price tag—those other Christians
would have to accept the exalted Johannine christology of preexistence if there was to be one sheep herd, one flock. If this did
not happen, one may argue, the Johannine Christians would reject
the Apostolic Christians from *koinōnia* even as they had previously rejected the Jewish Christians. Yet we are spared discussing
that theoretical possibility, for in fact the larger church did adopt
Johannine pre-existence christology, as we shall see in the next
chapter. Some scholars may ponder on the luck of the Beloved

---

171. "Glimpses" (n. 316 below in Appendix I) 171-72.

Disciple that his community's Gospel was not recognized for the sectarian tractate that it really was. But others among us will see this as a recognition by Apostolic Christians that the Johannine language was not really a riddle and the Johannine voice was not alien—a recognition facilitated by strains of pre-existence christology among non-Johannine communities.[172] What the Johannine Christians considered to be a tradition that had come down from Jesus seems to have been accepted by many other Christians as an embraceable variant of the tradition that they had from Jesus.

---

172. See pp. 45-46 above for pre-existence motifs in Paul and in Hebrews.

PHASE THREE:
WHEN THE EPISTLES WERE
WRITTEN
Johannine Internal Struggles

The story of the community of the Beloved Disciple is continued after the Gospel period in the Epistles. Let me begin by a summary description of the Epistles and the reasons for dating them after the Gospel.

The Second and Third Epistles of John are one-page letters written by the same man, who calls himself "the presbyter." In II John, while he is associated with one church (v. 13),[173] he writes directions to another church (v. 1: "the Elect Lady and her children") about the exclusion of people who may arrive denying that Jesus Christ has come in the flesh (vv. 7,10-11). In III John, the presbyter writes to Gaius praising him for the hospitality that he has shown to traveling missionaries (vv. 1,5-8) and telling him to receive Demetrius who is about to come (v. 12). The reason for the presbyter's addressing himself to Gaius is that his previous letter to "the church" (v. 9) had been ignored by Diotrephes who likes to be a church leader. In fact, Diotrephes refuses to welcome any missionaries and is expelling from the church anyone who does (v.

---

173. The term "church" is justified by its usage in III John 6,9,10.

10b). In both letters the presbyter promises to visit soon; but in III John he warns that, if he comes, he will bring up the matter of Diotrephes' hostility toward him (v. 10a).

The author of the First Epistle of John never identifies himself, and his work is more of a tractate than a personal note. His dominant concern is to reinforce the readers against a group that is doing the work of the devil and the antichrist (2:18; 4:1-6), a group that has seceded from the community (2:19) but is still trying to win over more adherents. Their errors are both christological and ethical. By not acknowledging Jesus Christ come in the flesh, they negate the importance of Jesus (4:2-3); and although they claim communion with God, they do not see any importance in keeping commandments and pretend to be free from the guilt of sin (1:6,8; 2:4). In particular, they do not show love for the brethren (2:9-11; 3:10-24; 4:7-21).[174]

This brief description of the Epistles leaves obvious questions. Is the presbyter of II and III John also the author of I John? What is the chronological order of the Epistles, and how are they related to the Gospel? What was the history of the secession? Every commentator debates these points, and in my own forthcoming commentary on the Johannine Epistles[175] I shall give detailed arguments for the positions that I adopt here.

I am going to assume that all three Epistles were written by one man whom I shall call interchangeably the author and the presbyter.[176] The fact that the same doctrinal and moral issues are being combatted in I and in II John and that both II and III John are concerned with the acceptance of traveling teachers interlocks the Epistles and makes it likely that all three have come from the same

---

174. The First Epistle stresses love heavily in order to reinforce inner community adhesion against conversion by the secessionists.

175. Volume 30 in the Anchor Bible (Garden City, N.Y.: Doubleday, 1981), in sequel to the two volumes of Gospel commentary already published (n. 12 above). All references in this chapter continue to be to the Gospel commentary.

176. It would not affect my interpretations greatly if the presbyter of II-III John were distinct from, but a close companion to, the author of I John.

phase of Johannine history.[177] As for the author, it is reasonably
certain that he was not the Beloved Disciple.[178] "The presbyter"
would be an unexpected self-designation for the Beloved Disciple;
and one can scarcely imagine members of the Johannine community ignoring their founding figure to the extent to which the secessionists ignore the author of I John, and Diotrephes ignores the
letters of the presbyter. While there are major stylistic and theological similarities between the Gospel and the Epistles, there are also
minor differences which make it dubious that the author of the
Epistles was the evangelist (i.e., the main writer of the Gospel). A
more popular thesis has been to identify the author with the redactor of the Gospel. Obviously the proof for that contention depends
on what parts of the Gospel one attributes to the redactor.[179] In
those most often attributed (Prologue, chap. 21) I do not find the
sharp internal conflict motif that marks the Epistles;[180] and so I
would say that, if the same man was involved, the respective

---

177. As will become apparent, I think III John was the last to be
written. It is usually assumed that II John was written to a church not yet
infested by the secessionists who had already divided the community of I
John. However, Langbrandtner, *Weltferner Gott* (n. 322 below in Appendix I), thinks that II John was written when the signs of trouble were just
appearing, and then I John after the trouble had developed.

178. It will be remembered that I do not think that the Beloved
Disciple wrote the Gospel either. Thyen, "Entwicklungen" (n. 41 above),
identifies the presbyter and the Beloved Disciple, but only at the price of
denying that the latter is the founder of the community or an eyewitness of
the ministry of Jesus.

179. For instance, while many attribute chaps. 15, 16, and 17 to the
redactor, J. Becker in several articles devoted to the Last Discourse
(*ZNW* 60 [1969] 56-83; 61 [1970] 215-46) finds evidence for three or more
different theological views and writers in these chapters. Similarities in
theme between the Last Discourse and I John do not prove identity of
author—the Last Discourse concerns Jesus' relation to "his own" and so
is closer in subject matter to the Epistles than is any other section of the
Gospel, without, however, the element of strife that marks the Epistles'
treatment of Johannine life.

180. I do not think that John 1:14, "And the Word became flesh," is
markedly anti-docetic, as some would argue (see n. 215 below). There is a
greater possibility that chap. 21 may have some internal reference; see
pp. 161-62 below.

writing was done at different periods in his life.[181] It is just as possible that the author of the Epistles was neither the evangelist nor the redactor but was one of the minor contributors to the Gospel or was not involved in writing the Gospel at all. Below I shall develop the thesis of a Johannine school of writers who shared a theological position and style, to which the evangelist, the redactor, and the author of the Epistles all belonged.

A more important question for our purpose is the relative chronology of the Gospel and the Epistles. Some have pointed to the presence of early-Christian motifs in the Epistles which are not prominent in the Gospel (final eschatology, stress on the humanity of Jesus, sacrificial quality of his death, etc.) and have argued for an early date for the Epistles. Similarly, the "Jewish" features of the Epistles (verbal parallels to the Dead Sea Scrolls; use of categories like false prophets, antichrists, idolatry) have contributed to an argument that the Epistles were addressed to Greek-speaking Jewish Christians[182]—despite the three Greco-Roman personal names in III John (Gaius, Diotrephes, Demetrius). Such conclusions reflect the fallacy of dating the composition of a work by its earliest strata of thought and vocabulary. I agree thoroughly that there are both early and Jewish motifs in I John; but that is because the author, in order to correct his opponents, professedly emphasizes what was proclaimed "from the beginning" (1:1). Such evidence tells us only that the Johannine tradition had earlier forms and arose among Jewish Christians; it tells us nothing about when and for whom the Epistles were written. Another argument for dating the Epistles before the Gospel is that I John ignores some of the higher christological stresses of the Gospel and plays down the role of the Spirit-Paraclete. This is true but again it tells us nothing about dating. The opponents of I John, as we shall see, have

---

181. I do not see much indication of internal strife in the redactor's view of Johannine community life; but even Langbrandtner (who does— see Appendix I below) recognizes that a schism takes place between the time of the redaction and that of the Epistles and that the seriousness of the situation is greatly advanced in the Epistles.

182. J.A.T. Robinson, "The Destination and Purpose of the Johannine Epistles," *NTS* 7 (1960-61) 56-65. See my remarks in n. 30 above about Robinson's methodology.

concentrated on the high christology of the Johannine tradition and are defending their (exaggerated) christology by appealing to the Spirit who teaches; and so it is quite understandable that the author does not emphasize elements which favor his opponents. Again it is claimed that the Prologue of I John (1:1-4) is not as advanced as the Prologue of John. I would claim that the opponents are making much of the pre-existence motif of the hymn that we call the Gospel Prologue, and so the Epistle's Prologue is meant almost as a corrective to be read alongside the community hymn to prevent misinterpretation of it.

The really decisive issue in the question of dating is that, while the Gospel reflects the Johannine community's dealings with outsiders, the Epistles are concerned with insiders. The secessionists now stand for the world (I John 4:5); and they, rather than "the Jews," arc castigated as children of the devil (3:10). If the Epistles were written before the Gospel, it would have been an already divided and decimated Johannine community that was struggling with the outsiders when the Gospel was written; and we get no indication of that. On the other hand, I shall try to show that it is precisely the message enshrined in the Gospel which has led to the split of the community because two groups interpreted it in different ways. Psychologically it is easy to explain why the struggle with outsiders has disappeared from view in the Epistles; for, when a community splits sharply within, that quickly becomes the primary battle for survival. Therefore, it seems best to work with the hypothesis that the Epistles were written after the situation envisaged by the evangelist in the Gospel. If the latter's work is dated *ca.* A.D. 90, the Epistles might be dated *ca.* A.D. 100, midway between the Gospel and the writings of Ignatius of Antioch (*ca.* A.D. 110), who will figure importantly in our discussions.

THE LIFE-SITUATION ENVISAGED IN THE EPISTLES

I shall discuss here three aspects of Johannine community life and history presupposed by the Epistles: (A) Its geographical spread into different churches; (B) The teaching role played by the Johannine school; (C) The nature of the division that had taken place between the author and the secessionists.

A. The Johannine Churches

The Second and Third Epistles of John are written to different churches at a distance from the author (who intends to visit them), and so we know that the Johannine community was not all in one geographical place. Different cities or towns must have been involved.[183] And since this was the period when Christian communities met in house churches that could not have held very many members, in a given town or city there may have been several house churches of Johannine Christians.[184] It is a serious possibility, then, that the Gaius and Diotrephes of III John, although living in the same town, belonged to different Johannine churches,[185] and that the presbyter was trying to obtain hospitality for his emissaries in one church after having been turned down by the head of another. The general geographic area can scarcely have been a "backwater", for the Gospel would cause us to think that in the same region there were non-Johannine churches (Jewish Christians, Apostolic Christians), as well as synagogues and some followers of JBap.

Much of this evidence could be explained if there were a large metropolitan center (Ephesus?) with many house churches of Johannine Christians to which I John was primarily addressed; and within reasonable traveling range there were also provincial towns with Johannine churches to which II and III John were addressed.[186] I posit a traveling range because of the journeys men-

---

183. Christianity was an urban phenomenon until its spread into the countryside in the second century. See A. Malherbe, *Social Aspects* (n. 114 above) 63.

184. Paul seems to envisage a number of house churches in the Roman community (Rom 16:5,14,15) and perhaps in Thessalonica as well (I Thess 5:27). This topic is treated in chap. 3 of Malherbe's *Social Aspects* 60-91; and by P. Stuhlmacher, *Die Brief an Philemon* (EKK; Zurich: Benzinger, 1975) 70-75.

185. A. Malherbe, "The Inhospitality of Diotrephes," in the Dahl Festschrift (n. 85 above) 222-32, esp. 226-27. Notice that Gaius has to be informed about what Diotrephes is doing.

186. So also R. Schnackenburg, "Die johanneische Gemeinde und ihre Geisterfahrung," in *Die Kirche des Anfangs* (H. Schürmann Festschrift; ed. R. Schnackenburg *et al.*; Leipzig: St. Benno, 1977) 277-

tioned in III John for which financial help is asked. The struggle between the author and the secessionists would have taken place in the large center, so that I John was meant to reinforce those loyal to the author there.[187] Evidently the secessionists began trying to win over the provincial communities as well; and so the author sent II John to one such community,[188] warning it of dangerous missionaries teaching false ideas. I shall hypothesize that in another town Diotrephes had decided that he wanted emissaries neither from the author nor from his opponents; and so III John was sent to another house church in the same town to gain hospitality for the author's emissaries.

B. The Johannine School

What was the function in these churches of the author who calls himself "the presbyter"?[189] By the end of the first century in many areas there was developing a church structure in which groups of "presbyters" were responsible for the administration

306, esp. 281. He suggests that we should use the term "Johannine community" for the group in the large center, and "Johannine Christianity" for the whole complexus, including the provincial towns.

187. Eventually he may have sent copies of it to the communities in the provincial towns when they were affected by secession. What is excluded is the thesis of W. G. Kümmel, *Introduction to the New Testament* (rev. ed.; Nashville: Abingdon, 1975) 437, that specific persons may not have been addressed in I John, and that it may have been a tractate meant for the whole of Christianity. The whole history of the Johannine community and its literature points to a very specific situation, even though the issues have wider import. Better balanced is the view of E. C. Hoskyns, *The Fourth Gospel* (ed. F.N. Davey; 2d ed.; London: Faber & Faber, 1947) 55: "Thus in his concern with one particular group of Christians, he enunciates the ultimate truths of the relation between God and man. . . . It is a Catholic Epistle even though written for certain Greek-speaking Christians."

188. Notice his delicate handling of this other Johannine church: "To the Elect Lady and her children."

189. "Elder" is another translation of *presbyteros*, a term which simply means "older man," although it has connotations of dignity and experience as well. Seemingly, an interchangeable designation for *presbyteros* was *episkopos*, variously translated as "overseer, superintendent, bishop."

and pastoral care of a church.[190] That the author of II-III John was just one of a group of presbyters responsible for the pastoral care of the Johannine community in the main city does not adequately explain his self-designation as "*the* presbyter," nor his dominant role in the battle against the secessionists, nor how he could be interfering in churches other than his own which presumably had their own presbyters. An attempt has been made to answer these objections by claiming that he was "*the* most important presbyter in a regional network of churches."[191] However, that would presuppose almost a "single bishop" model of church structure— indeed a single archbishop. We do not have that model attested elsewhere in the NT or before the second century, and I would hesitate to posit its earliest development in a community that otherwise seems to pay little attention to defined structure. The fact that, as we shall see, "the presbyter" cannot really discipline his opponents is a fatal objection to this theory, in my opinion.

To explain the title in the Epistles, another use of *presbyteros* has been invoked, as attested in different second-century forms in Papias and Irenaeus.[192] The term can be used to designate the generation of teachers *after* the eyewitnesses—people who could teach in a chain of authority because they had seen and heard others who, in turn, had seen and heard Jesus.[193] Any such concept of authoritative teacher in the Johannine tradition would have

---

190. Attested in Acts 14:23; 20:17,28-30; I Pet 5:1; Jas 5:14; I Tim 3:1-7; 5:17-22; Titus 1:5-11; *I Clem.* 44; *Did.* 15:1 (bishops). For a description of the situation, see my *Priest and Bishop: Biblical Reflections* (New York: Paulist, 1970) 34-40, 63-73.

191. K.P. Donfried, "Ecclesiastical Authority in 2-3 John," in *L'Evangile de Jean* (n. 41 above) 325-33, esp. 328.

192. W.C. van Unnik, "The Authority of the Presbyters in Irenaeus' Works," in the Dahl Festschrift (n. 85 above) 248-60. While the position of Irenaeus is clear, that of Papias is less so, as pointed out by J. Munck, "Presbyters and Disciples of the Lord in Papias," *HTR* 52 (1959) 223-43; nevertheless, even for Papias the presbyters are authoritative teachers.

193. This role of presbyters is not necessarily contradictory to the first role discussed above as pastors, for I Tim 5:17 would give double honor to a presbyter who labors in preaching and teaching. The term may have shifted in meaning, and the administrative, pastoral role may have been a secondary development.

a sharply modified nuance, however, since the Paraclete, the Holy Spirit, is the teacher par excellence (John 14:26; 16:13). The human teacher, even the Beloved Disciple himself, could serve only as the one who testifies to the tradition which the Paraclete interprets (19:35; 21:24; I John 2:27). Probably, in fact, the Johannine community learned existentially of the Paraclete through the work of the Beloved Disciple because the Paraclete was the moving Spirit behind the interpretation of the tradition as passed on by the Beloved Disciple. After the death of the Beloved Disciple, the community understood that the work of the Paraclete continued in the disciples of the Beloved Disciple who passed on the tradition and helped to formulate it.[194]

This second sense of *presbyteros*, modified by the Johannine optic, could explain why the presbyter of the Johannine Epistles speaks as part of a collective "we" who bear witness to what was seen and heard from the beginning (I John 1:1-2); and this brings us into the whole issue of "the Johannine school." Recently R. A. Culpepper has studied the term "school" as employed for other groups in antiquity (Pythagoreans, Plato's Academy, Aristotle's Lyceum, Essenes, etc.), and he has developed a set of characteristics appropriate to the term—characteristics which are met in the Johannine situation.[195] In fact, Culpepper wishes to extend the term "school" to the whole of what we have been calling the Johannine community, where all share the tradition that came from the Beloved Disciple and all bear witness (John 15:27). I recognize that there is a Johannine communality of discipleship that gives support to Culpepper's position.[196] That is why when the

194. See H. Schlier, "Der Heilige Geist als Interpret nach dem Johannesevangelium," *Internationale Katholische Zeitschrift* 2 (1973) 97-108. Also Culpepper, *Johannine School* (n. 9 above) 265-70.

195. *Ibid.*, 258-59, 288-89. The criteria include groups of disciples tracing their origins to a founder and preserving his teaching, with rules and practices concerning membership and continuity.

196. *Ibid.*, 274-75. Culpepper stresses the importance of the community setting in the composition of the Gospel. I think, however, he goes too far in making the community the author of the Gospel. The evangelist was a remarkably gifted thinker and dramatist. It is he who was the author, not the community, whence the need to distinguish between school and community.

author of the Epistles uses "we," many times he is including his
readers on an equal level—they are his "brothers" (a designation
which occurs fifteen times in I John). However, there are other
times when his "we" represents tradition-bearers and interpreters
who are distinct from a "you" that is addressed (I John 1:1-5)—
those addressed are the author's "little children" (a designation
that occurs seven times in I John). Despite a sincere Johannine
effort at a democracy of discipleship,[197] inevitably some would
have been closer historically to the Beloved Disciple, even as some
were more active in writing and bearing witness. It is for this group
that I reserve the term "Johannine school" within the wider
"Johannine community." In particular, I use it for those who felt so
close to the Beloved Disciple that they sought to pass on his
tradition through written interpretation. These include the
evangelist, the redactor of the Gospel (and any other writers involved in it), the author of the Epistles, and the tradition-bearers
with whom they associated themselves in their writing—in short,
the "we" of John 21:24 ("We know his testimony is true") and of I
John 1:1-2 ("What we have heard . . . we proclaim to you").

It is as a long-lived representative of such a Johannine school
that "the presbyter" speaks. He can say "what was from the
beginning . . . we have heard . . . seen with our own eyes . . .
looked at . . . felt with our own hands," not because he was an
eyewitness himself, but because of the closeness of the Johannine
school of disciples to the Beloved Disciple. In a chain reaction,
Jesus has seen God; the Beloved Disciple has seen Jesus; and the
Johannine school shares in his tradition.[198] At the time when the
Gospel was written the testimony of the Beloved Disciple was
sufficient,[199] and the community was united in accepting that

---

197. See P. Moreno Jiménez, "El discípulo de Jesu Cristo según el
evangelio de S. Juan," *Est Bib* 30 (1971) 269-311.

198. M. de Jonge, *Jesus* (n. 24 above) 205: "The *pluralis apostolicus*
passes over into the *pluralis ecclesiasticus*, and the *pluralis ecclesiasticus*
is inconceivable without the *pluralis apostolicus*."

199. Notice 19:35 and especially 21:24: "It is this same disciple who
is the witness for these things; it is *he who wrote these things*; and his
testimony, we know, is true." Most scholars think that the Beloved Disciple did *not write* the Gospel any more than the author of the Epistle

testimony over against outsiders. But, as we are now about to see, when the Epistles were written, *both* sides claimed to be interpreting the tradition of the Beloved Disciple; and so the presbyter tries to correct his adversaries by speaking as part of a Johannine school of disciples who really know the mind of the Beloved Disciple and therefore are witnesses to "what was from the beginning" (I John 1:1).

C. The Intra-Johannine Schism

The author of the First Epistle says that a group has gone out from the ranks of his community (2:19). Who are they? Before I seek to answer that question, I remind the reader that we are looking at them from the author's point of view when we call them adversaries, secessionists, or schismatics.[200] If their writings had been preserved, I suspect that they would have claimed that the author and his group went out from *their* ranks; and in point of fact, I John 4:5 hints that ultimately they may have become the larger group of Johannine Christians.

Our only knowledge of them is derived from the assumption that they held the opinions against which the author of I John argues,[201] and such a mirror-image approach has many perils. For

---

touched Jesus with his own hands (I John 1:1: "What we felt with our own hands"). However, vicariously the experience of the Beloved Disciple is the experience of the disciples of his school (the Beloved Disciple did touch Jesus); and what they do, he does (one of them did write the Gospel). See the quotation from Moody Smith related to n. 43 above.

200. One must interpret carefully the whole of 2:19: "It was from our ranks that they went out—not that they really belonged to us; for if they had belonged to us, they would have remained with us." This does not imply that they were recent converts who apostatized. Rather, it reflects John's attitude toward divine choice: the good and bad already exist when the light comes into the world, and the proclamation of Jesus' revelation simply reveals what people already are. The leaving of the secessionists shows a secret orientation that they had long before.

201. I am rejecting the theory that the author drew the statements with which he disagreed from an earlier written source (so von Dobschütz, Bultmann, H. Braun)—a theory with little following today. Those who hold this theory dispute whether the source was gnostic (Bultmann),

instance, it is uncertain that every idea that the author opposes in the Epistle is accepted by the secessionists. The author may be using the Epistle to correct wrong ideas no matter who held them. Nevertheless, it is a working hypothesis to separate the statements against which the author directly polemicizes[202] and to see whether, taken together, they present a consistent body of thought. It is my contention that they do, and in the pages that follow I shall reconstruct the christology, the ethical stance, the eschatology, and the pneumatology (i.e., doctrine of the Spirit) of the Johannine secessionists seen through the eyes of the author of I John. Presumably the disputes that caused the secession led the adversaries to shape lapidary statements expressive of their thought. The author has gathered these statements almost as slogans and used them in his rebuttal. Such an adversary procedure has inevitably hardened and presented without nuance the theology of the secessionists. Therefore, in presenting their views I shall seek to show that they were not without logic and a certain persuasiveness, *given their presuppositions*. I do this not out of any personal sympathy for their position as I reconstruct it, but so that the reader can see the inner motivations of Johannine thought on both sides of the battle line in this civil war.

But what were the presuppositions of the secessionists? What catalyzed the theological division that we find so sharply etched in I John? In many attempts to sketch a background that would explain secessionist theology there is posited an outside influence which led to their deviation from the true Johannine Gospel. Also it has been fashionable to identify the secessionists with some known second-century heretical movement,[203] e.g., gnosticism. Of

moderately gnostic (H. Braun), or relatively "orthodox" with the author as the gnosticizer (von Dobschütz). Kümmel, *Introduction* (n. 187 above) 439-40, makes eminent sense: "The supposition that there was a *Vorlage* [source] is therefore unproved and improbable. . . . I John in the form in which we have it is the work of a single author."

202. This is done competently by J. Bogart, *Orthodox and Heretical Perfectionism in the Johannine Community as Evident in the First Epistle of John* (SBLDS 33; Missoula: Scholars Press, 1977) 126-31.

203. "Heretical" (or heterodox) as judged by writers like Irenaeus whose position prevailed in the church—we need not think that these movements understood themselves as departing from orthodoxy. Let me

course, no one denies that the reconstructed thought of the opponents of I John has certain similarities to gnostic thought known to us in the second century.[204] But did the secessionist movement become gnostic after the schism, or did gnostic intruders influence secessionist theology before the schism? Recently, K. Weiss[205] has pointed out that some of the most characteristic marks of the gnostic systems are conspicuously absent in the thought of the secessionists, which, in fact, contains features opposed by later gnostics. A refinement of the gnostic theory is that the secessionists were docetists who denied the reality of Jesus' humanity. Cerinthus has been proposed as their leader on the basis of late second-century traditions that he was the enemy of John, son of Zebedee. We shall discuss these suggestions in more detail below (under christology), but I would stress here that reconstructed secessionist thought does not fit exactly either docetist or Cerinthian thought as we know it from the later evidence.[206] Its closest parallels are found in the thought of the opponents of Ignatius of Antioch (reconstructed from his criticisms of them)—something

---

caution that W. Bauer, *Orthodoxy and Heresy in Earliest Christianity* (Philadelphia: Fortress, 1971; German orig. 1934) was knocking down a straw man when he refuted the simplistic idea that what was regarded as orthodoxy in the late second century had been held from the beginning. A more important question, which Bauer never really answered, is whether what won out as orthodoxy was truer than its opposite to *the implications* of what was held from the beginning (see p. 80 above). For more perceptive treatments of this question, see J.D.G. Dunn, *Unity and Diversity in the New Testament* (London: SCM, 1977); D.J. Hawkin, "A Reflective Look at the Recent Debate on Orthodoxy and Heresy in Earliest Christianity," *Eglise et Théologie* 7 (1976) 367-78.

204. W.S. Vorster, "Heterodoxy in 1 John," *Neotestamentica* 9 (1975) 87-97, warns against the tendency to label as gnostic any divergent NT thought.

205. "Die 'Gnosis' im Hintergrund und im Spiegel der Johannesbriefe," in *Gnosis und Neues Testament* (ed. K.-W. Tröger; Berlin: Evang. Verlagsanstalt, 1973) 341-56. The secessionists claim to know God (I John 2:4), and the gnostic God is unknowable; the world goes after them (4:5), and the gnostic is antiworldly; they betray no strong eschatological thrust, etc.

206. Good on this point is K. Weiss, "Orthodoxie und Heterodoxie im 1. Johannesbrief," *ZNW* 58 (1967) 247-55, esp. 253-54.

that is not surprising if Ignatius was dealing with church situations only some ten years after the Johannine Epistles were written.

Leaving aside the gnostic issue for the moment, let us examine the thesis that the peculiar secessionist ideas came from a new group that had been admitted into the Johannine community. Sometimes the blame is placed on an influx of pagans or Gentiles,[207] often with the erroneous assumption that there were no Gentiles in the Johannine community when the Gospel was written. Others think of a Greek-speaking Jewish group whose ideas would have contained a mélange of Hellenistic philosophical religion.[208] Because of the mention of false prophets (I John 4:1) and the urging by the author to test the spirits, still others have thought of an invasion by wandering charismatics. There is no way to disprove such hypotheses, but they are little more than guesses. The author is very critical of his opponents, but never once does he suggest that there was outside influence upon them—a polemic point he would scarcely have overlooked were it true. And so I prefer to leave aside any such assumption of alien intrusion and to explain the secessionist thought completely within the Johannine framework.

In my judgment the hypothesis that best explains the positions both of the author of the Epistles and of the secessionists is this: *Both parties knew the proclamation of Christianity available to us through the Fourth Gospel, but they interpreted it differently.*[209]

---

207. J. Painter, *John: Witness and Theologian* (London: SPCK, 1975) 115.

208. Bogart, *Orthodox* (n. 202 above) 19, following Robinson (n. 182 above), describes secessionist thought thus: "Deductions drawn from the teaching of the fourth gospel by a gnosticizing movement within Greek-speaking diaspora Judaism." M.H. Shepherd, Jr., "The Jews in the Gospel of John. Another Level of Meaning," *ATR* sup. series 3 (1974) 95–112, thinks that the Johannine opposition to "the Jews" involved more than the issues which are clear in the Gospel, for the opponents in I John were a Jewish group of docetist leaning (as in Colossians and Ignatius—but see n. 303 below).

209. I have phrased this deliberately to avoid claiming that the opposing parties knew the Fourth Gospel itself. I am made cautious by the failure of the Epistles to quote John directly with any frequency (I John 1:4 = John 15:11; I John 3:11 = John 15:12), and so I prefer to confine myself

The adversaries were not detectably outsiders to the Johannine community but the offspring of Johannine thought itself, justifying their positions by the Johannine Gospel and its implications. I am not saying that inevitably the Johannine Gospel led either to their position or to the position of the author; nor is it clear that either position is a total distortion of the Johannine Gospel. The subsequent church, by accepting I John into the canon of Scripture, showed that it approved the author's interpretation rather than that of his adversaries; and, as a believing Christian, I accept that judgment.[210] Nevertheless, I suspect that the Johannine Gospel, as it came to both the author and to the secessionists, was relatively "neutral" on some of the points that were now coming into dispute, i.e., it did not contain direct answers, for these were new questions. In the tradition there were texts on both sides of the issue; so each of the disputing parties was making the claim that its interpretation of the Gospel was correct.[211]

I would stress that this hypothesis explains not only the secessionists' views (as we shall see below systematically), but also the author's style of argumentation. For instance, he does not deny the main slogans of his opponents but qualifies them. If the affirmations of the secessionists are drawn from Johannine tradition, they are truth for the author also; and so he must seek to show that his adversaries are not living out the implications of these principles (see I John 2:4,6,9, etc.). Of course, this means that the author is handicapped in his argumentation, and his refutations are curiously oblique.[212] My hypothesis is also consonant with the au-

---

to speaking of their dependence on the Johannine Christianity now known *to us* through John. That is what I mean in the following pages when I speak of the "Johannine Gospel."

210. Technically, canonization does not make it clear whether the author's true teaching results from preserving the correct implications of the Gospel against distortion by his opponents, or from his own correction of dangerous tendencies found in the Gospel itself.

211. See my article "The Relationship to the Fourth Gospel Shared by the Author of I John and by His Opponents," in *Text and Interpretation* (M. Black Festschrift; ed. E. Best and R. McL. Wilson; Cambridge Univ., 1979) 57-68.

212. Noteworthy too is the lack of reference in the Epistles to anything from the Synoptic Gospels, even when a citation from the ethical

thor's almost frustrated appeal to *what was from the beginning* (1:4; 2:7; etc.). His opponents may sound as if they know the Johannine Gospel, but in his judgment they are distorting it precisely because they are ignorant of the tradition underlying it. In the years just before the schism Johannine thought was shaped by battles with outsiders and particularly with "the Jews"; consequently what came to the fore was mostly what the outsiders denied. The thought of the secessionists is based on that one-sided outlook and is not faithful to those presuppositions of the tradition which never entered into the dispute with the outsiders. And so by appealing to the beginnings, the author reaches back to strains which find only minor emphasis in the Fourth Gospel[213] but which were part of the early community heritage—incidentally, a heritage shared with other Christian groups (as discussed on pp. 27-28 above). He sums up this position in the lapidary formula of 1:5: "Now this is the Gospel that we have heard from him [Jesus Christ] and declare to you,"[214] a slogan which implies that the contrary interpretations of the secessionists, despite their surface plausibility, are novel distortions rather than the authentic Johannine Gospel. The "we" is important in that slogan, for it brings to the author's side the authority of the Johannine school.

I now turn to a detailed discussion of the positions of the author and of the secessionists. On each point I shall diagnose the secessionist position to see whether it can have been derived from the Johannine Gospel. Then I shall see whether the way in which the author opposes the secessionists on this point is more intelligible if he is giving a contrary interpretation of the same Johannine Gospel. In establishing the Johannine Gospel I shall call upon John *exactly as we have it*. It is tempting to exclude certain pas-

---

content of those Gospels would have greatly strengthened the author's argument. Either those Gospels were not known or were not authoritative for the Johannine community.

213. E.g., final eschatology, use of apocalyptic language, salvific death, lower christology.

214. In 1:5 and 3:11 the term *aggelia* is used. The more familiar word for "gospel," *euaggelion,* never appears in the Johannine writings (cf. Rev 14:6), and I suggest that *aggelia* may be the technical Johannine equivalent.

sages from the Fourth Gospel on the grounds that they were probably not in the tradition known to the secessionists but were added by the redactor (either later or as anti-secessionist revision).[215] However, that could leave me with a circular argument: I would be proving that the secessionists drew upon Johannine tradition because I would have excluded from my main source of that tradition (the Fourth Gospel) every statement that seems to contradict the position of the secessionists. I prefer for the moment to ignore the possibility (nay certainty) of redaction in the Fourth Gospel in order to test whether the position of the secessionists makes sense if they held as Gospel the whole of the Johannine tradition known to us in the Fourth Gospel.

THE AREAS OF DISPUTE

The areas of christology, ethics, eschatology, and pneumatology were, in my judgment, the main points of conflict between the author and his opponents. One learns a great deal about people by discerning what they deem important enough to fight over. As the two Johannine offspring argue over their heritage, we see some of the strengths and some of the weaknesses of the community of the Beloved Disciple.

A. Christology

A very high christology was the central issue in the historical struggles of the Johannine community with the Jews and with other Christians, as we have seen from our discussion of the situation at the time the Gospel was written. A belief in the pre-existence of God's Son was the key to the Johannine contention that the true

---

215. G. Richter (see Appendix I) thinks that John 1:14, "The Word became flesh," was added by the redactor as an attack on the opponents of I John who did not acknowledge "Jesus Christ come in the flesh" (4:2; also II John 7). I shall try to explain the secessionist position even if that phrase was in the Johannine community hymn (Prologue) known to them. K. Berger, "Zu 'Das Wort ward Fleisch' Joh. I 14a," *NovT* 16 (1974) 161-66, argues against Richter from second-century evidence that such a phrase could easily be read: The Word appeared in the flesh.

believer possessed God's own life; and the Fourth Gospel had been written to bolster the faith of Johannine Christians on that very point (20:31). Inevitably, a belief defended so ardently would have been passed down within the community as the chief Christian message, and one might expect two side-effects from such a theological background. First, the emphasis on the divinity of Jesus sharpened through polemics would overshadow presuppositions that provoked no struggle (the humanity of Jesus[216]). Second, the fact that the community had been willing to take a tremendous punishment for their christology (exclusion from mother Judaism and persecution) would mean that very little tolerance might be expected toward inner Johannine deviations about christology—if people had literally died for a christological stance, devotion to christology could become all-consuming and suspicious. An understanding of these side-effects will help to make intelligible the positions and history I shall now reconstruct.

1. Position of the Secessionists

The following statements in I John are indicative of the christological conflict that exists between the author and his opponents:

Who then is the teller of lies? None other than he who denies that Jesus is the Christ. (2:22—see also 2:23 where the denial concerns the Son)

We are to believe in the name of His Son, Jesus Christ. (3:23)

Whenever anyone acknowledges that Jesus is the Son of God, then God abides in him and he in God. (4:15)

Everyone who believes that Jesus is the Christ has been begotten by God. (5:1)

---

216. In earliest Christianity there were no disputes about the humanity of Jesus: those who saw him live and die would have had no reason to question it, and the Jews never denied it. The problem for Christians was one of coming to understand the relation of the man Jesus to God (his divinity). Only after they came to believe in Jesus' divinity did his humanity become a problem for Christians.

The conqueror of the world is none other than he who believes
that Jesus is the Son of God. (5:5)

Clearly the author insists that Jesus is the Christ (Messiah), the Son
of God; and anyone who denies that is a liar and an antichrist
(2:22). How then does the message of the Epistle differ from that of
the Gospel which was written to stress "faith that Jesus is the
Christ [Messiah], the Son of God" (20:31)? Despite the similarity
of formulas[217] there is a real difference. The Gospel described the
earthly career of Jesus in order to identify this Jesus of the ministry
as the pre-existent Son of God, over against others who knew of
Jesus but denied any such identity. The issue there was: Is the
Jesus of whose life and death we know the (pre-existent) Son of
God? The Epistle is written in a context where both the community
addressed and the opponents commonly use the terminology
"Christ," "Son of God"; and the dispute is centered on how that
terminology should be related to the earthly career of Jesus. The
new issue here is: Is it important that the Son of God lived and died
as Jesus did? The Gospel stressed that Jesus is the *Son of God*; the
Epistles stress that *Jesus* is the Son of God. The issue of dispute is
well expressed in 4:2-3:[218]

Everyone who acknowledges Jesus Christ come in the
     flesh
reflects the Spirit which belongs to God,
while everyone who negates the importance of Jesus
reflects a Spirit which does not belong to God.

But what does it mean to "negate the importance of Jesus"

---

217. This similarity is intelligible according to my hypothesis because
the author had to remain faithful to the formulas that had come down in
Johannine tradition even if they were not originally intended to solve the
problem he was now facing. To use them as arguments against his opponents he had to reinterpret them.

218. I accept as original for the third line the Greek *pan pneuma ho
lyei ton Iēsoun* over against the more common reading *pan pneuma mē
homologei ton Iēsoun*, "while everyone who does not acknowledge
Jesus." My choice is also that of Zahn, Harnack, Büchsel, Preisker,
Bultmann, and Schnackenburg.

or to deny "Jesus Christ come in the flesh," which is presumably what the secessionists are doing? It must mean that the opponents so stress the divine principle in Jesus that the earthly career of the divine principle is neglected. All scholars could agree on this, but they do not agree on the extent to which the secessionists minimalized the earthly career of Jesus. Were they thoroughgoing docetists who denied any reality to the humanity of Jesus, in the sense that his visible career was a deceiving appearance or that his most human emotions were only apparent? We now have much more evidence of such Christian docetism in the gnostic works discovered in Egypt in the mid-1940s.[219] The *Trimorphic Protenoia* (XIII 50:12-15), written *ca.* 200, shows a heavenly Word saying aloud: "I put on Jesus. I bore him from the cursed wood and established him in the dwelling places of his Father. And those who watch over their dwelling places did not recognize me." In the third-century *Apocalypse of Peter* (VII 81:15-25) a living Jesus laughs at persecutors who torment the external Jesus. The *Tripartite Tractate* (I 113:37), which has affinities with Valentinian gnosticism, speaks of an "unbegotten, *impassible* Word [*Logos*] who came into being in the flesh." In particular, scholars have thought of the adoptionistic docetic theory attributed to Cerinthus by Irenaeus:[220] "After Jesus' baptism the Christ, coming down from that Power which is above all, descended upon him in the form of a dove. . . . In the end, however, the Christ withdrew again from Jesus . . . the Christ, being spiritual, remained unable to suffer." It has been argued that I John 5:6 was meant to refute such a notion: "Jesus Christ—he is the one who came by water and blood, not in water only, but in water and in blood."

---

219. These works, written in Coptic and dating from the fourth century, are translations of earlier Greek works. They are collected in *The Nag Hammadi Library* (ed. J.M. Robinson; New York: Harper, 1977).

220. *Adversus Haereses* I xxvi 1. Elsewhere (III iii 4) Irenaeus tells us that John the disciple of the Lord called Cerinthus "the enemy of truth"—information said to have come from Polycarp of Smyrna. I think that Irenaeus preserves a correct memory that Cerinthus played a role in Johannine history; but, as I shall explain below (p. 152), Cerinthus reflects a further stage of secessionist docetic development *after* the schism described in the Epistles.

The great obstacle to identifying the thought of the secessionists with such later-attested views is that the author of the
Epistle should then have had no difficulty whatsoever in refuting
his opponents from the Johannine Gospel. There is not the
slightest suggestion in the Fourth Gospel that Jesus had only a
seeming body, or that the Word (or Christ) and Jesus functioned as
two separate entities during the ministry. The scene with Thomas
in 20:24-29, which refers to the marks of the nails and the wound
in the side, shows that in Johannine thought Jesus' body was real
even after the resurrection. How could the opponents have ever
been part of a community which knew of this tradition and yet
have held the type of docetism we have been discussing?[221] And
furthermore, if they were Cerinthians, why in refuting them
would the author say that Jesus Christ "came by water," which
could only affirm an adoptionistic view of the baptism? I judge it a
wrong approach to interpret the Johannine secessionists through
a knowledge of later heresies.

A more fruitful approach is to ask whether from the Fourth
Gospel itself one can derive an interpretation of the earthly career
of Jesus that would make sense of the christological affirmations
of the secessionists and explain why the author found them
dangerous. I maintain that the secessionists believed that *the
human existence of Jesus, while real, was not salvifically significant.* Let me reconstruct this belief in a few summary sentences
before I enter into a detailed explanation of how I think it can be
related to information supplied by the Gospel and Epistles. For
the secessionists the human existence was only a stage in the
career of the divine Word and not an intrinsic component in re-
demption. What Jesus did in Palestine was not truly important for
them nor the fact that he died on the cross;[222] salvation would not
be different if the Word had become incarnate in a totally different

---

221. Even the docetism combatted in the Ignatian Epistles seems too
systematic and advanced to have been held on the basis of John without
intervening developments. In *Trall.* 9-10 and *Smyrn.* 2 Ignatius attacks
"unbelievers" who say that Jesus' suffering was only in semblance.

222. Weiss, "Die Gnosis" (n. 205 above) 342-43, 348, contends that
the secessionists had no sense of salvation history, and their theology was
a soteriological vacuum.

human representative who lived a different life and died a different death. The only important thing for them was that eternal life had been brought down to men and women through a divine Son who passed through this world. In short, theirs was an incarnational theology pushed to exclusivity. Now let me show in two steps how such an interpretation might have been based on Johannine thought as we know it in the Fourth Gospel.

First, John gives a portrait of Jesus that somewhat relativizes his humanity. (Let me remind the reader once more that I am not explaining what the evangelist meant, but how the Gospel could have been read by the secessionists, at times contrary to the presuppositions of the evangelist.) In discussing Johannine christology theologians have often turned in isolation to John 1:14ab: "The Word became flesh and made his dwelling among us." However, this affirmation cannot be divorced from the following lines: "And we have seen his glory, the glory of an only Son coming from the Father" (14cd). There is no doubt from 1:14 that the Johannine Jesus has a real humanity[223] but the stress is on the glory of God which shines through this humanity. In the Synoptic Gospels only at the transfiguration does the glory of Jesus as God's Son shine through transparently to three disciples who do not fully understand it. But for John the very first miracle that Jesus performed "revealed his glory and his disciples believed in him" (2:11). One may say that for John the whole life of Jesus was a transfiguration. I need not repeat here all that I said above about the uniquely high Johannine christology of pre-existence (pp. 45-46), so high that Jesus can use the divine name "I AM" and his Jewish opponents accuse him of making himself God. Rather, let me now concentrate on how pre-existence christology colors the Johannine portrait of Jesus' earthly life.

The Johannine Jesus seems scarcely to eat or drink in the normal sense, for when he discusses food (4:32), bread (6:33ff.), or water (4:7-14; 7:38; 9:7), they are symbolic of spiritual realities. He loves Lazarus but with a love strangely lacking in human sympathy; for he does not hasten to Lazarus when he is ill (11:5-6), and Lazarus' death becomes a joyful moment for teaching

---

223. Yet see the opinion of Berger in n. 215 above.

about belief (11:11-15). The sight of Lazarus' sister weeping seems to make him angry (11:33), and it is not clear whether his own weeping (11:35) is from sorrow over a friend or over the lack of belief.[224] The Johannine Jesus knows all things (16:30), so that he cannot ask for information. When he says to Philip, "Where shall we ever buy bread for these people to eat?" (6:5), the evangelist feels impelled in the next verse to insert parenthetically: "Actually, of course, he was perfectly aware of what he was going to do, but he asked this to test Philip's reaction." The Fourth Gospel has its own explanation of the crux involved in the choice of Judas—this was not the mistaken choice of a disciple who looked promising but turned out poorly. Rather, the very first time Judas is mentioned we are told, "Jesus knew from the beginning the one who would hand him over" (6:64,70-71).[225]

The Johannine Jesus is one with the Father (10:30), and so he cannot really pray to the Father in the sense of seeking a change in the divine will. When he speaks to God on the occasion of the raising of Lazarus,[226] he says, "Father, I thank you because you heard me. Of course, I knew that you always hear me; but I say it because of the crowd standing around, that they may believe that you sent me." The Synoptic tradition has Jesus pray in Gethsemane, "Father, all things are possible for you; remove this cup from me; yet not what I wish but what you wish" (Mark 14:36; Matt 26:39; Luke 22:42). The Johannine Jesus has a very different attitude: "What should I say?—'Father, save me from this hour?' No, this is precisely the reason why I came to this hour. 'Father, glorify your name!'" (12:27-28). In other words the Johannine Jesus refuses to pray in the manner in which the

---

224. See my AB commentary, I, 425-26, 435.

225. In Mark 14:17-21, even at the Last Supper, while Jesus knows that one of the Twelve will betray him, it is not clear that he knows which one.

226. R. Bultmann, *The Gospel of John* (Philadelphia: Westminster, 1971; German orig. 1941) 408, points out that Jesus' attitude in 11:41-42 is not arrogant, since his assurance of being heard comes from his always standing before God in an attitude of petition. This is true, but the petition is always heard because of a unity of will and, in that sense, a total communion between Jesus and the Father.

Synoptic Jesus prays because in the Fourth Gospel there is no distinction between Jesus' will and the Father's will, and the Father's name has been given to Jesus.[227]

E. Käsemann has described the christology of the Fourth Gospel as a naïve, unreflected docetism which has not yet been recognized as such by the evangelist and his community.[228] I think that Käsemann has mistakenly gone beyond the evidence in judging this to be the christology of the Gospel itself,[229] and he is anachronistic in applying the term docetism to the Gospel.[230] Yet he shows how the Gospel *can* be read, and he may well have approximated in the twentieth century the way in which the opponents of I John interpreted the Johannine tradition in the first century, namely, in terms of an earthly career that did not really involve an appropriation by Jesus of the limitations of the human condition.

Second, there are elements in John that lessen the salvific import of the public ministry of Jesus. In Johannine theology the Word brought eternal life down from God to men and women on

---

227. The correct reading of John 17:11 is probably: "Keep them safe with your name which you have given to me" (also 17:12).

228. *Testament* (n. 17 above) 26.

229. Smalley, *John* (n. 99 above) 55-56, criticizes Käsemann perceptively: "While elements in the Johannine portrait of Jesus are capable of a docetic interpretation if taken by themselves, the total effect can scarcely be regarded as of 'divinity without humanity.' "

230. If one must be anachronistic in discussing the Johannine situation in terms of the full-blown theological positions of a later period, I would see in John's description of Jesus more the danger of monophysitism than of docetism. The humanity of the Johannine Jesus is neither a false appearance nor temporary; yet it is not like ours. The Johannine Jesus is not "one who in every respect has been tempted as we are, yet without sinning" or "one who has learned obedience through what he suffered, being made perfect" (Heb 4:15; 5:8-9). More adeptly than John, the Epistle to the Hebrews has kept in tension a high christology (n. 82 above) and full humanity. The recognition that John's christology is not perfect when judged by the later standards of the Council of Chalcedon does not cause a conflict with an intelligent understanding of the inspiration of the Fourth Gospel—no biblical author caught the whole mystery of Jesus. The church that spoke at Chalcedon of true God, true man, like us in everything except sin, was a church that had both John and Mark in its canon of Scripture.

earth, but the secessionists may have thought that this eternal life was made available simply through the presence of the Word in the world and not through dependence on what the Word did while present. The really important factor for them would be that the Word became flesh, not the kind of life he lived or death he died. In 17:3 the Johannine Jesus says, "Eternal life consists in this: that they know you, the one true God, and Jesus Christ, the one whom you sent." And 17:8 stresses, "They knew in truth that I came forth from you, and they believed that you sent me." Such statements center salvation in the sending by God rather than in any actions of the Son on earth.

The author of I John aims a particular attack at the christology of his opponents in the obscure statement of 5:6 where he praises Jesus Christ: "He is the one who came by water and blood, not in water only, but in water and in blood." It is generally thought that "by water and blood" emphasizes the baptism and death of Jesus.[231] The author was not stressing these events to prove that Jesus was human (p. 113 above); rather he was using them as the framework of the salvific ministry of Jesus.[232] It is important that the Son came into the world, but his salvific coming involved his baptism and his death as well. If the opponents placed little or no emphasis on Jesus' baptism and death as salvifically important, can they have justified their position from what we know of Johannine tradition in the Fourth Gospel?

Actually, John is the only one of the four Gospels that does not describe the baptism of Jesus. An oblique reference (1:30-34) makes the baptism the moment of the revelation of the presence of God's pre-existent Son, for JBap says, "After me is to come a man who ranks ahead of me, for he existed before me. I myself never recognized him, though the very reason why I came and baptized with water was that he might be revealed to Israel." The baptism administered by JBap is no longer seen as a baptism of

---

231. Any reference to the sacraments of baptism and the eucharist would be secondary and more closely related to 5:7-8.

232. Notice how the baptism and death are used in Mark (1:11; 15:39): at the baptism God reveals to the reader who Jesus is (namely, God's Son); at the death it is revealed to a participant in the Gospel story who Jesus is.

repentance for the forgiveness of sins (Mark 1:4); it now confirms the revelation of pre-existence found in the Prologue hymn.[233]

The passion and death in the Fourth Gospel also differ in implication from the same events in other NT works.[234] We note this already in chap. 2 of John. The Synoptic Gospels make Jesus' attitude toward the Temple the direct cause for his being put to death (Mark 11:15-18;14:55-61); but John places the cleansing of the Temple early in the ministry and totally separates it from the passion. For John the Temple scene relates to Jesus' resurrection (2:19,21-22). This sets a tone whereby the passion and death are going to be reinterpreted as victory. There is no victimizing of the Johannine Jesus in the passion, for he says, "I lay down my life in order to take it up again. No one has taken it away from me; rather, I lay it down on my own accord. I have power to lay it down, and I have power to take it up again." This affirmation of Jesus in 10:17-18 is quite different from the view in Heb 5:8 that Jesus *learned obedience* through suffering. The Johannine Jesus nevers falls to earth in supplication in Gethsemane (Mark 14:35); rather, Roman soldiers and Jewish police fall to the earth of the garden before him as he utters the majestic "I AM" (18:6). In the trial scene the Johannine Jesus makes it clear that Pilate has no independent power over him (19:11), and we are told that the judge was afraid of the one being judged (19:8)! On the cross Jesus is already surrounded by an initial group of disciples (19:25-27), the beginnings of the church. He is in such control that only when he affirms, "It is finished," does he bow his head and hand over his Spirit (19:30).[235] This sovereign affirmation is far from the cry

___

233. In fact, in 1:15 John brings JBap's testimony to pre-existence back into the Prologue as a commentary on "the Word became flesh" (1:14). See below p. 153.

234. R.E. Brown, "The Passion According to John," *Worship* 49 (1975) 126-34.

235. In many ways the crucifixion is for John both an ascension and a pentecost. John does not deny the older tradition that the giving of the Spirit came after the glorification of Jesus (see 20:22). But since he sees the death or "lifting up" of Jesus as part of the glorification, he has a proleptic communication of the Spirit on the cross. The *handing over* (not "giving up") of the Spirit by the dying Jesus (19:30) and the flow of blood and water from the pierced side of the crucified corpse (19:34) must be read in the

of the Marcan Jesus, "My God, my God, why have you forsaken me?" (15:34)—a cry that would have been inconceivable on the lips of the Johannine Jesus who claimed in the face of desertion by his disciples, "I am never alone because the Father is with me" (16:32). In his death on the cross the Johannine Jesus is already being "lifted up" in triumph and drawing all men to himself (12:32-33; cf. 3:14-15). This is a very different picture from the Pauline hymn where death on the cross is the lowest point in the humiliation of the servant (Philip 2:8). The notion of sacrifice has yielded to that of revelation, as T. Forestell[236] makes clear: "The cross of Christ in Jn is evaluated precisely in terms of revelation in harmony with the theology of the entire Gospel, rather than in terms of vicarious and expiatory sacrifice for sin."

If John stresses the baptism and the passion as moments of revelation, the secessionists seem to have interpreted that in an exclusive way. The baptism is now only a public reminder that the Son has come into the world. The death is only the essential return of the Son to the Father—a passing from this world to the Father's presence and to the glory he had before the world existed (13:1; 17:4-5). How would they have dealt with a Johannine saying like: "I lay down my life for these sheep" (10:15)?[237] Presumably they would have seen themselves as those sheep who recognize Jesus' voice and whom he knows (10:4,14-15). They might have interpreted his laying down his life for them and *his taking it up*

---

light of 7:38-39 and the promise of Jesus to fulfill the Scripture, "From within him shall flow rivers of living water." John explains that promise for us: "He was referring to the Spirit which those who came to believe in him were to receive. For as yet there was no Spirit, since Jesus had not been glorified."

236. *The Word of the Cross: Salvation as Revelation in the Fourth Gospel* (An Bib 57; Rome: Biblical Institute, 1974) 191. Also S. Talavero Tomar, *Pasion y Resurrección en el IV Evangelio* (Salamanca: Universidad, 1976) esp. 173-223: The passion is a revelation of Jesus as the king who came into the world but whose kingdom is not of the world. U.B. Müller, "Die Bedeutung des Kreuzestodes Jesu im Johannesevangelium," *KD* 21 (1975) 49-71: The physical death of Jesus has no particular relevance except as a manifestation of *doxa* ("glory").

237. This is a more ambiguous statement than Mark 10:45: "The Son of Man came . . . to give his life as a ransom for many."

again (10:17) in light of 14:2-3: "I am going off to prepare a place for you; and when I do go and prepare a place for you, I am coming back to take you along with me." His death showed them that they too would pass from this world to the Father.

2. Refutation by the Author

How can the author of I John refute opponents who are proposing a christology that is not an impossible interpretation of the Johannine Gospel? Certainly he cannot dissent from a tradition which for him as well as for the secessionists constitutes "Gospel." For example, he is not free to deny the pre-existence of the Son of God, even though the secessionists may have drawn upon such a conception to lessen the importance of the career of Jesus in the flesh. The author too believes that "Eternal life, such as it was in the Father's presence, has been revealed to us" (I John 1:2), that "the Son of God revealed himself" (3:8), that "God has sent His only Son into the world" (4:9,14), that Jesus is the one who *came* (5:5,20), and that Jesus is "true God" (5:20).[238] However, the author will challenge the wrong conclusions that his opponents have drawn from this commonly admitted incarnational theology, and so he is careful to accompany statements implying pre-existence with other statements stressing the career of the Word-made-flesh—a stress more formal and explicit than what is found in the Fourth Gospel.

A good example of this shift of emphasis may be found by comparing the Prologue of the First Epistle with the Prologue of the Gospel. Many of the same terms appear in both ("beginning," "word," "life") but with a different significance. Whereas for the Gospel (1:1) the "beginning" is before creation, for the Epistle (1:1) "what was from the beginning" is parallel to "what we have heard . . . seen . . . looked at . . . felt"—in other words, the beginning of the ministry when Jesus first set up a relationship

---

238. In my opinion, the best reading of this verse applies the designation "true God" to Jesus; see my *Jesus God and Man* (Milwaukee: Bruce, 1967; or New York: Macmillan, 1972) 18-19.

with his disciples.[239] The author of I John is not violating the Johannine tradition in giving such a meaning to "beginning," for it appears in the Gospel in 2:11; 6:64; and 16:4. In fact, a particularly good parallel for I John 1:1 is John 15:27: "You too should bear witness because you have been with me from the beginning." What he is really doing in order to refute his opponents is giving preference to one Johannine usage of "beginning" and thus offsetting their overemphasis on another (namely, on the before-creation meaning and its implications for pre-existence). As for the terms "word" and "life," in the Gospel Prologue we are first told (1:1-5) that the Word was in God's presence and that what came to be in him was life (echoing the creation story of Gen 1–3). Only later in the Gospel Prologue do we have a reference to the incarnation when the Word became flesh (1:14). But in the Epistle Prologue (1:2) the author stresses eternal life, not only "as it was in the Father's presence," but also as it "has been revealed to us." Indeed, the first reference in the Epistle to "the word of life" (1:1) makes it equivalent to "that which we have heard," a "life visibly revealed as we have seen and bear witness." In other words, for the author of the Epistle the "word of life" is the Gospel message of the life-giving career of Jesus among men and women. Finally, even the emphasis on the incarnation is different in the two Prologues, as can be seen when we compare the Gospel's comment upon the Word-made-flesh in 1:14c, "We have seen his glory," to the Epistle's comment in 1:1, "We have heard, and seen with our own eyes . . . we looked at, and felt with our own hands." The emphasis is now on the observable and tangible quality of the proclamation and hence on the human career of Jesus,[240] as assured by the testimony of the Johannine school.

---

239. See I. de la Potterie, "La notion de 'commencement' dans les écrits johanniques," in the Schürmann Festschrift (n. 186 above) 379-403, esp. 396-402. This is also the meaning of "beginning" in I John 2:7,24; 3:11; II John 5,6. Of course, the epistolary author is aware of the Genesis (and creation) background of the term as well, e.g., I John 3:8 which may be compared to John 8:44 as a joint echo of Gen 2:17; 3:19.

240. P. Bonnard, "La première épître de Jean est-elle johannique?" in *L'Evangile de Jean* (n. 41 above) 301-5, is excellent on this point.

How does the presbyter deal with the failure of the secessionists to give salvific value to the death of Jesus? There is no
doubt, as we have seen, that the main stress in the Gospel is on
the death as revelation. But scattered through the Gospel (6:51;
11:51-52; 12:24; 18:14) there are minor references to the salvific
import of Jesus' death which could serve the author's purposes.[241] In particular, we may remember that in John 1:29 JBap
describes Jesus as "the Lamb of God who takes away the world's
sin." The secessionists may have interpreted this simply as Jesus
destroying sin by bringing light; but the author of I John would
undoubtedly see here a reference to the redemptive death of Jesus, whether he thought of the imagery as pertaining to the Suffering Servant or to the Paschal Lamb.[242] This would confirm his
theology of expiation: "The blood of Jesus, His Son, cleanses us
from all sin" (1:7); "He himself is an expiation for our sins, and
not only for our sins but also for the whole world" (2:2; cf. John
11:51-52). The statement in I John 3:16, "This is how we have
come to know what love means: for us Christ laid down his life,"
shows us how the author would comment on John 10:15, "For
these sheep I lay down my life," the passage discussed above
from the secessionist viewpoint. The author sees Jesus' laying
down his life, not simply in order to take it up again, but for
expiation: "In this, then, does love consist, not that we have
loved God but that He loved us and sent His Son as an expiation
for our sins" (I John 4:10). The importance of the shedding of
blood in the career of Jesus is underlined in the passage we have
already noted: Jesus Christ "came by water and blood, not in
water only, but in water and in blood" (5:6).[243] A truly human

---

241. G. Richter, "Die Deutung des Kreuzestodes in der
Leidensgeschichte des Johannesevangeliums (Joh 13-19)," *Bib Leb* 9
(1968) 21-36, maintained that there were two interpretations of the death
of Jesus in John. Besides the one already discussed (n. 236 above), there
was another view which saw the death of Jesus as a moral example of
love and humility; and I John's outlook was closer to the second.

242. See my AB commentary, I, 58-63, for three different interpretations of "the Lamb of God."

243. This passage is often thought to be related to John 19:34 where
blood and water flow from the dead Jesus. The secessionists could have
interpreted such a flow as a symbol that death had not affected Jesus'

Jesus who was baptized and shed his blood is the one whom the author characterizes as "the true God and eternal life" (5:21). Much more clearly, then, than in the Gospel, the Jesus of I John is a redeemer, even if as a true Johannine the author never forgets the role of Jesus as a revealer: "Christ revealed himself to take away sins" (3:5).

The importance of the theme of belief is obvious in the Fourth Gospel with ninety-eight occurrences of *pisteuein*, "to believe," averaging about five times a chapter. Probably the secessionists had no difficulty with believing in Jesus, and so there is no reason for the Epistle to emphasize belief (nine occurrences of *pisteuein* or about twice a chapter). In the Epistles the emphasis has shifted to *homologein*, "to confess," a word that is not foreign to the Gospel (three times) but is proportionately much more frequent in the Epistles (six times). The author and his opponents could agree that eternal life consists in knowing that Jesus Christ is the one who was sent by God (John 17:3), but the author is trying to weed out his opponents by insisting on a public *confession* that this sending or coming was in human flesh (I John 4:2; II John 7). Without that human modality, he maintains, eternal life would not have been revealed to us (1:1-2).

B. Ethics

If christology was the main battleground between the author and the secessionists, there were also skirmishes on the implications of christology for Christian behavior. From the condemnations of ethical positions that the author of I John considers false, we may reconstruct in mirror fashion three aspects of the thought of the secessionists. First, the opponents claimed an intimacy with God to the point of being perfect or sinless. The following boasts quoted in I John seemingly reflect their views:

If we boast, "We are in communion with Him"(1:6)
If we boast, "We are free from the guilt of sin" (1:8)

---

life-giving power. However, 19:35 is a parenthetical addition stressing the realism of the incident; and many scholars think that a redactor added this parenthesis in harmony with I John 5:6. See pp. 95-96 above on the relationship between the redactor and the author of the Epistles.

If we boast, "We have not sinned" (1:10)
The person who claims, "I know Him" (2:4)
The person who claims to remain in Him (2:6)
The person who claims to be in the light (2:9)
If anyone claims, "I love God" (4:20)

Second, the opponents do not put much emphasis on keeping commandments (2:3-4; 3:22,24; 5:2-3). Third, the opponents are vulnerable on the subject of brotherly love. Let us consider each of these points in turn, seeking the rationale in John for the secessionist position, and then observing how the author of the Epistles responds, also in fidelity to John.

1. Intimacy with God and Sinlessness

Most of the above-listed "boasts" or "claims" can easily be justified from the Fourth Gospel. To be in communion with God and to remain or abide with Him is one of the great gifts that the Johannine Jesus gives to those who believe in him.[244] His final prayer is: "That they all may be one, just as you, Father, in me and I in you, that they also may be [one] in us . . . so that the love you had for me may be in them and I may be in them" (17:21,26; also 6:56: 14:23; 15:4-5). The claim "I know God" is not surprising in a tradition where Jesus promises that those who really know him will know the Father too (14:7; 17:3,25-26). The claim to be in the light is understandable when Jesus is "the light who has come into the world" (3:19) and anyone "who acts in truth comes into the light" (3:21). As Jesus himself assures, "No follower of mine shall ever walk in darkness; no, he will possess the light of life" (8:12; also 12:35-36).

But in I John 1:8,10 there is a twofold claim of the opponents to sinlessness that at first glance may seem foreign to the Johannine tradition.[245] It is phrased thus: "We are free from the guilt of

---

244. For the Johannine concept of divine indwelling, see my AB commentary, I, 510-12.

245. All the other secessionist claims listed above are denied by the author only when an ethical condition is missing. For example, he denies the claim to be in communion with God only when the person who makes

sin" (*ouk ekomen hamartian*) and "We have not sinned" (*ouk hēmartēkamen*). The first form of the claim is the easier to relate to the Fourth Gospel when we recall that the terminology "guilty of sin" and "slaves of sin" is used there for non-believers. In John 8:31-34 Jesus addresses Jewish opponents thus: "Amen, amen, I say to you, everyone who acts sinfully is a slave of sin," whereas, "If you abide in my word, you are truly my disciples; and you will know the truth, and the truth will set you free." Since, by contrast with the non-believer, the believer is freed from sin, the secessionists are really only rephrasing slightly when they claim to be free from the guilt of sin. Indeed, there occurs in the scene with the blind man the very expression "guilty of sin" (*echein hamartian*). The man who was born blind (and therefore accused of being born in sin: 9:34) is enlightened. The Pharisees, on the other hand, are told that if they recognized their blindness, they would not "be guilty of sin," but because they claim to see, their sin remains (9:41). A logical assumption is that the blind man who did recognize his blindness is not guilty of sin, and his sin does not remain.[246] The evangelist wished the Gospel reader to identify himself with the blind man, and the secessionists have done just that in regarding themselves as those who have been enlightened and thus not guilty of sin.

But could the secessionists justify from the Johannine Gospel the other form of the claim to sinlessness, "We have not sinned"? Does this claim mean that they have never sinned in their lives, or that they have not sinned since they became believers?[247] The

---

it continues to walk in darkness. But the author seems to deny outright the twofold claim to be free from the guilt of sin and not to have sinned, for he mentions no ethical condition that could be met to make the boast correct.

246. See also John 8:24: "Unless you come to believe that I AM, you will surely die in your sins"; 15:22: "If I had not come and spoken to them, they would not be guilty of sin"; and 16:8-9: The Paraclete will prove the world wrong "about sin—in that they refuse to believe in me." All of these imply that believers will no longer be guilty of sin.

247. The distinction would be meaningless to those who would read John 3:17-21 to mean that the light brought by Jesus merely makes visible what people already are, so that "he who acts in truth" refers to one who has been sinless when he encounters Jesus.

latter claim could have a basis in John by an analogy between the Christian and Jesus. Jesus is the Son of God; those who believe in him are children of God (John 1:12). The secessionists may have claimed that by becoming children of God, they became sinless, even as the Son of God was sinless (8:46): "Can anyone of you convict me of sin?" Were not all Johannine Christians taught they had received the Spirit which gives a power over sin (20:22-23)?[248] Were they not taught that whoever believes in the Son is not judged (3:18; 5:24)? After all, Jesus had told Peter, "The man who has bathed has no need to wash . . . he is clean all over" (13:10).

That the Johannine tradition lends itself to a thesis of sinlessness after becoming a believer is illustrated graphically by the fact that, while the author of the First Epistle rejects the claim of the opponents, "We have not sinned" (1:10), he comes fairly close to making the same claim himself *precisely in imitation of the sinlessness of Christ*. In 3:5-6 he says, "You know well that Christ revealed himself to take away sins, and there is nothing sinful in him. Everyone who abides in him does not commit sin." In another text he associates the challenge to sinlessness with being begotten by God: "Everyone begotten by God does not act sinfully because God's seed remains in him; and so he cannot be a sinner because he has been begotten by God" (3:9). If both the opponents and the author seem to claim a sinlessness and a perfectionism, what is the difference between them? The author sees sinlessness as the proper implication of divine begetting and therefore as an *obligation* incumbent on a Christian. I understand his "cannot be a sinner" to mean cannot *consistently* be a sinner, for elsewhere he recognizes that Christians may fall short of the "should." In refutation of his opponents' perfectionism he says, "My little children, I am writing this to keep you from sin. But if anyone does sin, we have Jesus Christ, who is righteous, as an intercessor before the Father" (2:1). The opponents, on the other hand, in their perfectionism see sinlessness as a realized truth and not simply as an obligation. For them, the believer is sinless, and

---

248. For the meaning, extent, and exercise of the power over sin involved in this text, see my AB commentary, II, 1041-45.

they cannot allow the possibility of the exception, "If anyone does sin."[249]

Parenthetically, let me remark that I make these observations partly in agreement and partly in disagreement with J. Bogart's recent book on the subject (n. 202 above). We both recognize the seeds of perfectionism in the Fourth Gospel itself, and a development of perfectionism in different ways in the author and in his opponents (ways that Bogart calls orthodox and heretical). But I disagree with a trend in Bogart's thought which he phrases thus (p. 134): "Is heretical perfectionism *inherent* here [in the Gospel of John]? Did it develop *naturally* out of it? No, because the theology (i.e., the doctrine of God and creation), anthropology and soteriology underlying the Gospel of John are not gnostic." Later (p. 135) Bogart makes explicit his assumption: "By the time I John was written, some Johannine Christians had become gnostics . . . perhaps the Johannine community suffered an influx of pro-gnostic gentiles who had never accepted the basic biblical doctrines of God and man." This assumption is quite unprovable and, in my judgment, quite unnecessary. (He is really introducing into the period between the Gospel and the Epistles a development that we can document only in the period *after* the Epistles; he is reading into the beginning of the schism the fate of the secessionists after the schism.) I think too that Bogart is missing a middle road between his two alternatives; either the Fourth Gospel leads inherently and naturally to heretical perfectionism, or there has been an outside influx to account for the heretical perfectionism. The real question is whether the incipient perfectionism in the Gospel could plausibly (even if wrongly) have been interpreted so as to produce the perfectionism of the secessionists. I have tried to show that it could; but it also could be read so as to produce the perfectionism of the author, and so I agree with Bogart that there is no inherent direction toward secessionist thought in the Gospel.

---

249. Even for the secessionists, however, the inability to sin would come from belief in Jesus. As we shall see on pp. 151-52 below, a further step on the road they had taken would be to posit an ontological sinlessness stemming from the fact the enlightened came into the world as a spark of the divine; and that step would bring the secessionists into gnosticism.

2. Keeping the Commandments

Another way by which the author of I John challenges the perfectionism of the opponents is by relating it to "keeping the commandments" (2:3; 3:22,24; 5:2-3). Without further ado he dubs the person a liar who claims, "I know God," without keeping the commandments (2:4). What does the charge of not keeping the commandments tell us about secessionist ethics? Let us first distinguish between practice and theory. In practice, were the secessionists libertinarians, living an immoral life? There is a passage in I John (2:15-17) where the author warns against worldliness: "carnal allurement, eye-catching enticement, the glamorous life." But it is very difficult to be sure that this passage is directed against the opponents,[250] since it may be simply a general pastoral warning to his own followers. Otherwise the author never mentions any special vices of the secessionists, and this at a time in Christianity where catalogues of vices are well attested, especially in polemic writing.[251] The author calls his opponents "false prophets" (4:2), the same charge leveled in II Pet 2:1 against the opponents of the Petrine author; but there is nothing in I John to resemble even remotely the oratory that II Pet 2:13-14 directs against the behavior of the opponents: "They are blots and blemishes, reveling in their dissipation, carousing with you. They have eyes full of adultery, insatiable for sin. . . . They have hearts trained in greed." Such Johannine reticence raises the possibility that the secessionists are at fault primarily in theory. Their theory, of course, might ultimately be translated into practice, and that danger may be why the author rails so strongly against the theory.

The most plausible explanation of the secessionist attitude toward commandments is that they gave *no salvific importance to*

---

250. Commentators generally remark that the meaning "world" in this passage, caught by the English "worldliness," is not precisely the same as the meaning in 4:5 where the opponents are said to belong to the world, i.e., the diabolic realm.

251. Gal 5:19-21; I Cor 6:9-11; II Cor 12:20; Rom 13:13; I Pet 4:3. It is likely that such catalogues were pre-Pauline and part of early Christian teaching (*JBC* art. 79, #161).

ethical behavior and that this stance flowed from their christology. If they did not attribute salvific importance to the earthly career of Jesus, to the way he lived and died, why should the earthly life of the Christian be pertinent to salvation? After all, had not the Johannine Jesus said, "You do not belong to the world, for I chose you out of the world" (15:19), and "They do not belong to the world any more than I belong to the world" (17:16)? If eternal life consists in knowing God and the one whom He has sent (17:3), claims of intimacy with God might well have been made without stress on what one does in the world.

I have never agreed with Rudolf Bultmann[252] that the Johannine Jesus is a revealer without a revelation. But the fact that Bultmann could make such a charge indicates the extent to which christology dominates the Johannine proclamation. In a massive work on the Johannine concept of truth, I. de la Potterie[253] shows that the Hebrew concept "to do truth" (OT, Qumran), which meant to do the prescriptions of the Law faithfully, has been interpreted in Johannine literature to refer to adhesion to the truth of Jesus. The early Christian struggle over the relation between faith and works (Paul, James) is resolved by John 6:28-29 so that faith in Jesus is the one work of God. The Fourth Gospel is notably deficient on precise moral teaching when compared with the Synoptic Gospels. Matthew can gather the ethical demands of Jesus into the Sermon on the Mount, thus fashioning the eschatological law code of the Messiah; but no such collection is found in John. In Matt 7:16 the criterion of behavior is stressed: "By their fruits you will know them"; in John 15:5 this language of fruit-bearing is shifted over to adherence to Jesus: "He who remains in me and I in him is the one who bears much fruit."[254] In all three Synoptics discipleship is marked by *doing* the will or word of God (Mark 3:35; Matt 12:50; Luke 8:21), but for John 8:31: "If you abide in my word, you are truly my disciples." The

---

252. *Theology of the New Testament* (2 vols.; New York: Scribners, 1955) II, 66: He "reveals nothing but that he is the Revealer."

253. *La vérité dans Saint Jean* (2 vols.; AnBib 73-74; Rome: Biblical Institute, 1977) I, 480-83, 516.

254. John too knows the importance of good deeds and bad deeds, but it is curiously intertwined with christology (3:19-21; 9:3).

stress on repentance/reform (*metanoia/metanoein*) that is so much a part of the Synoptic proclamation of the kingdom (Mark 1:4,15; 6:12) is not found in John;[255] what cleanses is the word spoken by Jesus (15:3). No specific sins of behavior are mentioned in John, only the great sin which is to refuse to believe in Jesus (8:24; 9:41). Especially interesting, if we reflect on its implications, is the Johannine Jesus' statement about the world (15:22): "If I had not come and spoken to them, they would not be guilty of sin." It is quite possible then, that the secessionist lack of interest in commandments may have been shaped by the dominance of christology and the lack of specific ethical directions in the Johannine tradition.

How can the author of the Epistle refute them when he too is bound by this tradition? It is interesting that he does not attempt to quote specific ethical directives, presumably because he has none that would be accepted as authoritative.[256] Rather he appeals to the general example of Jesus' earthly life as a model for the life of the Christian, an argument that is in harmony with the difference between his christology and that of his opponents. He does not and cannot deny the possibility of abiding in God—that is Gospel for him as well as for his opponents—but he makes correlative to such indwelling the need to "walk *just as* Christ walked" (I John 2:6). He does not deny the hope to see God as He is, but he demands that the person who entertains this hope should "make himself pure *just as* Christ is pure" (3:3). The mark of one who is not a child of the devil is to act righteously "*just as* Christ is righteous" (3:7). This *kathōs* ("just as") ethic, while helpful, is noticeably vague on details; and so here we have a graphic illustration of what I meant when I said that the author was handicapped in refuting his opponents. The tradition itself did not give clear rebuttals to the new issues raised by the secessionists.

---

255. The idea of repentance or change of life seems presupposed in John 5:14: 8:34.

256. See n. 212 above on the signal failure of the author to quote the Synoptic tradition.

3. Brotherly Love[257]

If the opponents put no salvific emphasis on commandments, could they really justify their position from the Johannine Gospel, since the Johannine Jesus did speak about commandments for his disciples? However, such references in John are always tied into the demand to love (13:34-35; 14:15,21; 15:10,12,17). It is as if for the Johannine tradition there was only one commandment which subsumed all others: "This is my commandment: 'Love one another as I have loved you'" (15:12). "By this will all identify you as my disciples—by the love you have for one another" (13:35). The author of the Epistle too, although he talks about commandments (plural), translates this into brotherly love (3:22-24; 4:21–5:3). The only specific commandment that he can cite is "that we are to love one another just as He gave us the command" (3:23); "The commandment we have had from Him is this: Whoever loves God must love his brother as well" (4:21). It is the "old commandment" that the community has had from the beginning (2:7); indeed he can identify it as the Johannine "Gospel" (3:11—n. 214 above). Consequently, the only specific wrongdoing which the author mentions in attacking the secessionists and their disregard for keeping the commandments is their failure to love the brethren (2:9-11; 3:11-18; 4:20).

Yet let us press the matter farther: if the opponents hated their brethren, how could they justify that attitude from the Johannine Gospel? In fact, however, were the secessionists disobedient to the Johannine Jesus' command to love one another, and did they really acknowledge that they hated their brethren? Some scholars would answer affirmatively, hypothesizing that

---

257. I use the expression "love (and hate) of *brothers*," conscious that it would be better in modern usage to speak of brothers and sisters. The female section of the community is presupposed in Johannine thought, but to constantly stress it here by mentioning sisters might suggest that there was an anti-feminist issue involved in the schism; and there is no evidence for that. In the next section (Phase Four) I shall suggest that some of the secessionists may ultimately have gone over into Montanism, where the prominence of women prophets became a matter of polemics.

the secessionists saw no connection between the love of brethren and the love of God. Other scholars suggest that the secessionists so emphasized the individual's relation to God that they had no sense of community. I think it far more likely that they had as much sense of community as had the author of I John[258] and that they claimed to love their brethren just as the Johannine Jesus had commanded. The key to the problem lies in the definition of "brethren." For the author of the Epistles "brethren" were those members of the Johannine community who were in communion (koinōnia) with him and who accepted his interpretation of the Johannine Gospel;[259] the secessionists had left and were no longer brethren. Indeed, their very leaving was a sign of lack of love for the brethren of the author. Almost surely the exact same sentiments could be found among the secessionists. For them the brethren would be those united *against* the author and his group; the latter were no longer brethren since they had departed from the authentic Johannine tradition as taught by the secessionist teachers. And it was the author and his group that did not keep Jesus' command to love the brethren, for they had broken koinōnia by separating. The harsh tone of I John toward the secessionists would have been tangible proof that its writer did not love the brethren.

Here we come upon the great anomaly of the First Epistle. No more eloquent voice is raised in the NT for love within the Christian brotherhood and sisterhood; with evangelical fervor he affirms: "Whoever has no love for his brother whom he has seen cannot love the God he has never seen" (4:19). Yet that same voice is extremely bitter in condemning opponents who had been members of his community and were so no longer. They are demonic, antichrists, false prophets, and serve as the embodiment of eschatological lawlessness or iniquity (*anomia*; 2:18,22;

---

258. The tendency of the author and of other Johannine writers to speak as "we" (p. 102 above) is found also in the statements attributed to the secessionists (I John 1:6,8,10), and it is the whole tone of the Epistle to treat the opponents as a group that all seceded at the one time.

259. There is no personal arrogance in this attitude, since the author regards himself as part of the "we" of the Johannine school of tradition-bearers and witnesses.

4:1-6; 3:4-5). Although the members of the community are exhorted to love one another, the way they should treat dissenters is illustrated by II John 10-11: "If anyone comes to you who does not bring this teaching, do not receive him into your house, for whoever greets him shares the evil he does."[260] The members of the community are urged to pray for their brethren when they sin but "only for those whose sin is not deadly" (I John 5:15-17); the deadly sin which should not be prayed for is surely the apostasy that the author has been attacking.[261]

If the opponents had virtually the same theology of "love of brethren" that the author of the Epistles had, we are once again seeing in both groups the development of tendencies present in the Johannine proclamation of Christianity. Just as Johannine christology known to us in the Fourth Gospel could become heady when worked out to the "nth" degree, so also the dualistic tendencies present in that proclamation could become dangerous when transplanted into inner-Christian debate. The Matthean Jesus says, "Love your enemies and pray for those who persecute you" (Matt 5:44), but there is no such maxim in the Johannine tradition. The command to love is *not* in terms of love of neighbor (as in Matt 19:19) but in terms of loving *one another* (John 13:34-35; 15:12,17); and John 15:13-15 allows that "one another" to be interpreted in terms of those who are disciples of Christ and obey the commandments. The attitude of the Johannine Jesus who refused to pray for the world (17:9) is easily translated in the First Epistle (5:16) into a refusal to pray for other Christians who have committed the deadly sin by apostasizing from the Johannine community.

Indeed, when we compare the Gospel and the First Epistle,

---

260. Diotrephes of III John 9-10 treats the emissaries of the presbyter in exactly the same way that the presbyter urges the church of II John to treat the emissaries of the secessionists; and, of course, the presbyter does not like that one bit.

261. The "deadly" character of the sin suggests that, for in 3:12-14 the secessionists are connected with death and murder. The passage in 5:16-17 is the Johannine form of the Synoptic tradition about a blasphemy against the Holy Spirit which will not be forgiven (Mark 3:29 and par.).

we see that the dualistic language once employed by Jesus in his attack on the world or on "the Jews" (love/hate; light/darkness; truth/falsehood; from above/from below; of God/of the devil) has been shifted over to an attack on Christians with whom the author disagrees. (And if I am right it is probably also being used by his opponents in their attack on him.) Let me illustrate this terminological shift. In the Gospel Jesus assures his followers that they do not walk in darkness (8:12; 12:46), for "darkness" is the realm of those who do not accept Jesus (1:5; 3:19-21; 12:35). But in the Epistle those who do not agree with the author's ethics, even though they claim to be followers of Christ, are said to walk in darkness (I John 2:9-11). In the Gospel the Paraclete proves the *world* wrong about justice (John 16:8,10). In the Epistle the opponents claim to be just (I John 3:7); but the author offers a criterion to prove who is really just or righteous (3:7-8; 2:29), with the clear implication that the secessionists do not meet that criterion. In a bitter passage of Gospel dialogue, Jesus attacks Jews who believe in him (Jewish Christians) by telling them that they belong to the devil, their father, who is a murderer and liar (John 8:44). In the Epistle, at the same moment when he is speaking about the need for love of the brethren (3:10-11), the author uses this very same terminology for the secessionists:[262] they are the devil's children; they are like Cain who belonged to the Evil One who was a murderer from the beginning; they have the spirit of deceit and are the tellers of lies (3:8-15; 4:1-6; 2:22). The Gospel (12:39-40) applies Isa 6:10 to "the Jews"—God has blinded their eyes—but the Epistle (2:11) applies it to the secessionists: "The darkness has blinded their eyes." Certainly the ethical battle in the Epistle is fought with the same terminological weapons employed in the Gospel.

When we discussed the Gospel, we found a sense of estrangement, of "us" against "them," especially toward those who had made the Johannine Christians suffer. As understandable as this sense is, its dualistic articulation is dangerous; and in fact it encouraged Christians of later centuries to see a dualistic division

---

262. Its use in the Gospel for Jews *who believed* may have facilitated its use against Christians who believed.

of humankind into believers (Christians) and non-believers, into an "us" who are saved and a "them" who are not. Inevitably such a dualistic outlook will shift over to divisions within the "us," and the cannons that once pointed outwards to protect the fortress of truth against the world will be spun around to point inwards against those betray the truth from within (for whom there is always a more special hatred). Those who believe that God has given His people the biblical books as a guide should recognize that part of the guidance is to learn from the dangers attested in them as well as from their great insights. As I shall show below, the author of the Epistles did the church a great service in preserving for it the Fourth Gospel; he did this by showing that the Gospel did not have to be read the way the secessionists were reading it. In his struggle against the secessionists he had to take stern means. Nevertheless, one must recognize that his defense of the truth as he saw it was at a price. In his attitude toward the secessionists in a passage like II John 10-11 he supplied fuel for those Christians of all times who feel justified in hating other Christians for the love of God.

C. Eschatology

When we turn to this subject, we are somewhat handicapped because there are no clear eschatological statements that the author condemns. However, there are eschatological implications in the claims of the opponents to perfection which were listed in our discussion of ethics (pp. 123-24 above). Those claims are harmonious with the realized eschatology that we saw dominant in the Gospel (p. 50 above), an eschatology stressing what God has already done for those who believe in His Son. They are already judged favorably and do not need to face further judgment (John 3:18; 5:24); they have come into the light (3:21; 8:12; 11:9; 12:46); they already have eternal life (6:54; 8:12; 10:10,28; 17:3); they are children begotten by God (1:13; 3:3-8); they are in union with Him and Jesus (6:56; 14:23; 15:4-5; 17:21); they already know and see God (3:3; 12:45; 14:7,9; 17:3). The secessionists would have read such Johannine affirmations as harmonious with their christology and ethics: all this realized salvation was accomplished by the descent of the Word into the world, and Christians who have received such privileges need not worry about what they do in the world. Presumably there would have been no place in secessionist theology for future eschatology. Through knowing Jesus they already had eternal life, and they would take literally John 11:26: "Everyone who has life and believes in me shall never die at all"—they would simply pass from this world to which they never really belonged (17:14) to join Jesus in the mansions which he had prepared for them (14:2-3).

Since the author of the Epistles is also loyal to the Johannine tradition, it is no surprise that he too holds a realized eschatology. He too professes that:

> the Evil One is already conquered (I John 2:13-14)
> eternal life has been revealed (1:2)
> we already walk in the light (1:7; 2:9-10)
> divine love has reached perfection (2:5)
> there is communion with God (1:3)
> we are truly God's children (3:1)
> God abides in the believer (4:15)

But the author takes two steps to prevent such realized eschatology from rendering comfort to his adversaries. *First,* he attaches an ethical requirement to the claims of realized eschatology. Yes, we are in communion with God if we walk in light (1:7). Divine love has reached perfection in one who keeps God's word (2:5). It is the person who loves his brother who really remains in the light (2:10). Those who act justly belong to God and are God's children (3:10). *Second*, he appeals to future eschatology. Such an eschatology is not foreign to the Fourth Gospel as we have seen (pp. 50-52 above), even though it is a minor note there. I suggested that it was an older motif that the evangelist had reinterpreted in the light of his exalted christology. After all, there was no need to convince "the Jews" that God had future blessings in store for His people. What really needed to be emphasized in debates with them is that God had already sent His Son and therefore many of His blessings were already realized. But now in the internal Johannine disputes that gave rise to the Epistles the author once more revives the earlier stratum of Johannine thought which had been presupposed in the Gospel, and which was a minor note precisely because it was not in dispute.[263]

Let us look briefly at the manner and motif of the author's appeal to final eschatology. In 3:2 in loyalty to the main tradition of the Gospel, the author of the First Epistle says, "Yes, dearly beloved, we are God's children right now." But his real point is in what he adds to the affirmation: "What we shall be has not yet been revealed. Yet we know that at this revelation we shall be like Him, for we shall see Him as He is." Why is he stressing the hope of a future revelation? He goes on to explain in the next verse (3:3): "Everyone who has this hope based on God makes himself pure even as Christ is pure." In other words, he is stressing future blessings because they are contingent on the way Christians live, and future eschatology can therefore be employed as a corrective of the secessionist ethics. A similar ethical motive is inherent in 2:28: "Little children, do abide in Christ so that, when he reveals himself, we may have confidence and not draw back in shame from him at his coming." Similarly in 3:18-19: "Little children, let us show our love, not only in words, eloquently, but in deeds and truthfully—that is the way we shall know that we belong to the truth and indeed before God shall convince our hearts" (see also 4:17). For the author of the Epistles, the gifts acclaimed in Johannine realized eschatology are not an end in themselves (as they are for his opponents) but the source of confidence for the future, provided that those who are already God's children continue to live a life worthy of the Father whom they shall one day see face to face.

The seriousness of the schism lends a somber tone to the author's future eschatology, as he resorts to the language of Jewish and Christian apocalyptic. The opponents with their false teaching are the antichrists and the false prophets who are the

---

263. It is noteworthy, however, that in appealing to future eschatology, the author of the Epistles never quotes the future eschatology passages from the Gospel. Was it because they were not in the Gospel as he knew it (an explanation which would favor the redactional approach to those passages, an approach rejected in n. 89 above), or was it because they had been neutralized in the Gospel by being reinterpreted in the light of realized eschatology?

traditional heralds of the last times (2:18,22; 4:1-3).[264] Their indif-
ference to sin is the definitive lawlessness (*anomia*) of the final
struggle (3:4). In such imagery he approaches Mark 13:22, "False
christs and false prophets will arise"; and II Thess 2:1-12 which
speaks of "the mystery of lawlessness." These signs all constitute
proof that "it is the last hour" (I John 2:18); they serve as a warning
to those who think little of commandments that a time of judgment is coming when Christ will reveal himself (2:28). But for
those who hold on to the true Gospel which has been proclaimed
from the beginning there is encouragement: "The darkness is
lifting, and the real light is already shining" (2:8).[265]

D. Pneumatology

The author of I John assures his audience, "You have no
need for anyone to teach you" (2:27) and warns that, since "many
false prophets have gone out into the world," they should put
manifestations of the spirit to the test to see if the spirit they
reflect belongs to God (4:1). This leads us to suspect that the
opponents may have designated themselves as teachers and
prophets and have claimed to speak under the guidance of the
Spirit. In his list of charisms or manifestations of the Spirit, Paul
(I Cor 13:28) lists prophets and teachers in the second and third
places after apostles; and Acts 13:1 shows prophets and teachers
in the leading role at the church at Antioch where there were no
apostles.[266] It is not clear whether such an arrangement also prevailed in the Johannine house-churches and whether there were

---

264. The author assumes that the reader already knows of such
apocalyptic signs: "You heard that the antichrist is to come" (2:18).
Presumably such knowledge, not attested in the Fourth Gospel, would
have come from an early period of Johannine tradition. This raises the
question of whether Revelation (Apocalypse) is another witness to the
survival of a Johannine apocalyptic strain (see n. 5 above).

265. In John 3:19 light and darkness are present simultaneously; I
John envisions a sequence. G. Klein. " 'Das wahre Licht scheint schon,' "
ZTK 68 (1971) 261-326, uses this difference as an indication of distinct
authors.

266. At least there were no members of the Twelve, which is what
Luke usually means by "apostles."

prophets and teachers in the author's community or just among the secessionists. (In the latter case the very existence of such figures may have been seen as an untraditional aberration by the author.[267])

Could the secessionist prophets and teachers who claimed to speak by the Spirit justify their roles by appealing to the Johannine tradition that we know through the Fourth Gospel? The Spirit appears prominently in many NT books, but the personal role of the Spirit in the Fourth Gospel under the title of "Paraclete" is unique. I have shown elsewhere[268] that the Paraclete so resembles the Johannine Jesus that we may say that the Paraclete is the abiding presence of Jesus after Jesus has gone to heaven, and that the Paraclete plays the same revelatory role in relation to Jesus that Jesus played in relation to the Father. The concept of the Paraclete who remains forever (14:16) relativizes in Johannine thought the delay of the parousia. It is not so tragic that Jesus has not yet returned, for in a very real way he has returned in and through the Paraclete. The Johannine Jesus says to his disciples: "It is for your own good that I go away; for if I do not go away, the Paraclete will never come to you" (16:7). It is the Paraclete, the Holy Spirit, who teaches the believer everything (14:26) and guides the believer along the way of all truth (16:13). And it is the Paraclete who bears witness to Jesus in coordination with the Johannine believer (15:25-26). Presumably the secessionist prophet or teacher would justify his christological proclamation in terms of such Spirit-guided witness that is very much a part of the Johannine tradition.

Parenthetically let me remark that I find no evidence for assuming that the secessionist prophets and teachers were charismatics in the sense of being enthusiasts, ecstatics, or mantics. Certainly the author of the Epistle never indicates that. (Sometimes the suggestion reflects a misunderstanding of the

---

267. The denial of the need for teachers in I John 2:27 is aimed at protecting the author's community from the secessionist teachers but is not an absolute indication that there never have been teachers in the previous history of the community.

268. Appendix V in my AB commentary, II, 1135-44.

Pauline notion of charism; in I Cor 14:1-2 the charism of the prophet is kept clearly distinct from the more ecstatic experience of speaking in tongues.) I would judge that in both time and atmosphere the Johannine situation may be close to that described in the *Didache* where, although there are both prophets and teachers (13:1-2; 15:2), the line of demarcation is thin,[269] since the prophet teaches (11:10-11). Indeed, the prophet may differ from the teacher only in being a teacher who is not residential (10:7–11:1), so that there is not always a prophet in a community (13:4). I suggest that teaching by word or deed, not ecstasy, is the mark of the prophet in both *Didache* and among the Johannine secessionists.[270]

How does the author of the Epistles deal with the claim of the secessionist prophets and teachers to be guided by the Spirit in their teaching? Truly noteworthy is what he does *not* say. The first aspect of his eloquent silence is the failure of I John to mention the Spirit with any frequency, so that the writer is not offering the opponents any consolation. The Spirit is mentioned only in two sections of the Epistle. The first is 3:24–4:6,13 when the author is insisting on a test and criteria for distinguishing between the Spirit of God and the diabolic spirit of deceit. The second is 5:6-8, a passage again aimed at his opponents, where the testimony of the Spirit is tied to the testimony given by the baptism and the death of Jesus. Otherwise the First Epistle passes over in silence many of the roles given to the Spirit in the Gospel. For instance, in the Gospel the Christian is a child of God through begetting by God (1:13) or through begetting by the Spirit (3:5-8); in I John only begetting by God is mentioned (3:9; 4:7; 5:1,18). Presumably the author would not deny that the Spirit was the

---

269. The line of demarcation is also thin between the apostle and the prophet in *Didache* 11:3-6: the apostle who stays three days is a false prophet.

270. H. Conzelmann. "'Was von Anfang war,'" in *Neutestamentliche Studien für Rudolf Bultmann* (BZNW 21; Berlin; Töpelmann, 1954) 194-201, esp. 201, n. 22, is correct over against Käsemann on this. The *chrisma* or anointing of I John 2:20,27 that every Johannine believer has from Christ is not some form of enthusiastic charism, but a Spirit-guided ability to interpret the tradition.

Paraclete, but he never mentions it. Rather he emphasizes what is only hinted at in the Gospel, namely, that Jesus is the Paraclete (see John 14:16: "another Paraclete"). We see this in the only epistolary reference to the Paraclete (2:1-2) which portrays Jesus in this role as he intercedes for us before the Father and has expiated our sins.

The second aspect of the author's eloquent silence is his failure to correct the teaching of his opponents by the authoritative "I" statement of a church officer entrusted with the responsibility of guarding the faith. When we discussed the churches of the Apostolic Christians (pp. 86-87 above), we saw the increasing institutionalization of ecclesiastical offices at the end of the first century. In particular, the teaching gap resulting from the death of the apostles was filled in many places by the emergence of groups of presbyter-bishops in every town. The presbyter was admonished that he "must hold firm to the sure word as taught, so that he may be able to give instruction in sound doctrine and also to confute those who contradict it" (Titus 1:9). We saw that the Johannine community differed from the Apostolic churches on this point, for in the Johannine tradition the position of the Paraclete as the authoritative teacher and the gift of the Paraclete to every believer would have relativized the teaching office of any church official.[271] I think that this situation explains the inability of the author of the Epistles to correct his opponents in function of his office, even though he calls himself a presbyter. He must rather appeal to that inner guidance of the Christian which is in conformity with the Johannine tradition: "Your anointing is from the Holy One, so all of you have knowledge" (I John 2:20);[272] "The anointing received from Christ abides in your

---

271. While the witness of the Beloved Disciple was very important for the Johannine community (John 19:35; 21:24), he is never referred to as an apostle. Since the efficacy of his witness was attributed to the Paraclete, there was no feeling of an acute need to replace him when he died (21:20-23).

272. In this translation I give preference to the reading *pantes* (masc. nominative: "all people") over *panta* (neuter accusative: "all things"). Those who accept the latter reading translate: "so you know all things."

hearts; and so you have no need for anyone to teach you" (2:27). If the opponents are claiming to be Spirit-guided teachers, the author is reminding his audience that every Johannine Christian is a teacher through and in the Paraclete-Spirit (which he names only indirectly as "anointing" because his opponents stress their special possession of the Spirit[273]). He takes this approach rather than to claim that he himself is a special Spirit-guided teacher. If he has his own teaching importance, it is by inclusion in the "we" of the tradition-bearers of the Johannine school, a group that does not supplant the Paraclete but is the instrument of the Paraclete. The secessionists are wrong, not because of an authoritative "I say you are wrong" on the part of the author,[274] but because they have broken communion (koinōnia) with believers who are all anointed by the Word and the Spirit, and who therefore instinctively recognize the truth when those writers and preachers who have been intimately associated with the Beloved Disciple speak and say, "We proclaim to you the Gospel we have had from the beginning."

This is a very indirect method of correction, and quite obviously it would be countered by the secessionists who advanced their own "we" as justification for their interpretation of the tradition and who could appeal to the Johannine believers in virtue of their "anointing" to recognize the working of the Spirit in the secessionist teachers. Faced with that, all the author can do is demand a test of the manifestations of the Spirit to prove which side is right, which side reflects the Spirit of God as opposed to that of the antichrist (4:1-3). Probably in making this demand, the

---

273. All scholars agree that the Spirit is involved in this "anointing" or "chrism" (chrisma), although some think that the anointing is directly through the Spirit, while others think that it is through the word received from Jesus and that the role of the Spirit is in the interiorization of the word. See J. Michl, "Der Geist als Garant des rechten Glaubens," in Vom Wort des Lebens (NTAbh 1, Ergänzung; M. Meinertz Festschrift; ed. N. Adler; Münster: Aschendorf, 1951) 142-51. The clause in I John 2:27, "His anointing teaches you about all things," seems to echo John 14:26: "The Paraclete, the Holy Spirit, that the Father will send in my name, will teach you all things."

274. The one who uses the authoritative "I" in Johannine tradition is Jesus, the "I AM."

author was taking a desperate risk, for he was exposing himself to the charge of blasphemy against the Holy Spirit (Mark 3:29 and par.). Even though the church of the *Didache* is also afflicted by false prophets and teachers, the author of that work refuses to make a test: "Do not tempt or judge any prophet who speaks in the Spirit; for every sin shall be forgiven, but this sin shall not be forgiven" (*Did*. 11:7). In any case, the test that the Johannine presbyter offers is a doctrinal one that favors his own position: "This is how you can distinguish the Spirit of God: everyone who acknowledges Jesus Christ come in the flesh reflects the Spirit which belongs to God, while everyone who negates the importance of Jesus reflects a spirit which does not belong to God" (4:2-3). Inevitably the opponents would have paid little attention to such a criterion which, as the author frankly admits, is tantamount to agreement with him and his side of the Johannine spectrum: "We belong to God and anyone who has knowledge of God listens to us, while anyone who does not belong to God refuses to listen to us" (4:6).

That the author's test was ineffectual is seen in his admission that "the world" is listening to his opponents (4:5). "The world" is standard Johannine opprobrium for non-believers, but now it has been shifted over from outsiders who refuse to believe in Christ to the secessionists who refuse to believe in Christ as proclaimed by the author: "Those people belong to the world; that is why theirs is the language of the world" (4:5); "Many deceitful men have gone out into the world, men who do not acknowledge Jesus Christ as coming in flesh" (II John 7). But beyond mere opprobrium these references to success in the world seem to indicate that numerically the opponents are gaining over the author's adherents.[275] In their own estimation, of course, the secessionists would not have thought of their success as pertaining to the world. After all, the world consisted of those who

---

275. As for the cause of this success, one may theorize that the secessionist christology and ethics were less offensive than a Gospel interpretation that stressed the cross and the commandments. The idea that salvation came simply through the presence of the Word in the world may have attracted the devotees of the mystery religions and of various Hellenistic religious philosophies.

preferred darkness to the light (John 3:19) and the secessionists claimed to be in the light (I John 2:9). Success would have proved to them that they were the true Johannine community fulfilling the prayer of Jesus who foresaw a chain of conversions (John 17:20). They would have been convinced that their converts were the gift of the Father to Jesus who was thus continuing to make his name known as a sign to the world (17:23,26). On the losing side of the statistics, the author sees the success of his opponents in another light. Since the Paraclete is "the Spirit of truth whom the world cannot accept since it neither sees nor recognizes him" (14:17) and is a Spirit that proves the world wrong (16:8-10), secessionist success in the world is a sign that they have failed the test of the spirits. Theirs is not the Spirit of Truth; they belong to the Prince of this World. Jesus had warned his followers, "If the world hates you, bear in mind that it has hated me before you. If you belonged to the world, the world would love its own" (15:18-19). Success is a sign that the opponents do not belong to Christ; it is a sign adding to the author's pessimistic conviction that "the last hour" is at hand (I John 2:18).

PHASE FOUR:
AFTER THE EPISTLES
Johannine Dissolution

The author of the Epistles seems to have been prophetic in proclaiming that the split between his adherents and the secessionists marked "the last hour." The Johannine writings and some elements of Johannine thought are attested in the second century, but after the Epistles there is no further trace of a distinct and separate Johannine community. One cannot deny the possibility that a community descended either from the author's adherents or from the secessionists (or communities descended from both) did survive but left no traces in history; yet it is far more likely that the two groups were swallowed up respectively by the "Great Church"[276] and by the gnostic movement. The author's adherents would have made their own Johannine contribution to the Great Church; the secessionists would have made their Johannine contribution to gnosticism; but in each case the Johannine community would have so adapted its own heritage in favor of the larger

---

276. As I have previously explained, I am using this term for the church of the second century which has descended from the Apostolic Christians of the first century, and wherein the churches are being bound more closely together by an increasingly common structure of episcopate and presbyterate in mutual recognition. Ignatius. *Smyrn.* 8:2, says: "Wherever the bishop appears, let the congregation be present, just as wherever Jesus Christ is, there is the church catholic" (*hē katholikē ekklēsia*).

group that the peculiar identity of the Johannine Christianity
known to us from the Fourth Gospel and the Epistles would have
ceased to exist. I plan to marshal the evidence for this thesis step
by step, but for the convenience of the reader let me begin by
summarizing what I think happened.

If the author's branch of the Johannine community gradually
merged with the Apostolic Christians (pp. 81-88 above) into the
Great Church, it brought with it the high Johannine christology of
pre-existence, precisely because in his struggle with the secessionists the author of the Epistles had safeguarded that christology against any interpretation that would lead to docetism or
monophysitism. However, the very fact that a Paraclete-centered
ecclesiology had offered no real protection against schismatics
ultimately caused his followers to accept the authoritative
presbyter-bishop teaching structure which in the second century
became dominant in the Great Church but which was quite
foreign to Johannine tradition. The secessionists, deprived of the
kind of moderating influence that the author's adherents might
have supplied if the schism had not happened,[277] went further in
their ultra-high christology toward true docetism. Having thought
that Jesus' earthly career had no real salvific importance, they
now ceased to think of it as real at all. Having thought of themselves as children of God through faith in Jesus by God's choice,
they now began to move that choice back before their earthly
lives and thought of themselves as divine by origin in imitation of
Jesus. Like the Son, they too came into the world; but they had
lost their way while he had not; and it was now his role to show
them the way home to heaven. The fact that these secessionists
brought the Johannine Gospel with them offered to the docetists
and gnostics, whose thought they now shared, a new basis on
which to construct a theology—indeed, it served as a catalyst in
the growth of Christian gnostic thought. The Great Church, which
had accepted elements of the Johannine tradition when it accepted the Johannine Christians who shared the author's views,

---

277. Inevitably the reaction of the secessionists to the harsh word-
ing of I John would have been to move further in the direction condemned; after a schism positions tend to harden.

was at first wary of the Fourth Gospel because it had given rise to error and was being used to support error. Eventually, however, having added the Epistles to the Gospel as a guide to right interpretation, the Great Church (as illustrated by Irenaeus, *ca.* A.D. 180) championed the Gospel as orthodox over against its gnostic interpreters. Let me now turn to the evidence for the development I have thus summarized.

THE HISTORY OF THE FOURTH GOSPEL IN THE SECOND CENTURY

All our evidence points to the fact that a wide acceptance of the Fourth Gospel came earlier among heterodox rather than among orthodox Christians.[278] Our oldest known commentary on the Gospel is that of the gnostic Heracleon (A.D. 160-180).[279] The Gospel was greatly appreciated by the Valentinian gnostics (e.g., Ptolemaeus), so that in his refutation of them Irenaeus had to challenge their exegesis of John.[280] The *Odes of Solomon* have affinities to John, and many scholars think they are gnostic or semi-gnostic.[281] There is abundant evidence of familiarity with Johannine ideas in the recently published gnostic library from Nag Hammadi (n. 219 above). For instance, there is a Word (*Logos*) christology in the *Tripartite Tractate*, and "I AM" chris-

---

278. As applied to the early second century this terminology describes Christians who were *later* judged to be heterodox or orthodox, for instance, by the standards of Irenaeus (n. 203 above). Under "heterodox" I include a whole variety of gnostic, docetist, encratite, and Montanist elements.

279. There is a debate whether and to what extent Heracleon was a representative of *Valentinian* gnosticism. See E.H. Pagels, *The Johannine Gospel* (n. 12 above) 17-19.

280. *Adversus Haereses*, III xi. Similarly, in the Alexandrian tradition in the third century it was Origen whose commentary on John showed that Gospel to be capable of orthodox interpretation over against Heracleon.

281. Yet see J.H. Charlesworth, "The Odes of Solomon—Not Gnostic," *CBQ* 31 (1969) 357-69.

tology in the *Second Apocalypse of James;* also in *The Thunder, the Perfect Mind*, and in the *Trimorphic Protenoia* (where it is joined with a docetic account of the death of Jesus). Montanus (*ca.* A.D. 170), who in Asia Minor led a movement of ecstatic, Spirit-filled prophecy, considered himself the embodiment of the Johannine Paraclete.

On the other hand, it is difficult to prove clear use of the Fourth Gospel in the early church writings deemed to be orthodox. There is no specific citation of John in Ignatius of Antioch.[282] More curious is the absence of a citation in the letter of Polycarp of Smyrna to the Philippians (*ca.* A.D. 115-135); for Polycarp is said by Eusebius to have heard John, and Polycarp shows knowledge of some eighteen NT works. The closest Polycarp comes to the Johannine writings is an echo of I John 4:2-3 (II John 7): "Everyone who does not confess that Jesus Christ has come in the flesh is an antichrist" *(Phil.* 7:1). This choice is quite explicable if the Epistle was considered safer than the Gospel.[283] While Justin Martyr in mid-second century certainly knew a *Logos* christology, it is not clear once again that he knew or used the Fourth Gospel itself. Often it is noted that Tatian (*ca.* A.D. 170), a pupil of Justin, used the Fourth Gospel in his harmony of the Gospels, the *Diatessaron;* but Tatian was an encratite who played down the value of the flesh, and so he should be reckoned on the heterodox side of the usage of John.[284] The passages in the *Secret Gospel of Mark* quoted in a recently

---

282. F.-M Braun, *Jean le Théologien* (Paris: Gabalda, 1959) I, 270-82, gives a number of contacts between Ignatian and Johannine *thought* but admits there is no verbatim citation. Other scholars like J.N. Sanders and C.K. Barrett deny that Ignatius knew the Fourth Gospel. See my AB commentary, I, LXXXI,

283. Quite helpful on this history of the Fourth Gospel is N.K. Bakken, *The Gospel and Epistles of John: A Study of Their Relationship in the Precanonical Period* (New York: unpublished Union Seminary doctoral dissertation, 1963). He notes: "In so far as Polycarp touches on these matters he moves in the spirit of the Epistles of John, and on the side of the differences which distinguish them from the Gospel, but that he knew or used the Epistles is extremely doubtful."

284. R.M. Grant, "The Heresy of Tatian," *JTS* ns 5 (1954) 62-68.

discovered letter of Clement of Alexandria, which may reflect a knowledge of John in the mid-second century, should probably also be listed on the heterodox side of the ledger, since the *Secret Gospel* is somehow related to the Carpocratians.[285] Suspicions about elements in the Johannine corpus of writings is reflected in the attack of Gaius, a presbyter of Rome, on the orthodoxy of the Apocalypse (Revelation), and the related attack of the Alogoi ("no *logos*") on the Gospel, attributing it to Cerinthus.[286] The earliest indisputable orthodox use of the Fourth Gospel is by Theophilus of Antioch in his *Apology to Autolycus* (*ca*. A.D. 180). The acceptance of the Gospel into the canon before A.D. 200, as attested by the Muratorian Fragment, was only at the price of an assurance that it had apostolic origins. Irenaeus also takes pains to relate it to John the disciple of the Lord, and he carefully reads the Gospel through the looking glass of I John.[287]

This curious history of the Fourth Gospel would become quite intelligible if we posit that the larger part of the Johannine community, the secessionists, took the Gospel with them in their intellectual itinerary toward docetism, gnosticism, and Montanism, while the author's adherents carried the Gospel with them as they were amalgamated into the Great Church. This would explain why Johannine ideas but not quotations appear in the earlier church writings: because a majority of those who claimed the Gospel as their own had become heterodox, there would have been a reluctance among the orthodox to cite the Gospel as Scripture.[288] Nevertheless, the example of I John showed that there was an orthodox way to read the Gospel, and the Epistle's campaign against the secessionists ultimately encouraged writers like Irenaeus to employ the Gospel in a war

---

285. R.E. Brown, "The Relation of 'The Secret Gospel of Mark' to the Fourth Gospel," *CBQ* 36 (1974) 466-85.

286. Epiphanius, *Panarion* LI (GCS 31, 248ff.), drawing upon Hippolytus.

287. *Adversus Haereses* III xvi 5,8, citing I John 2:18.

288. J.N. Sanders, *The Fourth Gospel in the Early Church* (Cambridge Univ., 1943) 31, suggests that the vagueness of Justin's references to John may be explained by the Gospel's insecure standing.

against gnostics who were spiritual descendants of the secessionists.[289] Thus the ultimate contribution of the author of I John to Johannine history may have been that of saving the Fourth Gospel for the church.[290]

In this theory the tradition of Irenaeus about an opposition between John and Cerinthus (n. 220 above) and the attempts of scholars to identify the opponents of I John as followers of Cerinthus have an aspect of truth. Actually the heritage of the author of I John in interpreting John was used in the slightly later battle of the churches (before A.D. 120) against Cerinthus whose ideas may well have involved an exaggeration or hardening of the secessionist positions.[291] The attempt to trace the Fourth Gospel back from Irenaeus through Polycarp to the disciple John may be an oversimplified way of affirming that an orthodox reading of John came down to the church from the first century right through the second. In short, the Gospel was not a heterodox work being made orthodox for the first time at the end of the second century—even though it had been misused by gnostics throughout the second century. It had a pedigree of orthodoxy going back to "apostolic" times, a pedigree derived through the no-longer distinguishable descendants of the Johannine community that had been loyal theologically to the author of I John.

Moving from external evidence about the way the Fourth Gospel was received in the second century, let me now trace the possible theological development of the secessionist group into various forms of second-century heterodoxy, and then the possible development of the author's adherents.

---

289. By this I mean that some gnostics were influenced by the secessionist way of reading the Fourth Gospel.

290. Bakken (n. 283 above) saw much of this, but his claim that I John was written in order to make the Gospel acceptable to the orthodox reverses the proper chronology. The Epistle *de facto* played that function in history, but it was written before the great battles between the orthodox and the gnostics.

291. Little is known with certitude about Cerinthus or his dating, although he is consistently listed among the first gnostics. See G. Bardy, "Cérinthe," *RB* 30 (1921) 344-73.

THE SECESSIONISTS AND SECOND-CENTURY HETERODOXY

As I discuss a possible link between the secessionists of I John and the gnostics, docetists, Cerinthians, and Montanists of the second century, I wish to insist firmly on the word "possible." All that can be shown is how these heterodox groups *might* have derived some of their ideas from the Johannine tradition filtered through the secessionist optic.

Let me begin with that very diverse phenomenon known as gnosticism.[292] A common thesis in the gnostic systems involves the pre-existence of human beings in the divine sphere before their life on earth. In the Fourth Gospel only the Son of God pre-exists; others become children of God through faith, water, and Spirit during their earthly life. Their status as "not of this world" is a conferred one, not an ontological one. But as Wayne Meeks[293] has observed, there was a dynamism in this conception that could lead to the gnostic conception of a pre-existent relation to God. The Johannine stress on the pre-existence of Jesus and on his Sonship as the model for the Christian's status as child was the matrix out of which a gnostic thesis could be shaped. According to Irenaeus[294] the gnostic initiate connected his own status with a theology of pre-existence: "I derive being from Him who is preexistent and return to my own place from which I came forth." A particular catalyst in a development toward gnosticism may have been the Johannine insistence on the predestination of the chil-

---

292. M.F. Wiles, *The Spiritual Gospel: The Interpretation of the Fourth Gospel in the Early Church* (Cambridge Univ., 1960) 96-111, lists four aspects of John that would be very acceptable to gnostics: (1) the philosophical character of the Prologue; (2) dualism; (3) coming down from heaven; (4) determinism.

293. "Man from Heaven" (n. 8 above) 68ff., esp. 72: "Once the Fourth Gospel had identified Christ-Wisdom with the masculine Logos, and once the social dynamics of the anti-worldly sect were set in motion, all the forces were present for the production of a myth of the Valentinian type."

294. *Adversus Haereses* I xxi 5.

dren of light[295] so that they are already attracted to God before Jesus comes and he uncovers their predisposition (John 3:17-21). There is a sense of inevitability about those who come to believe because they have already been given by God to Jesus (3:27; 6:44, 64; 15:16). The gnostic would simply have had to move the orientation toward God and toward light back to pre-existence. Similarly the claim of the secessionists, "We have not sinned" (pp. 124-27 above), would in a gnostic milieu have been understood as stemming from the very being of the children of light rather than from belief in Jesus' word which sanctifies—like Jesus himself the believer would now by nature be opposed to sin. Although at the time of the First Epistle the secessionists spoke as a communitarian "we" (n. 258 above), the very secession may have led to a greater stress on the latent individualism in Johannine thought, so that salvation would become an individual matter (as with the gnostics), divorced from the idea of belonging to a saved people.[296]

If we turn from gnosticism in general to Cerinthus in particular, let us reflect on his position that Christ (a divine Power) descended upon Jesus after the baptism and withdrew from him before the crucifixion. In my judgment this goes beyond the detectable position of the secessionists in I John who seemingly accepted the reality but not the salvific significance of the baptism and the death (pp. 116-20 above). Nevertheless, once there was a tendency to deemphasize the two events, there were factors in John that might have led to Cerinthus' view. Too often we read John 1:14, "The Word became flesh," in the light of the Matthean and Lucan infancy narratives and assume that the moment of becoming flesh should automatically be interpreted as the conception/birth of Jesus. There is reason to believe that the evangelist himself regarded the whole human life of Jesus *from its*

---

295. H.M. Schenke, "Determination und Ethik im ersten Johannesbrief," *ZTK* 60 (1963) 203-15, contends that already in the Gospel there was a gnostic sense of determination.

296. E. Schweizer. *Church Order* (n. 6 above) 122-24 (11g-i), reads Johannine thought as highly individualistic.

beginning as the career of the Word-become-flesh.[297] However, Reginald Fuller[298] has done a service in pointing out that John could be read another way. The Gospel never clearly mentions the birth of Jesus. In the Prologue, before we are told that the light came into the world (1:9-10), JBap is mentioned. And immediately after the reference to the Word becoming flesh, there is another verse pertinent to JBap (1:15). If one isolated John's Gospel and read it with docetic spectacles, one might assume that the moment of the light's coming into the world and the moment of the Word's becoming flesh was right after the baptism of Jesus when the Spirit came upon Jesus, as JBap says, "I myself never recognized him, though the very reason why I came and baptized with water was so that he might be revealed to Israel. . . . I have seen the Spirit descend like a dove from the sky and it came to rest upon him" (1:30,32). We have evidence that this happened in the gnostic Nag Hammadi tractate, the *Testimony of Truth* IX 3 (30:24-28) which draws upon John's account of the events surrounding the baptism of Jesus: "And JBap bore witness to the (descent) of Jesus. For he is the one who saw the (power) which came down upon the Jordan river."

The other half of Cerinthus' docetic christology (i.e., that the divine element left Jesus before the crucifixion) might have stemmed from a misinterpretation of John's stress on the crucifixion as the "lifting up" of Jesus (12:32-33; 3:14; 8:28). John sees the crucifixion as the going of Jesus to the Father; but Cerinthus may have understood John to mean that, before Jesus died, the divine element had already gone heavenward. Remember that in 13:1, at the *beginning* of the Last Supper, John tells us that the

---

297. Notice that the *ginesthai* ("to become, be born") of John 1:14 is used in the christological descriptions of the *birth* of Jesus in Gal 4:4; Philip 2:7; Rom 1:3.

298. "Christmas, Epiphany, and the Johannine Prologue," in *Spirit and Light* (E.M. West Festschrift; ed. M. L'Engle and W.B. Green; New York: Seabury, 1976) 63-73. He proposes that the shift from the *Logos asarkos* (Word without flesh) to the *Logos ensarkos* (Word enfleshed) occurs in relation to JBap (69). He modifies this stance somewhat in the article cited in n. 95 above.

hour had come for Jesus to pass from this world to the Father; and frequent statements of imminent departure are found throughout the Last Supper (13:36; 14:2, 19, 28, 30, 31; 16:5, 7, 16ff.). Particularly striking in reference to Cerinthus' position are these Last Supper affirmations: "Now is the Son of Man glorified" (13:31); "I am leaving the world and I am going back to the Father" (16:28); "I have overcome the world" (16:33), especially when the last is read as an introduction to the great prayer of chap. 17 where Jesus seems suspended between heaven and earth. It is in that prayer (17:11) that Jesus says, "I am no longer in the world." Is it fantastic to assume that Cerinthus took that literally?

Even more obvious is a Johannine line of development to Montanus. We know that he read the Johannine promises of the coming, giving, or sending of the Paraclete (14:15, 26; 15:26; 16:7, 13) as a prediction of his own Spirit-inspired career. The Montanist stress on prophecy could be a continuation of the stress on prophecy among the secessionists (and, of course, of the stress on prophecy in the Book of Revelation). Montanus made use of two women prophets, Prisca and Maximilla, who ecstatically revealed the words of the Lord.[299] In Appendix II below I call attention to the extraordinary importance that John gives to women as proclaimers: the Samaritan woman by her word converts a whole village (4:39); Martha utters the solemn confession, "You are the Christ, the Son of God" (11:27), which Matt 16:16 attributes to Peter; Mary Magdalene, not Peter, becomes the first to see the risen Jesus (20:14) and the first to make the resurrection proclamation (20:18). It may be added that it was probably John's portrait of Mary Magdalene which sparked the gnostic Gospels to make her the chief recipient of post-resurrectional revelation and the rival of Peter.[300]

---

299. There is an attack on a false woman prophetess and teacher ("Jezebel") in Rev 2:20-22, and on the false-prophet figure of the beast from the land in Rev 13:11-18; 19:20. Montanus expected the coming of the heavenly Jerusalem to earth near Pepuza in Asia Minor, an expectation that echoes Rev 21:2.

300. In the *Gospel of Philip* II 3 (63:35–64:5) she has become the disciple whom Jesus loved most; in the *Gospel of Mary* BG 8502 I

We have now seen some possibilities and even probabilities of a lineal ideological descent from the secessionist interpretation of the Johannine tradition to second-century heterodoxy. Let us now look at the other half of the Johannine community.

THE AUTHOR'S ADHERENTS AND THE GREAT CHURCH

While there are no clear orthodox citations of the Fourth Gospel before the last quarter of the second century, Johannine ideas are acceptable much earlier.[301] We may concentrate on Ignatius (*ca.* A.D. 110). In discussing the state of the Johannine community when the Gospel was written, we saw that the "Jewish Christians of Inadequate Faith" (Group V) who appeared in the Gospel resembled in several ways the Jewish Christians against whom Ignatius fought twenty years later (pp. 79-80 above). Ignatius fought also against docetism and perhaps against emerging gnosticism (e.g., *Smyrn.* 4:1). Were these two adversaries, the Jewish Christians and the docetists, the same? While some scholars would answer affirmatively,[302] a serious case can be made that Ignatius was fighting on two fronts, and that both his adversaries were heterodox, but on opposite extremes.[303] This would

---

(17:7ff.) Peter becomes jealous of Mary even as he is jealous of the Beloved Disciple in John 21:20-23.

301. Two cautions should be observed here. I shall use *Logos* as an example of a *Johannine* idea when it is applied to Jesus, but theoretically it is possible that a second-century writer who used that term derived it from an unknown Christian source other than John. Also, when we speak of Johannine ideas being acceptable, one probably should make geographical distinctions. It has often been noted that, while Logos christology gained acceptance in the East in the first half of the second century, Rome seems to have resisted it longer as suspect of docetism.

302. E. Molland, "The Heretics Combatted by Ignatius of Antioch," *JEH* 5 (1954) 1-6; L.W. Barnard, "The Background of St. Ignatius of Antioch," *VC* 17 (1963) 193-206. This was a view held earlier by Lightfoot and Zahn.

303. V. Corwin, *St. Ignatius and Christianity in Antioch* (New Haven: Yale, 1960), esp. 59. This thesis has been defended again by P.J. Donahue, "Jewish Christianity in the Letters of Ignatius of Antioch," *VC* 32 (1978) 81-93, who maintains that in *Magnesians* and *Philadelphians* Ignatius carried on the Pauline dialectic against Jewish Christians but never accused those opponents of denying the reality of the incarnation.

correspond closely to the two fronts on which the Johannine community fought—during the Gospel period Jewish Christians were among those criticized by the evangelist because of their low christology; during the Epistle period the secessionists were criticized for inadequate emphasis on the humanity of Jesus. Thus there is a similarity of ambiance between the Johannine writings and the Ignatian letters.

In Ignatius we find elements of a high christology similar to John's. In *Magn.* 8:2 Ignatius speaks of "The one God who manifested Himself through Jesus Christ, His Son." This is not unlike John 17:3: "That they know you, the one true God, and Jesus Christ whom you have sent," combined with the thesis of 14:8 that whoever sees the Son sees the Father. The *Magnesians* passage continues by describing the Son as "God's Word proceeding from silence who in all things was pleasing to Him who sent him." Three elements here seem to be Johannine,[304] namely, the reference to Jesus as the "Word," the description of him as the one sent by God, and the idea of his having come forth, especially when the preceding chapter of *Magnesians* (7:2) makes it clear that he came forth from the Father (see John 16:28). It is fascinating that elsewhere (*Eph.* 19:1) Ignatius shows knowledge of the virginity of Mary, thus implying a christology of virginal conception, not known to us from John but from Matthew and Luke. This mixed christology of pre-existence (the Word) and virginal conception may be brought together in the eloquent phrase of *Eph.* 7:2: "both of Mary and of God." A similar mixed christology whereby a pre-existent figure becomes incarnate in the womb of the virgin Mary is attested in the first half of the second century in the *Apology* of Aristides (15:1) and in the *Apology* of Justin (I 21, 33). Another Ignatian mixture of the non-Johannine and the Johannine is found in *Trall.* 9:2: Jesus Christ "who was also truly raised from the dead , . . without whom we have no true [*alēthinos*] life." The latter clause with its characterization of eternal life as "true" over against earthly life is very Johannine; but the idea of Jesus' being raised from death[304a] is not Johannine,

---

304. Non-Johannine, however, is the image of proceeding *from silence*.

304a. For the seeming exception in John 2:22; 21:14, see my AB Commentary, I, 116.

for the Johannine Jesus takes up his own life again (John 10:17-18). I attach importance to these mixed patterns in Ignatius. When I was discussing the relationship between the Johannine Christians and the Apostolic Christians, I pointed out that the prayer of Jesus, "That they all may be one" (17:21), expressed the desire of the Johannine Christians for unity with the Apostolic Christians, if the latter would accept the high, pre-existence christology of the Fourth Gospel. Ignatius and the other second-century writers cited give evidence that the Great Church did accept that christology and indeed eventually gave preference to the thesis of a pre-existent Word, but only with the compromise of not rejecting the virginal conception and other lower christologies.

Another possible Ignatian echo of Johannine tradition would be the reference to the eucharist as the *flesh* and blood of Jesus (*Phld.* 4:1),[305] especially when that is combined with Ignatius' high sacramentalism wherein the eucharist is "the medicine of immortality, the antidote that we should not die, but live forever in Jesus Christ" (*Eph.* 20:2). This is quite close to John 6:51-58 where the flesh and blood of Jesus are real food and drink, and "the man who feeds on this bread will live forever." Thus John and Ignatius would have shared a common outlook on the two points on which they both disagreed with the Jewish Christian churches, namely, a high christology and a sacramental view of the eucharist.[306]

There are Ignatian parallels to themes in I John as well, showing that if Ignatius knew Johannine thought, he would have been sympathetic with the Epistles' emphases rather than with those of the secessionists (as we might expect from his anti-

---

305. I speak precisely of an echo of the "tradition" and not of the Fourth Gospel. Although in the NT only that Gospel refers to the eucharist as the flesh of Jesus, such terminology would undoubtedly go back to an earlier Semitic tradition which influenced both John and Ignatius.

306. If, as I have suggested, Ignatius fought on two fronts, he would also have battled his docetist enemies over the reality of the eucharistic flesh: "They abstain from the eucharist and prayer, because they do not confess that the eucharist is the flesh of our Savior Jesus Christ who suffered for our sins" (*Smyrn.* 7:1).

docetic attitudes). In *Trall*. 9:1; 10:1, Ignatius emphasizes the true humanity of Jesus who was born, ate, drank, and truly died. Ignatius claims that what he holds about this came from the beginning and is self-authenticating.

However, there is one very serious obstacle to the thesis that the group of Johannine Christians who sided with the author of the Epistle could have fitted into the type of churches addressed by Ignatius and have become part of what he calls "the church catholic" (the Great Church). There may be close similarities between Ignatius and John in matters of high christology and the eucharist, but they are very unlike each other in ecclesiology, especially in matters of church structure. We have seen that the Johannine community did not seem to have authoritative church officers (presbyter-bishops) who could control doctrine by the very nature of their office, and so differed in this aspect from the churches attested in Luke-Acts, the Pastorals, and Matthew.[307] Ignatian church structure has gone even further in the direction of authoritative church offices, and Ignatius insists on the role of the single bishop (who was now over the presbyters) almost to the point of obsession. The established hierarchy now had control over baptism and the eucharist (*Smyrn*. 8:1-2); human authority now became the visible sign of divine authority, as the following citations suggest:

> All of you, follow the bishop as Jesus Christ follows his Father; and follow those in the presbyterate as if they were the apostles; and reverence those in the diaconate as you would a commandment from God. (*Smyrn*. 8:1)

> It is good to know God and the bishop. He who honors the bishop has been honored by God; he who does anything without the knowledge of the bishop is serving the devil. (*Smyrn*. 9:1)

> Let us be careful not to oppose the bishop, that we may be subject to God. (*Eph*. 5:3)

---

307. Matt 18:15-20 shows the existence of clear authority in the Matthean church, even that of binding and loosing, although no name is transmitted for those who exercise it.

When you are obedient to your bishop as though to Jesus Christ, it is clear to me that you are living after the manner of Jesus Christ himself. (*Trall.* 2:1)

Could Johannine Christians have accepted such an ecclesiology wherein the bishop is given the prerogatives of the Paraclete? Certainly it could not have been seen as harmonious with Johannine tradition, but it might have been grudgingly tolerated for the sake of a greater good when Johannine dependence on the Paraclete-teacher had proved ineffectual. If the world listened to the opponents, as the author of I John admits (4:5); if the appeal to test the spirits was not successful in preventing more of his followers from being converted by the "progressives" (II John 8-10); if the majority of the Johannine churches were going into what the author considered christological and ethical error—in this case, may not some of the author's adherents have recognized that the truth could not be preserved by simply appealing to an anointing by the Spirit which teaches about all things (I John 2:27)? The lesson that the Pauline churches learned (as we see in the Pastorals) may also have been learned by some of the author's adherents in the Johannine churches, namely, that authoritative presbyter-bishops serving as teachers were a bulwark against those who presented a doctrine which "does not agree with the sound words of our Lord Jesus Christ and the teaching which accords with godliness" (I Tim 6:3). I am proposing, then, that while "the church catholic" exemplified by Ignatius may have accepted the high Johannine christology of pre-existence as a valid evaluation of Jesus, especially when it was accompanied by the stress on the earthly career of Jesus that we find in the Epistles, the Johannine adherents of the author of the Epistles may have had in turn to recognize that the hierarchy stressed by "the church catholic" was a valid teaching office, so long as it exercised its functions in the name of the Paraclete who is the teacher of all. And through this mutual recognition of value in the other's strength (which is the opposite of sectarianism), some of the Johannine Christians and the Apostolic Christians may have become "one sheep herd."

Signs of the acceptance of a more stringent church authority may have already occurred in the lifetime of the author of the

Epistles and probably to his chagrin, for one who held on so firmly to the Johannine tradition which came "from the beginning" may not himself have been able to accept this deviation. In III John we find the presbyter locked in struggle with Diotrephes "who likes to put himself first," apparently not over the doctrinal issues which separated the author from the secessionists, but over two styles of authority. It has long been suggested that Diotrephes was an emerging bishop on the Ignatian model,[308] although that suggestion has often been complicated by the attribution of heterodoxy either to the presbyter[309] or to Diotrephes. Rather, we may be encountering two proponents of the *same* Johannine christology and ethics who differed on how best to preserve the believers from false teaching.[310] The presbyter sends his emissaries to bear witness and he thinks they should be received; their testimonial is the fact that the presbyter sent them, for "you know that our witness is true" (III John 5-8, 12). Even at this juncture he can appeal only to the self-authenticating quality of his testimony, and to the implicit support of the Johannine school ("*our* witness"). He cannot correct or depose Diotrephes by simple order; he can only challenge, "If I come, I shall bring up what he is doing in spreading evil nonsense about us" (III John 10). But there are also false teachers and false emissaries wandering around, as the presbyter well knows; and he thinks they should be refused admittance to any house church (II John 10). Diotrephes, as the assembler of a house church, may have faced the practical difficulty of telling true teacher-emissaries from false teacher-emissaries, a situation we see verified in *Didache* 11; and he may have found the test of the spirits quite impractical and

---

308. A. von Harnack, "Über den dritten Johannesbrief," TU 15, #3 (1897) 3-27.

309. E. Käsemann, "Ketzer und Zeuge: Zum johanneischen Verfasserproblem." ZTK 48 (1951) 292-311; reprinted in his *Exegetische Versuche und Besinnungen* (Göttingen: Vandenhoeck & Ruprecht, 1960) I, 168-87.

310. Pastor, "Comunidad" (n. 6 above), 64-65, is right when he insists that the only clear controversy in III John is over the acceptance of emissaries, a controversy that exists in II John as well. Unfortunately, however, Pastor does not see the implications for church structure in this battle over missionaries.

inconclusive. In which case, his prudential decision would have been to exclude all emissary-teachers and to discipline those who received them (III John 10). His own interpretation of the tradition would then, de facto, have become the supreme authority for the church in which he made himself first (III John 9). In this hypothesis, it would have been a leader like Diotrephes, rather than the author of the Epistles himself, who made the transition to a structure or ecclesiastical polity which "the church catholic" could understand and accept.

There may be one last Johannine passage that casts light on how some of the doctrinal adherents of the epistolary author became part of the Great Church. As I pointed out above (pp. 95-96), the relationship between the redactor of the Gospel and the author of the Epistles is obscure, precisely because there is no scholarly agreement on how much of the present Gospel to attribute to the redactor. Were both the Gospel-redaction and the Epistles the work of the same man, and which came first? In general, in order to avoid the charge of manipulating the Gospel, I have preferred to treat the Gospel as a whole which antedated the Epistles; and thus implicitly I have worked with the thesis that even the final redaction came before I John was written. But if one allows the possibility that chap. 21 was written by the redactor after the main Gospel and therefore roughly contemporaneously with the Epistles,[311] some recent suggestions of E. Ruckstuhl are interesting.[312] This chapter certainly protects the memory and status of the Beloved Disciple, so that there is no betrayal of the Johannine heritage. The destiny of the Beloved Disciple was planned by Jesus; and he is not of lesser dignity than Peter, even if he did not die a martyr's death as Peter did. But the chapter also recommends Peter to the Johannine reader. I have

---

311. Thyen (n. 41 above) sees the redactor motivated by an aspect of the theological struggle so visible in the Epistles. Also Langbrandtner, *Weltferner Gott* (n. 322 below in Appendix I) 116: "We must presuppose a theological-dogmatic struggle within Johannine Christianity in which the redactor championed a particular stance under the name and with the adherence of the Beloved Disciple."

312. "Zur Aussage und Botschaft von Johannes 21," in the Schürmann Festschrift (n. 186 above) 339-62, esp. 360-61.

insisted that the rest of the Fourth Gospel was not anti-Petrine, although it made clear that Simon Peter (the paradigm of the Apostolic Christians) did not understand Jesus as profoundly as did the Beloved Disciple (the paradigm of the Johannine Christians). But chap. 21 goes out of its way to underline the pastoral role of Peter. It does not exempt him from the Johannine criterion of loving Jesus; but the threefold question and affirmation of love (21:15-17) assures the Johannine reader that he is a genuine disciple, and it is on that basis that Jesus himself has given him pastoral authority.[313] Since no similar pastoral role is given to the Beloved Disciple, we may be hearing a symbolic description of the structural difference between two types of churches. We can be sure that some of the adherents of the author of the Epistles (and perhaps the author himself) would have regarded an acceptance of the presbyteral-episcopal structure as an inadmissible betrayal of the Johannine tradition (and, in fact, it did lead to the end of this branch of the Johannine community as a distinct body of churches). In the redactional chap. 21 we may have a more moderate voice persuading the Johannine Christians that the pastoral authority practiced in the Apostolic churches and in "the church catholic" was instituted by Jesus and could be accepted without denigration of the specially favored place in history given by Jesus to the disciple(s) whom he loved most.

REFLECTION

I shall not insult the reader's intelligence by a long discourse on the church problems in the Johannine Gospel and Epistles as parallel to the church problems in our own times. Obviously, struggles between churches over a diversity of traditions and struggles within an individual church over diverse interpretations of the same tradition tend *mutatis mutandis* to follow the same

---

313. In these verses John uses *boskein*, "to feed," and *poimainein*, "to tend"; the second includes such duties toward the flock as guiding, guarding, and feeding, whether literally (Luke 17:7) or figuratively (Ezek 34:10; Acts 20:28; I Pet 5:2—the latter passages being associated with the work of presbyters). Equivalently it may mean "to rule, govern" (II Sam 7:7; Ps 2:9; Matt 2:6).

lines over the centuries. A familiar pattern, too, is the anguish over authoritative church offices and the reluctant recognition, even by groups committed to freedom under the Spirit, that some form of authority is the only way to protect against extravagant claims in the name of the Spirit. Sir Edwyn Hoskyns[314] phrased well the insight that Johannine history presents in microcosm the church struggles of the ages: "The modern reader will therefore not apprehend the Fourth Gospel as its author meant it to be apprehended if he concludes that it was against, say Gnosticism, or Docetism, or Ebionitism, or even against the Jews, and rests satisfied with that explanation, without at the same time recognizing that those ancient movements of religion are still deap-seated and destructive factors in our common life."

What I do want to reflect upon is the results for the Great Church of the amalgamation of Johannine Christians into its membership and of the acceptance of the Johannine writings into its canon of Scripture. At various times I have referred to the theology of the Fourth Gospel as challengingly different, volatile, dangerous, and as the most adventuresome in the NT. The history of the Johannine secessionists who laid claim to the Gospel should explain those adjectives. Over the centuries John's Gospel has provided the seedbed for many exotic forms of individualistic pietism and quietism (as well as the inspiration for some of the most profound mysticism). Johannine christology has nurtured a widespread unconscious monophysitism, popular even today, in which Jesus is not really like us in everything except sin, but omniscient, unable to suffer or to be tempted, foreseeing the whole future. (At the same time, Johannine christology has been the mainstay of the great orthodox faith of Nicaea.)

The ultimate check upon what Kysar calls the "maverick Gospel" has been the church's hermeneutical decision to place it in the same canon as Mark, Matthew, and Luke, Gospels which implicitly advocate the side opposite to many Johannine positions. This means that the Great Church, "the church catholic" of Ignatian language, whether consciously or unconsciously, has chosen to live with tension. It has chosen not a Jesus who is either God or man but both; it has chosen not a Jesus who is either

---

314. *Fourth Gospel* (n. 187 above) 49.

virginally conceived as God's Son or pre-existent as God's Son but both; not either a Spirit who is given to an authoritative teaching magisterium or the Paraclete-teacher who is given to each Christian but both; not a Peter or a Beloved Disciple but both. Tension is not easily accepted in ordinary life, and we usually try to resolve it. So too in church history—but because of the church decision about the canon, attempts at simple resolutions of these theological tensions into a static position on one side or the other are unfaithful to the whole NT.

This means that a church such as my own, the Roman Catholic, with its great stress on authority and structure, has in the Johannine writings an inbuilt conscience against the abuses of authoritarianism. (So also the "free" churches have in the Pastorals an inbuilt warning against abuses of the Spirit and in I John a warning against the divisions to which a lack of structured authority leads.) Like one branch of the Johannine community, we Roman Catholics have come to appreciate that Peter's pastoral role is truly intended by the risen Lord, but the presence in our Scriptures of a disciple whom Jesus loved more than he loved Peter is an eloquent commentary on the relative value of the church office. The authoritative office is necessary because a task is to be done and unity is to be preserved, but the scale of power in various offices is not necessarily the scale of Jesus' esteem and love. In this day when Catholics quarrel about how much respective authority pope, bishop, priest, and lay person should have, and when Christians quarrel about whether a woman should be an ordained minister of the eucharist, John's voice cries out its warning. The greatest dignity to be striven for is neither papal, episcopal, nor priestly; the greatest dignity is that of belonging to the community of the beloved disciples of Jesus Christ.

SUMMARY
CHARTS

CHART ONE
THE HISTORY OF THE JOHANNINE COMMUNITY

PHASE ONE: ORIGINS (mid-50s to late 80s)

ORIGINATING GROUP: In or near Palestine Jews of relatively standard expectations, including followers of JBap, accepted Jesus without difficulty as the Davidic Messiah, the fulfiller of the prophecies, and one confirmed by miracles. Among this group was a man who had known Jesus during the ministry and who would become the Beloved Disciple.

SECOND GROUP: Jews of an anti-Temple bias who believed in Jesus and made converts in Samaria. They understood Jesus against a Mosaic rather than a Davidic background. He had been with God, seen Him, and brought down His words to people.

The acceptance of the Second group catalyzed the development of a high, pre-existence christology, which led to debates with Jews who thought the Johannine community was abandoning Jewish monotheism by making a second God out of Jesus. Ultimately the leaders of these Jews had the Johannine Christians expelled from the synagogues. The latter, alienated from their own, saw "the Jews" as children of the devil. They stressed a realization of the eschatological promises in Jesus to compensate for what they had lost in Judaism. The Disciple made this transition and helped others to make it, thus becoming the Beloved Disciple.

GENTILE CONVERTS

PHASE TWO: GOSPEL (*ca.* 90)

Since "the Jews" were blinded, the coming of the Greeks was God's plan of fulfillment. The community may have moved from Palestine to the Diaspora to teach the Greeks. This contact brought out the universalistic possibilities in Johannine thought. However, rejection by others and persecution by "the Jews" convinced Johannine

Christians that the world was opposed to Jesus, and that they should not belong to this world which was under the power of Satan. Rejection of the high Johannine christology by Jewish Christians was seen as unbelief and led to a breaking of communion (koinōnia). Communications were kept open to the Apostolic Christians (see Chart Two) with hopes for unity, despite differences of christology and church structure.

The defensive concentration on christology against "the Jews" and the Jewish Christians led to a split within the Johannine community.

PHASE THREE:
EPISTLES
(ca. 100)

THE ADHERENTS OF THE AUTHOR OF THE EPISTLES: To be a child of God one must confess Jesus come in the flesh and must keep the commandments. The secessionists are the children of the devil and the antichrists. The anointing with the Spirit obviates the need for human teachers; test all who claim to have the

THE SECESSIONISTS: The One who has come down from above is so divine he is not fully human; he does not belong to the world. Neither his life on earth nor that of the believer have salvific import. Knowledge that God's Son came into the world is all important, and those who believe in this are already saved.

PHASE FOUR: Spirit.
AFTER THE EPISTLES
(2nd century)

UNION WITH THE GREAT CHURCH: Unable to combat the secessionists simply by appealing to tradition, and losing out to their opponents, some of the author's adherents accepted the need for authoritative official teachers (presbyter-bishops). At the same time "the church catholic" showed itself open to the high Johannine christology. There was a gradual assimilation into the Great Church which was slow, however, to accept the Fourth Gospel since it was being misused by gnostics.

ROAD TO GNOSTICISM: The larger part of the Johannine community seems to have accepted secessionist theology which, having been cut off from the moderates through schism, moved toward true docetism (from a not fully human Jesus to a mere appearance of humanity), toward gnosticism (from a pre-existent Jesus to pre-existent believers who also came down from the heavenly regions), and toward Montanism (from possessing the Paraclete to the embodiment of the Paraclete). They took the Fourth Gospel with them; it was accepted early by gnostics who commented on it.

CHART TWO
DIFFERENT RELIGIOUS GROUPINGS
OUTSIDE THE JOHANNINE COMMUNITY
AS SEEN THROUGH THE PAGES OF THE FOURTH GOSPEL

THOSE WHO DO NOT BELIEVE IN JESUS

I. The World

II. "The Jews"

III. The Adherents
of John the Baptist

Those who prefer darkness to the light of Jesus because their deeds are evil. By this choice they are already condemned; they are under the power of the Satanic "Prince of this world" and hate Jesus and his disciples who are not of this world. Jesus refuses to pray for the world; rather he has overcome the world. "The world" is a wider conception than "the Jews" (II) but includes them. This opposition gave the Johannine community an alienated sense of being strangers in the world.

Those within the synagogues who did not believe in Jesus and had decided that anybody who acknowledged Jesus as Messiah would be put out of the synagogue. The main points in their dispute with the Johannine Christians involved: (a) Claims about the oneness of Jesus with the Father—the Johannine Jesus "was speaking of God as his own Father, thus making himself God's equal"; (b) Claims that understanding Jesus as God's presence on earth deprived the Temple and the Jewish feasts of their significance. They exposed the Johannine Christians to death by persecution and thought that thus they were serving God. In John's view they were children of the devil.

Although some of JBap's followers joined Jesus or became Christians (including Johannine Christians), others refused, claiming that JBap and not Jesus was God's prime emissary. The Fourth Gospel carefully denies that JBap is the Messiah, Elijah, the Prophet, the light, or the bridegroom. It insists that JBap must decrease while Jesus must increase. Yet the adherents of JBap are pictured as misunderstanding Jesus, not hating him. There seems to remain hope for their conversion.

THOSE WHO (CLAIM TO) BELIEVE IN JESUS

IV. The Crypto-Christians

Christian Jews who had remained within the synagogues by refusing to admit publicly that they believed in Jesus. "They preferred by far the praise of men to the glory of God." Presumably they thought they could retain their private faith in Jesus without breaking from their Jewish heritage. But in the eyes of the Johannine Christians, they thus preferred to be known as disciples of Moses rather than disciples of Jesus. For practical purposes they could be thought of along with "the Jews" (II), although John was implicitly still trying to persuade them to confess their faith publicly.

V. The Jewish Christians

Christians who had left the synagogues but whose faith in Jesus was inadequate by Johannine standards. They may have regarded themselves as heirs to a Christianity which had existed at Jerusalem under James the brother of the Lord. Presumably their low christology based on miraculous signs was partway between that of Groups IV and VI. They did not accept Jesus' divinity. They did not understand the eucharist as the true flesh and blood of Jesus. In John's view they had ceased to be true believers.

VI. Christians of Apostolic Churches

Quite separate from the synagogues, mixed communities of Jews and Gentiles regarded themselves as heirs of the Christianity of Peter and the Twelve. Theirs was a moderately high christology, confessing Jesus as the Messiah born at Bethlehem of Davidic descent and thus Son of God from conception, but without a clear insight into his coming from above in terms of pre-existence before creation. In their ecclesiology Jesus may have been seen as the founding father and institutor of the sacraments; but the church now had a life of its own with pastors who carried on apostolic teaching and care. In John's view they did not fully understand Jesus or the teaching function of the Paraclete, but the Johannine Christians prayed for unity with them.

APPENDIX I
RECENT RECONSTRUCTIONS
OF JOHANNINE COMMUNITY
HISTORY

I warned the reader in the Preface that my reconstruction of Johannine community history carried at most probability. Therefore, I think it only fair as well as useful to summarize some other reconstructions in order to familiarize the reader with the range of scholarly opinion on this subject. In the introduction to my AB commentary on John (n. 12 above), by discussing many theories of composition, authorship, and destination, I have already surveyed the classic approaches to Johannine history;[315] and so here I shall confine myself to reconstructions that have appeared in the 1970s since my commentary was finished.

J. LOUIS MARTYN

For years Martyn has been most active in developing the thesis that the Fourth Gospel must be read on several levels, so that it tells us not only about Jesus but also about the life and

---

315. This is conveniently supplemented by the writings of R. Kysar: *The Fourth Evangelist* (n. 20 above); and "Community and Gospel: Vectors in Fourth Gospel Criticism," *Int* 31 (1977) 355-66.

struggles of the Johannine community (n. 18 above). It is significant that now he has attempted an elaborate reconstruction of Johannine church origins,[316] based on the following principle: "The literary history behind the Fourth Gospel reflects to a large degree the history of a single community which maintained over a period of some duration its particular and somewhat peculiar identity." Martyn distinguishes three periods of Johannine community history: Early, Middle, and Late.

I. THE EARLY PERIOD. (Before the Jewish revolt until some point in the 80s.) The pre-Gospel formation began with separate homilies, e.g., a homily underlying John 1:35-49 wherein a preacher sought to persuade (fellow) Jews, who had well-formed messianic expectations, to *come* to Jesus and *find* him to be the Messiah. The miracles of Jesus were narrated as signs that he was the Messiah. Success in conversions at first produced relatively little alienation from the Jewish heritage, viz., no debates about the validity of the Torah nor about the Gentile mission. The resultant Johannine group consisted of *Christian Jews* who stood "in a relatively untroubled stream of social and theological continuity precisely within the synagogue." One of the preachers in this inner-synagogue messianic group gathered the traditions and homilies about Jesus into a rudimentary written gospel, somewhat similar to the Signs Gospel or Signs Source posited by many scholars. "The possibility that the Beloved Disciple was a historical person who played a role in the Early Period cannot be pursued in the present essay."

II. THE MIDDLE PERIOD. (Presumably the late 80s.) Becoming suspicious of this rapidly growing messianic group, some in the synagogue demanded exegetical proof for what the group proclaimed about Jesus. This led to midrashic debates and to degrees of alignment within the synagogue for and against the group. Two traumas precipitated new developments. The first trauma occurred early in the Middle Period when the synagogue authorities

---

316. "Glimpses into the History of the Johannine Community," in *L'Evangile de Jean* (n. 41 above) 149-75. This is republished in his *The Gospel of John in Christian History* (New York: Paulist, 1979).

introduced the reworded *Birkat ha-Minim* (curse on the deviators) into the liturgical service in order to be able to identify and
eject those who confessed Jesus as the Messiah. Some of the
messianic group (and some attracted toward it) turned back to
remain safely within the synagogue community. Those who continued in the group now became *Jewish Christians* (no longer
Christian Jews), separate and alienated from the synagogue. The
second trauma occurred when the synagogue authorities, in order
to prevent further defections to the Jewish Christian group, put
on trial and executed some of the Johannine community's
evangelists on the charge that they were misleading Jews "into
the worship of a second god alongside Adonai" (see John 5:18;
10:33; 16:2). Expulsion and persecution led the Johannine community to new christological formulations; and instead of a simple
heilsgeschichtlich continuity with Jewish expectations, a dualism
of above/below came to the fore. Jesus was now presented as a
Stranger who had come from above (3:31) and been rejected by
"his own people" (1:11). Those who accept him are hated by this
world and are not of this world (17:14, 16); they are no longer
"Jews" but have become "true Israelites" (1:47) chosen by the
Stranger from above (15:16). By the judgment of the synagogue
itself, they are no longer disciples of Moses but disciples of Jesus
(9:28).

III. THE LATE PERIOD. (Not precisely dated by J.L.M.) This
complex period involved the increasing self-identification of the
Johannine community in relation to other Christian groups (and
not only in relation to the synagogue). *First*, a relationship to
Crypto-Christians who remained within the synagogue. The
Johannine group argued that one is either from above or from
below and that no fence straddling is possible. The Christian Jews
in the synagogue were judged unable to maintain a dual alle-
giance; they were equivalent to the hated "Jews" and were "disciples of Moses, not of Jesus." Moreover, the Crypto-Christians
seemed to have aided the synagogue authorities in their persecution of the Johannine Jewish Christians by informing on them.
Second, a relationship to other Jewish Christians who had left the
synagogue and were scattered by persecution. These were the
"other sheep" of 10:16 who would ultimately be joined with the

Johannine community into one flock under one Good Shepherd.
When the Gospel was written, at least a quadrilateral situation existed:

1. The synagogue of "the Jews."
2. Crypto-Christians (Christian Jews) within the synagogue.
3. Other communities of Jewish Christians who had been expelled from the synagogue.
4. The Johannine community of Jewish Christians.

* * *

By way of brief comment, it should be obvious to the reader of this book that I agree on many points with Martyn whose work I greatly respect. But let me note briefly my disagreements. First, he does not come to grips with the role of the Beloved Disciple, a figure who can scarcely be left in suspension if one wants to be faithful to the Gospel's own sense of history. Second, he does not explain why the Christian Jews from the early period developed a christology that led to their expulsion from the synagogue and their becoming Jewish Christians. What was the cause or, at least, the catalyst? Third, he dates the middle period too late. Granted that the most probable date for the introduction of the *Birkat ha-Minîm* was *ca.* A.D. 85, an opposition between the community and the synagogue must have been developing for a considerable period before that. The late 80s would be a better date for his *late* period. Fourth, Martyn needs to give more attention to the Gentile component, not only in the Johannine community (since simple Jewish terms are explained in the Gospel), but also in what he calls "other communities of Jewish Christians." By the end of the century the main churches were mixed.

GEORG RICHTER

The late G. Richter[317] proposed a reconstruction of Johannine history whose guiding principle is *prima facie* diametrically

---

317. "Präsentische und futurische Eschatologie in 4. Evangelium," in *Gegenwart und kommendes Reich* (A. Vögtle Schülergabe; ed. P. Fiedler and D. Zeller; Stuttgart: Katholisches Bibelwerk, 1975) 117-52. Eng. summary by A.J. Mattill, "Johannine Communities behind the Fourth Gospel: Georg Richter's Analysis," *TS* 38 (1977) 294-315. There are some similarities to Richter's approach in the articles and thesis of J. Becker (n. 179 above).

opposed to Martyn's guiding principle of continuity within the same community. Richter is not tracing the history of one community adapting itself to changing circumstances; for he finds in the Fourth Gospel traces of the theological views of four different communities, all of whom worked with and upon an early basic Johannine writing (*Grundschrift*):

I. MOSAIC-PROPHET CHRISTIANS. Rejecting the idea of a Davidic Messiah, a group of Jews, resembling the Ebionites, proclaimed Jesus as a prophet-like-Moses. Expelled from the diaspora synagogues in the area of North Palestine, Syria, and the Transjordan, this group produced a *Grundschrift*, a foundational gospel-like work, out of the traditions that were available (including a Signs Source and a non-synoptic passion account).

II. SON-OF-GOD CHRISTIANS. Part of this Jewish Christian community developed a higher christology of Jesus as the preexistent, divine Son of God, a figure who came down from heaven bringing salvation. This christology caused conflict with other members of the community who retained the earlier christology of the group. The Son-Of-God Christians split from the Mosaic-prophet Christians and rewrote the *Grundschrift* as a vehicle of their higher christology. For example, they added the *Logos* hymn of 1:1-13 and the pre-existence statements of the Johannine Jesus. The rewriter may be called the evangelist.

III. DOCETIST CHRISTIANS. Some of the Son-of-God Christians interpreted the evangelist's high christology in a docetic way: Jesus' divine origins were so stressed that he became a totally divine being whose earthly appearance was only an illusion. The docetist Johannine Christians withdrew from the communities of Group II, as attested in I John 2:19, but continued a missionary activity which produced strife. The gospel, as it had been revised by the evangelist, served the Johannine docetists as their gospel, and no new docetic revision was made—only a docetic interpretation.

IV. REVISIONIST CHRISTIANS. A redactor who was decidedly anti-docetic rewrote the *Grundschrift* by making additions (1:14-18; 19:34-35) and composed I John as an apologetic defense of a theology of Jesus as the Son of God come in the flesh. The result was that he and his congregation stood somewhere in-between the Johannine Christians of Group I and Group II; for, in rejecting the docetism of Group III, he had pulled back to a position that was less adventurous than that of the evangelist of Group II.

* * *

Like Martyn, Richter thinks the Johannine community arose among Jews who believed that Jesus had fulfilled well-known Jewish expectations, and at a later stage there developed within the Johannine community a higher christology that went beyond Jewish expectations. Let me note briefly my disagreements with Richter. First, on the basis of 1:35-51 Martyn is right over against Richter in seeing the originating group's expectations as more standard *Davidic* expectations. I would judge that the substitution of Mosaic expectations came later, after the contact with the Samaritans. Second, Richter is probably wrong in positing two totally different communities (I and II). As I pointed out in discussing chap. 4 of John, the disciples of Jesus accepted the new Samaritan converts without acrimony. Perhaps the correct position is between Martyn and Richter: a basic group underwent development (so there is continuity); but part of the development is attributed to the entrance of and amalgamation with a second group, who catalyzed the higher christology. Third, while Richter does a service in carrying the development beyond stage II (where Martyn stopped for all practical purposes), he is wrong in reading the struggle between docetist Christians and revisionist Christians into the Gospel. That struggle is documented in the period of the Epistles (after the Gospel). Fourth, the designations "docetist" and "revisionist" do not do justice to the subtlety of the issues involved in the struggle between the author of the Epistles and those who seceded.

OSCAR CULLMANN

For over thirty years and in scattered articles Cullmann has discussed aspects of Johannine community history, but only recently has he given us an overall and detailed picture of the development as he sees it. In one sentence[318] he sums up his thesis about a Johannine circle which embraces several writers (at least the evangelist and a redactor) and a community with a special tradition: "We thus arrive in the following line, moving back in time: Johannine community—special Hellenist group in the early community in Jerusalem—Johannine circle of disciples—disciples of the Baptist—heterodox marginal Judaism." These cannot be broken down neatly into I, II, etc., as with the previous reconstructions; but let me describe the direction of Cullmann's reconstruction.

At the font of Johannine life there is a strong but distinctive historical tradition and direct relationship to Jesus. The Fourth Gospel, which can be called a life of Jesus, was the work of the Beloved Disciple (who is thus the author or evangelist), an eyewitness of the ministry of Jesus. The original (unredacted stage) of John was composed "at least as early as the synoptic gospels and probably even earlier than the earliest of them." The differences between John and the Synoptics are explicable, at least in part, by the fact that Jesus had two different styles of teaching.

The Johannine movement drew its followers from among "heterodox" Jews, including those who were followers of JBap and then of Jesus, and those who were very close to or identical with the Hellenists of Acts 6. The community that emerged was not a small group polemicizing against a larger church, but a group with distinct origins that had its own peculiar components.

* * *

Obviously in my own reconstruction I am close to Cullmann on a number of significant points: the importance of the Beloved Disciple; origins among disciples of JBap; the importance of the Samaritans and of Jews *similar* to the Hellenists; a core historical tradition behind the Gospel. However, Cullmann overly simplifies the situation, leading me to list the following disagreements. First, it is fundamentally inadequate to explain the differ-

---

318. *The Johannine Circle* (Philadelphia: Westminster, 1976) 87. See the reviews mentioned in n. 57 above.

ences between John and the Synoptics on the basis of different styles of speech stemming from Jesus; those differences are the product of editorial and theological development. Second, precisely those differences make it most implausible (nay impossible) that the Fourth Gospel was written by an eyewitness of the ministry of Jesus; the role of the Beloved Disciple was therefore not that of the evangelist. Third, the term "heterodox Jews" is too much of an umbrella term bringing under the same cover movements that were more distinct. Moreover, it is inaccurate historically since it implies Jewish orthodoxy at the time of Jesus.[319] Fourth, more needs to be said about the shaping of Johannine thought by struggles with other Christians and by internal division.

MARIE-EMILE BOISMARD

The honors for the most elaborate and detailed reconstruction of Johannine literary history belong to Boismard whose volume on John is really a commentary on four hypothetical stages of composition.[320] Each stage is intricately involved with the life of the Johannine community:

I. DOCUMENT C. This was a complete gospel stretching from JBap to the resurrection of Jesus, written in Aramaic in Palestine about the year 50. This may have been composed by the Beloved Disciple (whether he was John Son of Zebedee or Lazarus). Its christology was primitive, with Jesus pictured as the Prophet-like-Moses or as the Danielic Son of Man. It had no pejorative attitude toward the Jews. The order of material in the document was close to that of the Synoptic Gospels, although it was more archaic than Mark.

II. JEAN IIA. Another writer (John the presbyter, mentioned by Papias) subsequently did two editions of Document C (and

319. If one accepts the testimony of Josephus (*Life* 10), in the Judaism before A.D. 70 the Pharisees, Sadducees, and Essenes were all Jewish sects, so that there was no standard Judaism until the Pharisees outlasted the others and their theology became orthodoxy.

320. *L'Evangile de Jean* (Synopse des Quatres Evangiles en français, III; ed. M.-E. Boismard and A. Lamouille; Paris: Cerf, 1977).

wrote the Epistles). He was a Jew who wrote this first edition in Palestine *ca.* A.D. 60-65. In it he added new material to C, and began to speak pejoratively of the world, as well as showing some opposition to the Jews—reflections of the changing life-situation of the community.

III. JEAN IIB. His second edition, done *ca* A.D. 90, drastically changed the order of the original to the order of the Gospel much as we now know it. He now knew all three Synoptic Gospels and some Pauline letters, and so had contact with other Christian groups. The writer had moved to Ephesus from Palestine, and this edition was in Greek. Persecution had left its trace in a strong aversion to "the Jews"; and Jesus was now presented as a pre-existent figure, clearly superior to Moses. Sacraments also came to the fore.

IV. JEAN III. Still a third writer, an unknown Jewish Christian of the Johannine school at Ephesus, was the final redactor early in the second century.

* * *

Although Boismard's reconstruction of such exact literary stages will probably not receive wide acceptance, there are aspects of real importance in his theory. By positing three Johannine writers, he portrays well the complexity of the Johannine school. Correctly he sees a shift from an original Jewish background and a more primitive christology to a Gentile setting and a higher christology; and he may well be right in connecting this to a geographical move (from Palestine to Ephesus) on the part of the main writer and presumably of some of the community.[321]

---

321. Smalley, *John* (n. 99 above) 119-20, gives a reconstruction with some points of similarity to Boismard: *Stage I*. John son of Zebedee (the Beloved Disciple) moved from Palestine to Ephesus where he handed on orally to disciples some accounts of the deeds and sayings of Jesus, including an account of the death and the resurrection. *Stage II*. A disciple or disciples committed to writing a first draft of these traditions. *Stage III*. After the death of the Beloved Disciple at Ephesus, there was a final edition with additions.

WOLFGANG LANGBRANDTNER

Another type of reconstruction, represented by this young scholar,[322] brings gnosticism into the heart of Johannine development. He distinguishes three community stages:

I. GRUNDSCHRIFT. There was an early basic Johannine composition which organized the Jesus-material thematically: John 1:1-13 was a statement of christology and soteriology; John 3 dealt with anthropology; John 4 and 6 dealt with the need for faith; etc. Jesus was portrayed as in the world but not known by the world, and signs were regarded as irrelevant to faith. The author of the *Grundschrift* had a gnostic, dualistic outlook, so that the modern scholarly attempts to interpret the Fourth Gospel as gnostic do more justice to this basic work than to the final Gospel. It was not written before A.D. 80, and the Johannine community that gave expression to its thought therein did not go so far back (as a social unit) as the Jewish War of the late 60s.

II. REDACTION. A complete reshaping of the *Grundschrift* both as to material and order gave us the Gospel as we now know it, with the journeys to Jerusalem and the calendar of feasts that runs through chaps. 5–10. Although the redactor was not the Beloved Disciple, he appealed to the Beloved Disciple (an aged man of great status and the living vehicle of the Paraclete) as the guarantor of the tradition. The redactor needed this support precisely because he was reinterpreting the *Grundschrift* in an anti-gnostic, anti-docetic way; and a major struggle was underway within the community. This redaction, which was done *ca.* A.D. 100, stressed the fleshly existence and bodily resurrection of Jesus, ethics, sacraments, and future eschatology.

III. EPISTLES. These were written in the order II John, III John, I John (n. 177 above). The redactor had gathered a group around him, including the presbyter of II-III John; and this "we" presented themselves as community teachers, while those who opposed the redacted Gospel had now seceded. Although relatively few years had passed since the Gospel was redacted, the

---

322. *Weltferner Gott oder Gott der Liebe: Die Ketzerstreit in der johanneischen Kirche* (Beiträge zur biblischen Exegese und Theologie 6; Frankfurt: Lang, 1977).

community of the redactor was moving in the direction of "early Catholicism." Some, however, like the Diotrephes of III John, thought the situation was still too ambiguous and more church order was demanded.

* * *

In my judgment there are some valuable observations in Langbrandtner's analysis, especially as to the final directions of Johannine history. However, I would have the following points of disagreement. First, he does not do justice to the pre-Gospel situation, to the tie between Jesus and early Johannine origins and tradition, and to the struggle with "the Jews." Second, his theory depends on his ability to reconstruct verse-by-verse the *Grundschrift* and the additions of the redactor. No firm theory can be built on so disputable a base, for every scholar will have a different assignment of verses to the putative *Grundschrift*. Third, he has moved back into the heart of the Gospel an inner-Johannine dispute that is attested clearly only in the Epistles, and so has neglected the major struggle of the Gospel with outsiders, whether Jews or other Christians. Fourth, he has overdone the gnostic orientation of the Fourth Gospel which he attributes to its earliest layer. The fascination of German scholarship with the gnostic orientation of John produces some contradictory results in terms of allotting the gnosticism to different stages of composition. Bultmann alloted it to Revelatory Discourse source (which few scholars now accept); Langbrandtner allots it to the *Grundschrift*; and both agree that the main writer of the Gospel was correcting the gnostic tendencies of the earlier material that came to him.[323] Other German scholars think that the main Johannine writer was the source of the gnosticism, so that he was introducing gnostic ideas into the material that came to him; for Käsemann he was "naïvely docetic"; for Luise Schottroff he was a rather developed

323. U.B. Müller, *Die Geschichte der Christologie in der johanneischen Gemeinde* (SBS 77: Stuttgart: Katholisches Bibelwerk, 1975) thinks that John 1:14,16 belonged to an early stage of Johannine christology with a one-sided emphasis on glory, which the main Johannine writer modified by introducing the notion of Jesus' death.

gnostic.[324] I would argue that, while the Gospel was capable of being read in a gnostic manner, it was the Johannine secessionists, mentioned in I John, who first began to go down the path toward gnosticism, and that at no period documented in either the Gospel or the Epistles can one yet speak of a real Johannine gnosticism.

NB

---

324. *Der Glaubende und die feindliche Welt* (Neukirchener Verlag, 1970); also M. Lattke, *Einheit im Wort* (SANT 41; Munich; Kösel, 1975) 44-53.

APPENDIX II
ROLES OF WOMEN
IN THE FOURTH GOSPEL

This appendix appeared originally as an article in *Theological Studies* 36 (1975) 688-99, and I am grateful to the editor of that journal for the permission to reprint it here. As will be apparent from the introductory paragraphs and from n. 328, it was originally intended as a contribution to the discussion of the ministry of women in the Roman Catholic Church today. However, since the Johannine attitude toward women was quite different from that attested in other first-century Christian churches, I think it important to include this study as part of the picture of the community of the Beloved Disciple. The unique place given to women in the Fourth Gospel reflects the history, the theology, and the values of the Johannine community.

* * *

There are several ways of approaching the biblical evidence pertinent to the contemporary debate about the role of women in the Church and about the possibility of ordaining women to the priesthood. One approach is a general discussion of first-century ecclesiology both in itself and in its hermeneutical implications for the present. How does one read the NT evidence about the foundation of the church and the institution of the sacraments, and to what extent is that evidence culturally conditioned? Following the teachings of the Council of Trent, Catholics have spoken of the institution of the priesthood at the Last Supper. Does that mean that at the Supper Jesus consciously thought of priests?[325] If he did not and if the clear conceptualization of the priesthood came only toward the second century, does the fact that men exclusively were ordained reflect a divine dispensation? Or are we dealing with a cultural phenomenon which can be changed? In other words, do we work with a "blueprint ecclesiology" wherein Jesus or the Holy Spirit has given us a blueprint of church structure in which virtually no changes can be made? While I regard the discussion of these questions as most important, I have written on them elsewhere and shall not repeat my observations here.[326]

---

325. In this question care is required in interpreting Trent: "If anyone shall say that by the words 'Do this for a commemoration of me,' Christ did not institute the apostles priests . . . let him be anathema" (Denzinger-Schönmetzer 1752). The fathers of Trent did not distinguish between the Jesus of the historical ministry and the developed christological picture of Jesus presented in the Gospel accounts of the ministry written thirty to sixty years later; thus they did not speak simply of Jesus but of Christ. Today, in loyalty to the 1964 statement of the Pontifical Biblical Commission on Gospel historicity (*JBC,* art. 72, #35), Catholics would have to acknowledge that the divinity of Jesus was recognized *after* the resurrection and that eventually it was this fuller appreciation of Jesus as the Christ, the Son of God, that was made part of the Gospel accounts of his ministry. Therefore, institution of priests by *Christ,* as taught by Trent, which cites words reported by Luke and Paul (but not by Mark and Matthew), implies more than was apparent at the historical Last Supper.

326. One of my Hoover Lectures delivered at the University of Chicago in January 1975 treated this subject; it is now published in *Biblical Reflections* (n. 19 above). To what I have said there I would add only a plea for accuracy. The statement is sometimes made that there were no women priests in NT times. Since in the NT itself the term "priest" is applied to Christians *only* in the broad sense of the priesthood of the people (I Pet 2:5; Rev 5:10—i.e., a priesthood of spiritually offering one's life as a sacrifice according to the demands of the gospel), it would seem warranted to affirm that the term "priest" was just as applicable to women as it was to men in NT times. If the more precise claim is made that women did not celebrate the eucharist in NT times, there is simply no way of proving that, even if *one may well doubt that they did.* We

A second approach to the biblical evidence is to discuss the explicit texts that refer respectively to the equality and the subordination of women in society and cult. I am not convinced of the usefulness of such a discussion, since for every text pointing in one direction there is usually a countertext. If Eph 5:24 states that wives must be subject in everything to their husbands, Eph 5:21 introduces that section by commanding "Be subject to one another." If I Cor 11:7 says that the man (*anēr*) is the image and glory of God, while woman is the glory of man, Gen 1:27 states that both man and woman are in the image of God. If I Cor 14:34 rules that women should keep silence in the churches,[327] I Cor 11:5 recognizes the custom that women pray and prophesy—and prophecy is the charism ranking second after apostleship (I Cor 12:28), to the extent that Eph 2:20 has the church, the household of God, built upon the foundation of apostles *and prophets*. I might continue listing contrary voices, but then we would still have the question of how to evaluate the voices that stress subordination. Once more we would have to ask: Is that purely a cultural pattern or is it divine revelation?

I prefer here to follow a third approach and to consider the general picture of women in one NT work, the Fourth Gospel, and in one NT community, the Johannine community.[328] I have

---

know very little about who presided at the eucharist in NT times. Yet, there is some evidence that prophets did, for prophets are said to be involved in liturgy (*leitourgein* in Acts 13:2) and to give thanks (*eucharistein* in *Didache* 10:7); and certainly there were women who prophesied (I Cor 11:5; Acts 21:9).

327. It is frequently argued that I Cor 14:34b-36 is not genuinely Pauline. H. Conzelmann, *1 Corinthians* (Philadelphia: Fortress, 1975) p. 246, states: "The section is accordingly to be regarded as an interpolation."

328. This paper is a development of remarks prepared for the session of the Pontifical Biblical Commission in April 1975. In treating the Gospel, while maintaining that the evangelist has tradition about the ministry of Jesus, I take for granted that he reports that tradition through the optic of his own times (p. 17 above), so that he tells us something about the role of women in his own community. I shall use the name "John" for the evangelist even though I do not think he was John son of Zebedee. All the narratives in the Gospel dealing with women will be discussed except the story of the adulteress in 7:53-8:11, which is a later and non-Johannine insertion into the Gospel.

chosen the Fourth Gospel because of the perceptive corrective that the evangelist offers to some ecclesiastical attitudes of his time—his should be a voice heard and reflected upon when we are discussing new roles for women in the church today. I presuppose[329] that the evangelist was an unknown Christian living at the end of the first century in a community for which the Beloved Disciple, now deceased, had been the great authority. I do not think that the evangelist was either antisacramental (in a Bultmannian sense) or antiecclesiastical. He knew that other churches of his time were stressing both structure and sacraments; yet he counteracted some of the tendencies inherent in that situation by writing a Gospel in which he attempted to root the Christians of his community solidly in Jesus. They may be members of the church, but the church does not give God's life; Jesus does. And so, in order to have life, they must inhere in Jesus (John 15:1-8). The sacraments are not simply church actions commanded or instituted by Jesus; they are the continuation of the power that Jesus exhibited in signs when he opened the eyes of the blind (baptism as enlightenment) and fed the hungry (eucharist as food). At the end of the first century, when the memory of the apostles (now more often identified with the Twelve) was being increasingly revered, the Fourth Gospel glorifies the disciple and never uses the term "apostle" in the technical sense,[330] almost as if the evangelist wishes to remind the Christian that what is primary is not to have had a special ecclesiastical charism from God but to have followed Jesus, obedient to his word. In short, it is a Gospel that seeks to make certain that in the structuring of the church the radical Christian values are not lost. What information does such a perceptive evangelist give us about the role of women?

VARIOUS WOMEN OF THE GOSPEL

There is not much information about church offices in the

---

329. The evidence for these presuppositions may be found in my AB commentary (n. 12 above); see the section on Johannine ecclesiology, I, CV-CXI.

330. See n. 150 above. *Apostellein*, "to send," occurs for sending on a mission, but women can be involved in a mission too. See n. 333 below.

Fourth Gospel[331] and, a fortiori, about women in church offices. Perhaps the only text that may reflect directly on this is 12:2, where we are told that Martha served at table (*diakonein*). On the story-level of Jesus's ministry this might not seem significant; but the evangelist is writing in the 90s, when the office of *diakonos* already existed in the post-Pauline churches (see the Pastorals) and when the task of waiting on tables was a specific function to which the community or its leaders appointed individuals by laying on hands (Acts 6:1-6).[332] In the Johannine community a woman could be described as exercising a function which in other churches was the function of an "ordained" person. But, except for that one passage, our discussion must center rather on the *general* position of women in the Johannine community.

Let us begin with the story of the Samaritan woman. In the sequence of reactions to Jesus found in the dialogues of chaps. 2, 3, and 4, there seems to be a movement from disbelief through inadequate belief to more adequate belief. The "Jews" in the Temple scene are openly skeptical about his signs (2:18-20); Nicodemus is one of those in Jerusalem who believe because of Jesus' signs but do not have an adequate conception of Jesus (2:23 ff.); the Samaritan woman is led to the brink of perceiving that Jesus is the Christ (Messiah; 4:25-26, 29) and shares this with others. Indeed, the Samaritan villagers believe because of the woman's word (4:39,42: *dia ton logon [lalian] pisteuein*). This expression is significant because it occurs again in Jesus' "priestly" prayer for his disciples: "It is not for these alone that I pray, but also for those who believe in me through their word" (17:20: *dia tou logou pisteuein*). In other words, the evangelist can describe both a woman and the (presumably male) disciples at the Last Supper as bearing witness to Jesus through preaching

---

331. Although John knows of the existence of the Twelve as a group during Jesus' ministry (6:70), their names are not listed, nor is there a description of their call as a group.

332. Originally this scene referred to the selection of leaders for the Hellenist Christian community. Although we do not know if titles were used at this early period, the closest parallel in the titulary used in later church structure would be "bishop." Luke looks back on the scene from the 80s, and he may have thought that their work was comparable to that done by the deacons in his time, especially if he had begun to think of the apostles as bishops.

and thus bringing people to believe in him on the strength of their word. One may object that in chap. 4 the Samaritan villagers ultimately come to a faith based on Jesus's own word and thus are not dependent on the woman's word (4:42). Yet this is scarcely because of an inferiority she might have as a woman—it is the inferiority of any human witness compared to encountering Jesus himself. A similar attitude may be found in chap. 17, where Jesus prays that those who believe in him through the word of his disciples may ultimately be with him in order that they may see his glory (17:24).

That the Samaritan woman has a real missionary function is made clear by the dialogue between Jesus and his male disciples which precedes the passage we have been discussing. In 4:38 we have one of the most important uses of the verb *apostellein* in John.[333] Jesus has just spoken of the fields being ripe for the harvest—a reference to the Samaritans coming out from the village to meet him because of what the woman has told them (4:35 following 4:30). This is missionary language, as we see from the parallel in Matt 9:37-38: "The harvest is plentiful, but the laborers are few; therefore pray to the Lord of the harvest that He send out laborers into the harvest." But curiously the harvest of the Samaritans verifies the saying "One sows, while another reaps" (John 4:37). Jesus explains this to his male disciples: "What I sent [*apostellein*] you to reap was not something you worked for. Others have done the hard work, and you have come in for the fruit of their work." Whatever this may have meant in reference to the history of the Samaritan church (see pp. 35-39 above), in the story itself it means that the woman has sown the seed and thus

---

333. See n. 330 above. Another usage of *apostellein* is in 17:18: "As you [Father] sent me into the world, so I sent them into the world," which precedes the prayer "for those who believe in me through their word" (17:20)—even as *apostellein* in 4:38 precedes the references in 4:39, 42 to those who believe in Jesus through the woman's word. A third significant usage of "send" (*apostellein* and *pempein*) is in the postresurrectional appearance of Jesus to the disciples: "As the Father has sent me, so do I send you" (20:21). In the next paragraph of this Appendix, I shall discuss the priority John gives to the appearance of the risen Jesus to a woman disciple.

prepared for the apostolic harvest. One may argue that only the male disciples are sent to harvest, but the woman's role is an essential component in the total mission. To some extent she serves to modify the thesis that male disciples were the only important figures in church founding.

The phenomenon of giving a quasi-apostolic role to a woman is even more apparent in chap. 20. Essential to the apostolate in the mind of Paul were the two components of having seen the risen Jesus and having been sent to proclaim him; this is the implicit logic of I Cor 9:1-2; 15:8-11; Gal 1:11-16. A key to Peter's importance in the apostolate was the tradition that he was the first to see the risen Jesus (I Cor 15:5; Luke 24:34). More than any other Gospel, John revises this tradition about Peter. Matthew 28:9-10 recalls that the women who were leaving the empty tomb were the first to encounter the risen Jesus, but in Matthew they are not contrasted with Peter. In John 20:2-10 Simon Peter and the Beloved Disciple go to the empty tomb and do *not* see Jesus (also Luke 24:12,24); in fact, only the Beloved Disciple perceives the significance of the grave clothes and comes to believe. It is to a woman, Mary Magdalene, that Jesus first appears, instructing her to go and tell his "brothers" (the disciples: 20:17 and 18) of his ascension to the Father.[334] In the stories of the angel(s) at the empty tomb, the women are given a message for the disciples; but in John (and in Matthew) Mary Magdalene is sent by the risen Lord himself, and what she proclaims is the standard apostolic announcement of the resurrection: "I have seen the Lord." True, this is not a mission to the whole world; but Mary Magdalene comes close to meeting the basic Pauline requirements of an apostle; and it is she, not Peter, who is the first to see the risen Jesus.[335] Small wonder that in some gnostic quarters Mary Mag-

---

334. A similar instruction to go and tell Jesus' "brothers" is found in the parallel appearance to the women in Matt 28:10.

335. The tradition that Jesus appeared first to Mary Magdalene has a good chance of being historical—he remembered first this representative of the women who had not deserted him during the passion. The priority given to Peter in Paul and in Luke is a priority among those who became official witnesses to the resurrection. The secondary place given to the tradition of an appearance to a woman or women probably reflects

dalene rather than Peter became the most prominent witness to
the teaching of the risen Lord (see n. 300 above). And in Western
Church tradition she received the honor of being the only woman
(besides the Mother of God) on whose feast the creed was recited
precisely because she was considered to be an apostle—"the
apostle to the apostles" (*apostola apostolorum*).[336]

Giving to a woman a role traditionally associated with Peter
may well be a deliberate emphasis on John's part, for substitution
is also exemplified in the story of Lazarus, Mary, and Martha.
The most famous incident in which Peter figures during the ministry of Jesus (and his other claim to primacy besides that of
witnessing the first appearance of the risen Jesus) is the confession he made at Caesarea Philippi, especially in its Matthean form
(16:16): "You are the Christ, the Son of the living God." Already
the disciples had generally confessed Jesus as a "Son of God" (no
definite article in Matt 14:33), but it is Peter's more solemn confession that wins Jesus' praise as a statement reflecting divine
revelation. The closest parallel to that confession in the four Gospels is found in John 11:27: "You are the Christ, the Son of
God,"[337] and it appears on the lips of a woman, Martha, sister of
Mary and Lazarus. (And it comes in the context of a major reve-

---

the fact that women did not serve at first as official preachers of the
church—a fact that would make the creation of an appearance to a
woman unlikely.

336. J.A. Jungmann, *The Mass of the Roman Rite* (New York: Ben-
ziger, 1950) 470, n. 55. The use of "apostle" of Magdalene is frequent in
the famous ninth-century life of her authored by Rabanus Maurus: Jesus
instituted her apostle to the apostles (*PL* 112, 1474B); she did not delay in
exercising the office of the apostolate by which she had been honored
(1475A); she evangelized her coapostles with the news of the resurrection of the Messiah (1475B); she was elevated to the honor of the apostolate and instituted evangelist (*evangelista*) of the resurrection (1479C).

337. In my AB commentary on John, I, 302, I show how the elements of Matthew's account of Peter's confession at Caesarea Philippi
are found scattered in John: e.g., Andrew, Simon Peter's brother, confesses Jesus to be the Messiah when Andrew is calling Simon to follow
Jesus, and on that occasion Jesus changes Simon's name to Cephas
(1:40-42); Simon Peter as spokesman of the Twelve confesses Jesus to be
the "holy one of God" (6:69); ecclesiastical authority is given to Simon
Peter in 21:15-17.

lation of Jesus to Martha; it is to a woman that the mystery of Jesus as the resurrection and the life is revealed!) Thus, if other Christian communities thought of Peter as the one who made a supreme confession of Jesus as the Son of God and the one to whom the risen Jesus first appeared, the Johannine community associated such memories with heroines like Martha and Mary Magdalene. This substitution, if it was deliberate, was not meant to denigrate Peter or deny him a role of ecclesiastical authority, any more than the introduction of the Beloved Disciple alongside Peter in crucial scenes had that purpose. If I interpret John correctly, at a time when the Twelve Apostles (almost personified in Peter, as in Acts) were becoming dominant in the memory of the ministry of Jesus and of church origins, John portrays Simon Peter as only one of a number of heroes and heroines and thus hints that ecclesiastical authority is not the sole criterion for judging importance in the following of Jesus.[338]

The importance of women in the Johannine community is seen not only by comparing them with male figures from the Synoptic tradition but also by studying their place within peculiarly Johannine patterns. Discipleship is the primary Christian category for John, and the disciple par excellence is the Disciple whom Jesus loved. But John tells us in 11:5: "Now Jesus loved Martha and her sister [Mary] and Lazarus." The fact that Lazarus is the only male in the Gospel who is named as the object of Jesus' love[339]—nothing similar is said of the Twelve—has led some scholars to identify him as the Beloved Disciple.[340] And so it is

338. Such an attitude can be detected in the Synoptic tradition as well. Matthew is the evangelist who gives Peter the most exalted role as the recipient of the keys of the kingdom of heaven (16:19), but Matthew would never make Peter first in the kingdom. That is a primacy specifically denied even to members of the Twelve (Matt 20:20-26). The criterion for primacy in the kingdom, as distinct from the church, is not ecclesiastical authority or power but total dependence on God, whence the model of the little child (18:1-4)

339. See also John 11:3,11,36, where *philein* and *philos* are used of Lazarus. The significance is not different from the use of *agapan* in 11:5; both verbs are used of the Beloved Disciple (*philein* in 20:2; elsewhere *agapan*).

340. See the discussion in my AB commentary, I, xcv.

noteworthy that John would report that Jesus loved Martha and Mary, who seem to have been better known than Lazarus.[341] Another proof that women could be intimate disciples of Jesus is found in chap. 20. In the allegorical parable of the Good Shepherd John compares the disciples of Jesus to sheep who know their shepherd's voice when he calls them by name (10:3-5). This description is fulfilled in the appearance of the risen Jesus to Mary Magdalene as she recognizes him when he calls her by her name "Mary" (20:16). The point that Mary Magdalene can belong to Jesus' sheep is all the more important since in 10:3-5 the sheep are twice identified as "his own," the almost technical expression used at the beginning of the Last Supper: "Having loved his own who were in the world, he loved them to the end" (13:1). It is clear that John has no hesitation in placing a woman in the same category of relationship to Jesus as the Twelve who are included in the "his own" in 13:1.

THE MOTHER OF JESUS

It is as a continuation of this idea that I now turn to John's treatment of the mother of Jesus, who appears in the Fourth Gospel at the first Cana miracle and at the foot of the cross. There are many symbolisms that John may have intended his reader to associate with the mother of Jesus; in my AB commentary on the two scenes I have explained some of them at length. But here I am concerned only with discipleship and with the relative importance of men and women in the Johannine community. I shall be concise, since I do not want this Appendix to be more than a note and since elsewhere I have given detailed arguments.[342]

341. Notice the order of names in 11:5. Moreover, in 11:1-2 Lazarus is identified through his relationship to Mary and Martha. The reason for this may be that the two women were known in the wider Gospel tradition (Luke 10:38-42), whereas Lazarus is a peculiarly Johannine character (at least as a historical figure; cf. Luke 16:19-31) who is introduced into the Gospel by being placed in a family relationship to Mary and Martha. This is not unlike the introduction of the Beloved Disciple into well-known scenes by placing him in a relationship to Peter.

342. In the last of the Hoover Lectures (the one on an ecumenical understanding of Mary) mentioned in n. 326 above and published in the same collection; there I approach the Johannine evidence concerning Mary from another angle—a quest for the historical Mary.

Let us begin with the wedding at Cana. Many theorize that there was a pre-Johannine form of the story. One form of this theory suggests that John drew the basic Cana miracle story from a tradition of the *preministry* career of Jesus—a tradition wherein the christology of the ministry was anticipated by describing Jesus as endowed with divine power and knowledge during his youth, when he was still living with his family.[343] In this tradition Jesus spoke freely of his divine mission and worked miracles in order to help family and friends. It is borne witness to in the apocryphal gospels of the second century (e.g., *The Infancy Gospel of Thomas*) and in one other place in the canonical Gospels, namely, the scene in Luke 2:41-50 where as a youth Jesus shows extraordinary knowledge and refers to the Temple as his Father's house.

---

343. This is a development of the thesis proposed by B. Lindars, *The Gospel of John* (London: Oliphants, 1972) 126-27. It supposes the legitimacy of several attitudes in modern Gospel research. First, in the course of early Christian preaching the christology developed "backwards": the role of Jesus as the Messiah, the Son of God, was first understood in relation to the future (the parousia), then in relation to the present (the resurrection), and finally in relation to the past (the ministry). As part of a reflection on what Jesus was before the resurrection, christology was pushed back to his youth and to his conception/birth. Thus, Mark, the oldest Gospel, has no infancy story but concentrates on Jesus as Son of God during the ministry; the later Gospels, Matthew and Luke, have infancy stories which took their final shape after the story of Jesus' ministry had been preached. In Luke 2:41-50 a once-independent story of Jesus as a youth has been appended to the story of Jesus' conception/birth, leaving us the awkward sequence wherein Mary who has been told that Jesus is the Son of God does not understand when he speaks about his Father (2:50). *Second*, the modern Roman Catholic exegete, following the directives of Pius XII, recognizes the existence of different types of literature in the Bible, including fiction and popular stories which can be inspired by God just as well as history. And so there is nothing contrary to Catholic teaching in supposing that an evangelist on rare occasions took over stories (of undefinable historicity) from popular traditions about Jesus—certainly that happened in both infancy narratives. Inerrancy comes into play, not in reference to either the origin or historicity of a story like that of Cana, but in reference to its teaching "that truth which God wanted put into the sacred writings for the sake of our salvation" (Vatican II, *Dei Verbum*, no. 11). As we shall see, John did adapt the story to make it conform to the genuine Gospel picture of Jesus' relationship to his family. All of this is treated in detail in the lecture referred to in the preceding note.

This background would explain many peculiar features in the story of the water changed to wine at Cana: Jesus is still up in the highlands of Galilee (where he does not work miracles in the Synoptic tradition); he has not yet left his home and moved to Capernaum, which will be the center of his public ministry (2:12); he is in the family circle of his mother and brothers (2:12) and he is attending the wedding of a friend of the family (2:1-2); his mother expects him to use his miraculous power to solve the shortage of wine at the wedding (2:3); the miracle he performs is particuarly exuberant (about 100 gallons of wine from the six stone jars mentioned in 2:6).

I have described one form of the theory that a pre-Johannine story underlies the present Cana narrative. There are other forms of this theory, but almost all propose that there was no response of Jesus such as now appears in 2:4—a response which makes the story very hard to understand. It is a seeming refusal; and yet Jesus' mother goes ahead as if he had not refused, and Jesus does what she requested. The substance of the pre-Johannine story may have gone thus:[344]

> Now there was a wedding at Cana of Galilee and the mother of Jesus was there. Jesus himself and his disciples had been invited to the wedding celebration. But they had no wine, for the wine provided for the wedding banquet had been used up. The mother of Jesus told the waiters: "Do whatever he tells you." There were at hand six stone water jars, each holding fifteen to twenty-five gallons. "Fill those jars with water," Jesus ordered. . . .

Such a popular picture of Mary's ability as a mother to intervene in Jesus' activities, to ask for a miracle for her friends and to have it granted, did not correspond with the oldest Gospel tradition

---

344. The best reconstruction of the pre-Johannine miracle material is found in R.T. Fortna, *Gospel of Signs* (n. 36 above), and I offer here a translation of the first part of his Greek reconstruction of the pre-Johannine Cana miracle story. I (and others) do not agree with Fortna that a whole pre-Johannine gospel can be reconstructed, but all admit that the best evidence for a pre-Johannine miracle collection is in the two Cana miracles which John himself numbers in sequence (2:11; 4:54).

about Jesus' attitude toward family. In Mark 3:31-35 we find Jesus strongly rejecting intervention by his mother and brothers in favor of obedience to God's will. And so, when John brought this miracle story into the Gospel, he modified it by inserting 2:4,[345] where Jesus carefully dissociates himself from his mother's interests ("Woman, what has this concern of yours to do with me?") and gives priority to the hour dictated by his heavenly Father ("My hour has not yet come").[346] Thus the Fourth Gospel agrees with the other three that Mary had no role in the ministry as Jesus' physical mother. The Jesus who asked his disciples not to give any priority to family (Mark 10:29-30; Matt 10:37; Luke 14:26) was not himself going to give priority to family. This interpretation of John 2:4 is valid whatever theory one accepts about the origins of the Cana story.

If one had just Mark 3:31-35, the only scene common to the Synoptics in which the mother and brothers of Jesus play a role, one might conclude that Jesus completely rejected them from his following. According to Mark, when Jesus was told that his mother and brothers were outside asking for him, he replied: " '*Who are my mother and my brothers?' And looking about at those who sat around him, he said: 'Here are my mother and my brothers!'* " He then stated that whoever did the will of God was his brother and sister and mother—in other words, his disciples take the place of his family. But this was not Luke's understanding of Jesus' intent. His version of the scene (8:19-21) omits the Marcan words I have italicized above and reads thus:

> Then Jesus' mother and his brothers approached him, but they could not reach him because of the crowd. He was given the message: "Your mother and your brothers are standing out-

---

345. Fortna points out that this verse, besides creating logical difficulties, is written in the characteristic prose of the evangelist, something that is not true of the pre-Johannine story Fortna has reconstructed. It is worth noting that in Luke 2:49 a similar modification of the parents' claims appears: "How is it that you sought me? Did you not know that I must be in my Father's house [about my Father's business]?"

346. The "hour" pertains to the heavenly Father's domain: "The hour had come for Jesus to pass from this world to the Father" (13:1).

side waiting to see you." But he replied: "My mother and my brothers are those who hear the word of God and do it."

For Luke, the hearers of the word of God do not *replace* Jesus' mother and brothers as his true family; for his mother and brothers hear the word of God and do it and so are part of the true family of disciples. Luke preserves Jesus' insistence that hearing the word of God and doing it is constitutive of his family, but Luke thinks that Jesus' mother and brothers meet that criterion. That this is a correct interpretation is confirmed by Acts 1:14,[347] where, among the 120 "brethren" who constitute the believing community after the resurrection-ascension, Luke lists "Mary the mother of Jesus and his brothers."

This is also John's understanding of the role of Jesus' mother in relation to discipleship, as we see from the other scene in which she appears (19:25-27). At the foot of the cross there are brought together the two great symbolic figures of the Fourth Gospel whose personal names are never used by the evangelist: the mother of Jesus and the Disciple whom Jesus loved.[348] Both were historical personages, but they are not named by John, since their primary (not sole) importance is in their symbolism for discipleship rather than in their historical careers. During the ministry, as we saw in the final Johannine form of the Cana story (especially 2:4), the mother of Jesus was denied involvement as his physical mother in favor of the timetable of the "hour" dictated by Jesus' Father;

---

347. Another confirmation is found in Luke 1:38 which dramatizes Mary's reaction to the christological proclamation about Jesus' divine sonship (formerly attached to the baptism of Jesus but now attached to his conception). Her response is drawn from Luke's positive understanding of the Marcan scene, namely, that she was one who heard the word of God and did it: "Let it be done to me according to your word." See R.E. Brown, "Luke's Method in the Annunciation Narratives of Chapter One," in *No Famine in the Land: Studies in Honor of John L. McKenzie* (ed. J.W. Flanagan and Anita Robinson; Missoula: Scholars Press, 1975).

348. John's failure to use the personal name of the mother of Jesus is striking because John is not shy of that name. "Mary" occurs some fifteen times in the Fourth Gospel: for Mary the sister of Martha, for Mary Magdalene, for Mary the wife of Clopas. His insistence on the title "the mother of Jesus" or "his mother" is probably because John is interpreting a tradition about what constituted her true motherhood.

but now that the hour has come for Jesus to pass from this world to the Father (13:1), Jesus will grant her a role that will involve her, not as *his* mother but as the mother of the Beloved Disciple. In other words, John agrees with Luke that Jesus' rejection of intervention by Mary did not mean that his natural family could not become his true family through discipleship. By stressing not only that his mother has become the mother of the Beloved Disciple, but also that this Disciple has become her son, the Johannine Jesus is logically claiming the Disciple as his true brother. In the Fourth Gospel, then, as well as in the Synoptic scene, Jesus has reinterpreted who his mother and his brothers are and reinterpreted them in terms of discipleship.[349] If in Acts 1:14 Luke brought back the mother and brothers of Jesus as disciples after the ascension, John chooses the "hour" when Jesus has been lifted up (12:32) to bring onto the scene the mother of Jesus who is made the mother of the Beloved Disciple, now Jesus' brother.

I pointed out earlier that discipleship is the primary Johannine category and that John included women as "first-class" disciples by telling us that Jesus loved Martha and Mary and that Mary Magdalene was one of "his own" sheep whom he called by name. John's treatment of the mother of Jesus is a step further in that direction. If the Beloved Disciple was the ideal of discipleship, intimately involved with that Disciple on an equal plane as part of Jesus' true family was a woman. A woman and a man stood at the foot of the cross as models for Jesus' "own," his true family of disciples.

I spoke earlier of the Samaritan woman to whom Jesus revealed himself as the source of life and the Messiah, a woman who in a missionary role brought men to him on the strength of her

---

349. I repeat what I stated at the beginning of the discussion of the mother of Jesus: this is not the only symbolism. It should be noted, too, that Mary does not become simply a disciple among many; she has an eminence as the mother of the ideal Beloved Disciple. While John and Luke move here in the same general theological direction, Luke is reinterpreting the role of Jesus' physical "brothers," i.e., relatives. John (7:5) treats the physical brothers as nonbelievers, and so he chooses to deal with the brotherhood of the Beloved Disciple, who is not a physical relative of Jesus.

word. In the scene in 4:27, we are told that when Jesus' male disciples saw him speaking to her, they were surprised that he was dealing in such an open way with a woman. In researching the evidence of the Fourth Gospel, one is still surprised to see to what extent in the Johannine community women and men were already on an equal level in the fold of the Good Shepherd. This seems to have been a community where in the things that really mattered in the following of Christ there was no difference between male and female—a Pauline dream (Gal 3:28) that was not completely realized in the Pauline communities.[350] But even John has left us with one curious note of incompleteness: the disciples, surprised at Jesus' openness with a woman, still did not dare to ask him, "What do you want of a woman?" (4:27). That may well be a question whose time has come in the church of Jesus Christ.

350. The rule that a woman should keep silence in the churches, if it was authentically Pauline (see n. 327 above), was scarcely in effect in the Johannine community, in whose gallery of heroes were the Samaritan woman who brought men to faith by her word and Mary Magdalene who proclaimed the good news of the risen Jesus.

BIBLIOGRAPHICAL INDEX

This is *not* an index of the discussions of views held by various authors; rather it lists the page for the first occurrence of an author's work(s) where full biographical information is supplied. In that information I have followed the standard abbreviations for periodicals and series employed by the *Journal of Biblical Literature* 95 (June 1976) 339-46 and by the *Catholic Biblical Quarterly* 38 (July 1976).

Achtemeier, P. J. 27

Bacon, B. W. 38
Bagatti, B. 76
Bakken, N. K. 148
Bardy, G. 150
Barnard, L. W. 155
Barrett, C. K. 53, 79, 86
Bauer, W. 105
Becker, J. 95
Berger, K. 109
Best, E. 19
Boismard, M.-E. 178
Bogart, J. 104
Bonnard, P. 121
Bornhäuser, K. 67
Bornkamm, G. 16
Bowman, J. 44
Braun, F.-M. 148
Brown, R. E. 5, 6, 15, 17, 19, 31, 70, 94, 100, 107, 118, 120, 149, 196

Brown, S. 15
Bultmann, R. 115, 129

Conzelmann, H. 140, 185
Coppens, J. 50
Corwin, V. 155
Cullmann, O. 177
Culpepper, R. 14

Davies, W. D. 22
de Jonge, M. 20, 31, 60, 72, 85, 86
de la Potterie, I. 121, 129
Dodd, C. H. 28, 76
Donahue, P. J. 155
Donfried, K. P. 100
Dunn, J. D. G. 105

Fiorenza, E. S. 6
Fitzmyer, J. A. 22
Forestell, T. 119
Fortna, R. T. 27, 39, 52

Freed, E. D. 38
Fuller, R. H. 53, 153

Grant, R. M. 148

Hahn, F. 54
Harnack, A. von 160
Hawkin, D. J. 83, 105
Hoskyns, E. C. 99

Jungmann, J. A. 190

Käsemann, E. 16, 160
Klein, G. 138
Kümmel, W. G. 99
Kysar, R. 18, 50, 52, 171

Langbrandtner, W. 180
Lattke, M. 182
Leroy, H. 61
Lindars, B. 50, 193

MacRae, G. 57
Malherbe, A. 65, 98
Martyn, J. L. 17, 30, 45, 80, 172
Matsunaga, K. 40
Mattill, A. J. 174
Meeks, W. 14, 38
Michl, J. 142
Molland, E. 155
Moloney, F. J. 50
Moreno Jiménez, P. 102
Müller, U. B. 119, 181
Munck, J. 100

Neirynck, F. 82
Nicol, W. 27

O'Grady, J. 87, 88

Pagels, E. H. 15
Painter, J. 106
Pancaro, S. 13, 67
Parker, P. 39
Pastor, F.-A. 13
Purvis, J. D. 38

Richter, G. 122, 174
Robinson, J. A. T. 22, 67, 96
Robinson, J. M. 112
Ruckstuhl, E. 161

Sabugal, S. 44
Sanders, J. M. 149
Schein, B. E. 77
Schenke, H. M. 152
Schlier, H. 101
Schnackenburg, R. 32, 33, 98
Schottroff, I. 181-82
Schweizer, E. 13
Scobie, C. H. 38
Scroggs, R. 14
Shepherd, M. H., Jr. 106
Smalley, S. 55
Smith, D. M., Jr. 14, 22, 30
Snyder, G. F. 16
Spicq, C. 49
Stuhlmacher, P. 98
Sundberg, A. C. 53

Talavero Tomar, S. 119
Thyen, H. 31

van Unnik, W. C. 67, 100
Vorster, W. S. 105
Vouga, F. 62

Weiss, K. 105
Wiles, M. F. 151
Wink, W. 30

SUBJECT INDEX

Alienation: see *Sectarianism*
Alogoi, 149
Apocalypse: see *Revelation*
Apostle (apostolic), 13, 16, 21,
    81, 185, 189-190
  apostolic churches (Christians),
    31, 32, 81-88, 98, 141, 145,
    146, 157, 159, 162
  contrast with disciple, 82, 84,
    86, 141, 186, 191
  succession to, 86-88, 141
  the Twelve, 18-19, 27, 30, 32,
    34, 38, 48, 74, 75, 81-82,
    85, 86, 186, 187, 191, 192
  woman as, 189-190
Authorship of Johannine writings,
    33-34, 94-96, 102-103, 138,
    150, 185-186

Baptism, 79, 88, 117, 140, 158,
    186
  of Jesus, 117-118, 119, 152-153
Beloved Disciple, 22-23, 31-34,
    89, 95, 101, 102-103, 141,
    161-162, 164, 177, 180, 186,
    191, 197
  and JBap, 32-33, 69
  and mother of Jesus, 196-197

  and Simon Peter, 31-32, 34,
    82-84, 90, 161-162, 164,
    189, 191, 192
  and "the presbyter," 95
  christology of, 33
  identity of, 33-34, 172, 177,
    178, 179, 191
Birkat ha-Minîm, 22, 173, 174
  see also *Judaism synagogue
    expulsion*
Brothers (physical) of Jesus,
    75-76, 89, 197
  James, 75, 76, 78-79, 80
  replaced by believers, 76, 189,
    195-197

Cerinthus, 24, 105, 112-113, 150,
    151, 152-154
Charismatics in I John, 106,
    139-140, 186
Christology, 16, 23, 25-26,
    109-123, 126-127, 133, 136,
    143, 159, 160, 163, 193
  higher, 25, 28, 29, 36, 45-47,
    49, 51, 53, 60, 77, 80,
    84-86, 96, 97, 109, 114-116,
    146, 156, 157, 175, 176, 179
  I AM, 45, 46, 57, 78, 86, 114,
    118, 142, 147

Jesus' human career, 114-119,
121-123, 146, 156, 159
lower, 25, 51, 53, 54, 80, 108,
156, 178
Messiah, 25, 26-27, 29, 38,
43-44, 47, 55, 69, 84, 111,
187, 193
Moses christology, 38, 44
pre-existence, 24, 26, 29, 37,
45-46, 54, 60, 78, 85, 90-91,
97, 109, 111, 114, 117-118,
120-121, 146, 151, 157, 159,
175, 179
Church (ecclesiology), 7, 13,
86-88, 93, 129, 183-184, 186
anti-institutionalism, 16, 87, 186
"catholic," 24, 145, 158, 159,
161, 162, 163
ekklēsia, 13, 21
Johannine churches, 93, 98-99
pluralism, 23, 73-74
structure: see Presbyter
Commandments, 90, 94, 128-132,
138, 143
Continuity (Johannine), 28-30,
51-54, 56, 63, 175-176, 181
see also Secession in I John
Crypto-Christians, 68, 71-73, 77,
78, 82, 89, 173

Dating of Johannine writings,
22-24, 59, 65, 93-97, 172,
177, 178-179, 180
Dead Sea Scrolls: see Qumran
Didache, 140, 143, 185
Diotrephes, 13, 31, 93-96, 99, 133,
160-161, 181
Discipleship, 84, 101, 102,
191-192, 197
women disciples, 86, 154, 188,
192, 197
see also Apostle; Beloved
Disciple
Docetism, 16, 24, 105, 106,
112-113, 116, 146, 155-158,
163, 175, 176, 180
Dualism, 30, 60, 133-135, 157

Ecclesiology: see Church
Ephesus, 56, 67, 70, 98, 179
Eschatology, 50-51, 52, 96, 108,
135-138, 180
Ethics (Johannine), 94, 107-108,
123-135, 136-137, 143, 159,
160, 180
sinlessness, 124-127, 152
see also Commandments
Eucharist, 21, 67, 74-75, 78-79,
88, 117, 157, 158, 164,
184-185, 186
Eyewitness, 21, 23, 31, 32, 100,
102, 177-178

Gaius of Rome, 149
Galilee, 39-40
Gentiles, 23, 25, 27, 48, 55-58,
63-65, 66, 81, 106, 127, 174
Gnosticism, 15-16, 24, 27, 70,
103-105, 106, 112, 127,
145-148, 150, 151-152, 154,
163, 180-182, 189
Gospel (aggelia), 108
"Great Church" (larger church),
76, 83, 90, 145-147, 149,
158-162, 163, 164, 177
see also Church "catholic"

Hebrews (Epistle) and John, 46,
49, 54, 73, 91, 116, 118
Hellenists, 36, 38-39, 48, 49, 56,
177
"Heterodox" (Heresy), 24, 36,
80, 104-105, 147, 178
Historicity, 21, 26, 32, 36, 41, 74,
75, 83, 177, 184, 189, 193

Ignatius of Antioch, 24, 75, 79,
97, 105-106, 113, 145, 148,
155-160, 163

Irenaeus, 16, 100, 104, 112, 147,
    149, 150, 151
Irony, 57
"Israel," 13, 48, 56, 58, 173

Jamnia, 22, 66
Jewish Christians, 73-81, 89, 98,
    155-157, 173, 175
    see also *Crypto-Christians*
"Johannine Gospel," 106-107
Johannine School: see *School of
    Johannine Writers*
John the Baptist (in John), 26,
    29-30, 58, 69
    followers of, 29-30, 35, 37, 57,
        69-71, 177
    see also *Beloved Disciple and
        JBap*
Judaism and John, 22-23, 35, 39,
    40-43, 55, 63, 66-69, 72-73,
    89, 134, 163, 178-179
    christological debates, 23, 43,
        46-47, 67, 78, 109-110
    cult and feasts, 37-38, 48-50, 73
    current relevance, 41-42, 68-69,
        73
    mission to the Jews, 67-68
    persecution of Christians, 23,
        42-43, 51, 78, 110, 173
    synagogue expulsion, 22, 23,
        41, 43, 51, 55, 63, 65,
        66-68, 71-73, 172-173, 175
    Temple opposition, 23, 35,
        38-39, 49, 118
    term "the Jews," 40-43
Justin Martyr, 42-43, 148, 156

Locale of Johannine writing, 39,
    56-57, 65, 66-67, 98, 175,
    178-179
    see also *Ephesus*
Love (Johannine concept of),
    60-61, 87, 90, 94, 131-135

Mary Magdalene, 154-155,
    189-190, 192, 197
Messiah: see *Christology*
Methodology of research, 15-21
Miracles (signs), 19, 27-28, 75,
    172, 180, 186, 193-194
Misunderstanding (Johannine
    technique), 61-62, 90
Monophysitism, 116, 146, 163
Montanism, 24, 131, 147, 148,
    149, 151, 154
Mother of Jesus, 19, 35, 75-76,
    192-198

Nag Hammadi, 112, 147-148, 153
    see also *Gnosticism*
Nicodemus 35, 61, 62, 72, 187

Odes of Solomon, 147
"Orthodox," 24, 36, 104-105, 147
    orthodoxy of John, 16, 24,
        147-150

Papias, 34, 100
Paraclete (Holy Spirit), 24, 28-29,
    39, 63, 87-88, 89, 96-97,
    101, 134, 138-144, 146,
    159, 180
    giving of Spirit, 118-119, 154
    Jesus as Paraclete, 141
    see also *Montanism*
Passion of Jesus, 96, 118-120,
    122, 153-154, 189
Peter: see *Apostle (the Twelve);
    Beloved Disciple and
    Simon Peter*
Phases of Johannine life, 22-24,
    166-167
Polycarp, 43, 148, 150
Pontifical Biblical Commission,
    17, 21, 184, 185
Pre-existence: see *Christology*
Presbyters:
    church officers (bishops), 16,
        87, 99-100, 141, 145, 146,
        158-162, 187

meaning of term, 99-103
"the presbyter," 31, 93-95,
    100-103, 178, 180
Prologues (Johannine), 32, 46, 54,
    70, 95, 97, 109, 118,
    120-121, 175
Prophets, 96, 106, 131, 137,
    138-140, 143, 148, 154, 185

Qumran (Dead Sea Scrolls), 5,
    30-31, 96

Redaction of Gospel, 16, 20, 23,
    31, 52, 95-96, 102, 109,
    123, 137, 161-162, 175-176,
    179, 180-181
Revelation (Book of),
    Apocalypse, 6, 65, 66-67,
    138, 154, 179

Sacraments, sacramentalism, 16,
    51-52, 79, 88, 117, 157,
    179, 180, 183-184, 186
Samaritans, 22-23, 35-40, 44, 48,
    56, 70, 77, 177
School of Johannine writers, 20,
    101-102, 108, 121, 132, 142,
    179
Secession in I John, 23-24, 74-75,
    97, 99, 103-109, 132, 175

Secret Gospel of Mark, 148-149
Sectarianism (Johannine), 7,
    14-16, 61-62, 89-91
    alienation, 64, 65-66, 89,
    134-135, 172, 173
    meaning of sect, 14-15
Signs: see Miracles
Sources (Johannine) 18, 20, 28,
    52, 103-104, 172, 175, 178,
    180, 182, 193, 194
Synagogue expulsion: see
    Judaism and John
Synoptics compared to John, 13,
    21, 26-28, 35-36, 41, 42, 45,
    50-51, 54, 70, 79, 85, 86,
    88, 107-108, 114-116,
    118-119, 163-164, 177,
    178-179, 189, 190-191,
    193-194

Tatian, 148
Temple opposition: see Judaism
    and John
Twelve: see Apostle

Virginal conception, 21, 85, 156

World (Johannine term), 14, 23,
    63-66, 105, 143-144, 179